E. M. Forster

A Passage to India

EDITED BY BETTY JAY

Series editor: Richard Beynon

macmillan

Published by
PALGRAVE MACMILLAN
Houndmills, Basingstoke, Hampshire RG21 6XS and
175 Fifth Avenue, New York, N. Y. 10010
Companies and representatives throughout the world

PALGRAVE MACMILLAN is the global academic imprint of the Palgrave
Macmillan division of St. Martin's Press, LLC and of Palgrave Macmillan Ltd.
Macmillan® is a registered trademark in the United States, United Kingdom
and other countries. Palgrave is a registered trademark in the European
Union and other countries.

First published 1998 by Icon Books Ltd

ISBN 1–84046–027–X

This book is printed on paper suitable for recycling and made from fully
managed and sustained forest sources.

A catalogue record for this book is available from the British Library.

Transferred to digital printing 2003

Printed and bound in Great Britain by
Antony Rowe Ltd, Chippenham and Eastbourne

Contents

By way of brief introduction to *A Passage to India*, this chapter begins by considering the work of Peter Burra, a critic whom Forster much admired. It goes on to summarise the main concerns of the criticism on Forster's text contained in the Guide, with particular reference to the establishment of Forster's reputation and attempts to decipher the complex codes that are a feature of his novel. These attempts include works by critics who focus on Forster's narrative technique, his sexual politics and the question of imperialism.

'A Delicious and Terrible Book': The Reception of *A Passage to India*

This chapter records the responses of Forster's contemporaries to the publication of *A Passage to India*. It highlights the strength of Forster's reputation in 1924 along with the problems and difficulties his readers negotiate as they engage with his newest novel. In addition to the spirituality and ideology inscribed in *A Passage to India*, questions relating to the text's ambiguity and realism are the focus of these early reviews.

'For Want of a Smile an Empire is to be Lost': Forster's Liberal Humanism

This chapter explores *A Passage to India* in relation to the claims and counter-claims made concerning Forster's liberal humanism. F.R. Leavis and Lionel Trilling are both critics who are closely associated with the liberal-humanist tradition and their response to Forster shows a keen awareness of his own relation to liberal humanism – a relation that each critic problematises. Malcolm Bradbury's assessment of Forster is also attentive to the difficulties of categorising his work, not least because of Forster's complex relation to both the Romantics and the Victorians. Taken together, these essays show how Forster's association with liberal humanism is far from absolute and can be qualified in many different ways.

This chapter focuses on the indeterminacy and ambiguity of *A Passage to
India*. It not only provides ways of reading Forster's textuality but also
relates his narrative techniques to the philosophical, spiritual and political
issues the text encompasses. The extracts from Gillian Beer and Robert
Barratt draw upon the insights of post-structuralist theory in order to
read Forster's textual strategies. Wendy Moffat, on the other hand,
foregrounds Forster's manuscript version of *A Passage to India* as a means
of reading the complex events that constitute the Cave sequence in the
final text. Jo Ann Hoeppner Moran uncovers in the details scattered
throughout Forster's novel an awareness of Jain spirituality and uses
this discovery to interpret the central scene of the novel – the alleged
rape of Adela.

This chapter focuses on the work of critics for whom issues relating to
gender and power are integral to an understanding of *A Passage to India*.
For Elaine Showalter, Forster's ambivalent relation to the institution of
marriage provides a way of understanding the fates of Adela and Fielding
in the novel. Her Anglo-American perspective on the text is developed
and also challenged by Frances L. Restuccia, who reads *A Passage to India*
from both Anglo-American and French feminist perspectives. The final
essay in the chapter, by Eve Dawkins Poll, centres on Forster's deploy-
ment of the ingenue figure and shows how Adela's status in the text
enables Forster to question the sexual and colonial ideologies of his time.

This chapter focuses on two critics who read *A Passage to India* in terms of
its engagement with British imperialism. In his reading of the text,
Jeffrey Meyers argues that Forster's political awareness in *A Passage to*

India has been either overlooked or ignored by critics. In order to redress this problem Meyers demonstrates how the history of British imperialism and Indian resistance to it is inscribed within Forster's text. In common with Jenny Sharpe, whose essay completes the Guide, Meyers is interested in the relation between history and fiction. Sharpe's reading of this relationship offers a way of understanding the complex interplay of sexual and racial politics in Forster's text.

INTRODUCTION

■ One grows accustomed to being praised, or being blamed, or being advised, but it is unusual to be understood. □   E. M. Forster[1]

A Passage to India was Forster's fifth novel and the last to be published during his lifetime. Its publication brought the immensely successful novelistic career of its author to a close for, although he continued to write, Forster confined his subsequent labours to other forms. At the time of his death in 1970, Forster was Honorary Fellow at King's College, Cambridge, a position he had assumed in 1945. This fortuitous residency returned him, in his own words, to the place 'that first set me off writing'.[2] Forster's long association with Cambridge, which led F. R. Leavis to identify him with the undergraduates in *The Longest Journey* (1907), suggests that he led a somewhat insular existence. Yet in his fiction, Forster is clearly at pains to move beyond the realms of the English middle classes and provincial life. He is not only concerned with the domestic and cultural lives of those who inhabit his own class and is perhaps best known, indeed, for his attempts to show what happens when the English travel. From *Where Angels Fear to Tread* (1905) to *A Passage to India* his concern with crossings between individuals and cultures is constantly in evidence. His texts record the terrible consequences of failed connection, of meetings that unsettle the surface calm of middle-class life and, ultimately, challenge its ideological foundations.[3]

Of Forster's six published novels, four appeared before the First World War and one was published posthumously. The most successful of all his novels, *A Passage to India* (begun in 1912) was not published until 1924, fourteen years after Forster's previous novel, *Howards End*. An immediate best-seller that also met with critical acclaim, *A Passage to India* was initially categorised as and understood to be a political novel, albeit one that challenges the reader's comprehension through its obfuscating narrative techniques.

Forster's own comments on the political function of the text are contradictory and in his commentary on the 1957 edition he gives centre stage to Peter Burra's interpretation of his 'purpose' in writing the text.[4] In this piece, Burra argues that the function of the artist is to select material from the chaos and formlessness of life, 'confining his impressions of that life into a space which is infinitely smaller than itself'. Echoing the words of T.S. Eliot, Burra understands that the artist must 'arrange the chaos into some sort of an order'.[5] A number of different factors govern Forster's selection process: his political commitments; his desire to tell a story; the advancement of a plot in order to develop character; and finally, the development of a novelistic rhythm. For Burra, Forster's rhythm manifests itself through phrases and images that create a pattern of connectedness within his work. This aspect of Forster's fiction is crucial to Burra who understands Forster to be 'a musician who chose the novel because he had ideas to utter which needed a more distinct articulation than music could make'.[6] When it comes to relating these novelistic elements to Forster's fiction Burra actually has very little to say about *A Passage to India*. He notes its 'propagandist element' and that 'the real theme of the book' is 'the friendship of Fielding and Dr Aziz'.[7] Beyond this, he summarises the novel as demonstrating Forster's 'interest in the clash of human beings, the struggle which any one individual must endure if he is to achieve intimacy with any one other'.[8] In *A Passage to India* 'the fundamental personal difference is again heightened by an external circumstance – the difference of race'. Despite the importance Forster accords to his critic, the comments Burra makes on *A Passage to India* only touch upon the novel's complexity. The most useful insight Burra offers to Forster's readers relates to his insistence that 'Forster has developed the art of clues and chains to an unusual extent'.[9] Inextricably linked to the process of 'selection', it is the significance of such 'clues and chains' that concerns the critics of *A Passage to India* included in this Guide. Forster's own selection process inevitably raises questions about the ideology of representation, while the 'clues and chains' that enable particular kinds of interpretation are themselves subject to analysis. If one takes Frances L. Restuccia's suggestion that the text obliges its reader to play at detective, then it is apparent that Forster's 'clues and chains' lead the critics to many and varied destinations. At the same time a great deal of common ground is traversed by these critics as they engage in their investigations of the text.

All of the essays in this volume engage with Forster's politics, from his liberal humanism through to his negotiations of sexual and colonial power. In this respect, the essays necessarily work in dialogue with Forster's contemporary readership. Often they resonate with debates that, though highlighted by Forster's text, return present-day readers to the unresolved concerns of the Victorians, the Edwardians and the Modernists. Such critical continuity, and the conflicting responses of Forster's critics to his text, demonstrate the powerful allure of *A Passage to India*.

The first chapter in this Guide looks at contemporary responses to Forster's text and lays the groundwork for the debates that engage subsequent generations of critics. Focusing on the politics of *A Passage to India* as well as the difficulties with which it confronts the reader, these early reviews illuminate those elements of the text that continue to confound and provoke. They contest the realism of Forster's text and in so doing highlight the conflict between the process of artistic selection in which Forster engaged and the political claims of the text.

In the second chapter, the attempt to categorise Forster's work and identify his cultural significance is problematised. Although both F.R. Leavis and Lionel Trilling associate Forster with liberal humanism they also qualify this judgement by drawing attention to Forster's ambivalence and his irony, the means by which he in fact signals his unease with liberal-humanist ideology. Malcolm Bradbury's attempt to place Forster within a literary and cultural tradition leads him to an assessment of the novelist's debt to the Victorians and Romantics – an issue integral to any assessment of Forster's Modernism. All three critics included in this chapter address Forster's reputation and examine the claims made on his behalf concerning his contribution to English literature.

The difficulties critics approaching *A Passage to India* must overcome as they negotiate its formal and linguistic structures are the subject of the third chapter. While Gillian Beer, Wendy Moffat, Robert Barratt and Jo Ann Hoeppner Moran share an interest in the formal properties of Forster's text, they draw very different conclusions about the way in which Forster's narrative strategies contribute to the overall signification of *A Passage to India*. Each of these critics focuses on Forster's ambiguities and indeterminacies. For both Beer and Barratt, these aspects of the text demonstrate its compatibility with the insights of recent critical and narrative theorists. A focus on the Marabar Caves as a site of indeterminacy leads Moffat and Moran respectively to investigate the crises of rationalism and of Western philosophy.

Although attentive to the aesthetic particularities of Forster's text, which cannot be disentangled from its subject matter, all of the critics whose work is included in the Guide's last two chapters focus on the political implications of *A Passage to India*. For Elaine Showalter, Frances L. Restuccia and Eve Dawkins Poll (in chapter four), an engagement with Forster's sexual politics not only enables one to grasp the way in which the text negotiates relations between the sexes but also to understand the conjunction of gender and race that operates within it. For Showalter, writing from an Anglo-American feminist perspective, *A Passage to India* records Forster's attempt to explore conventional marital ideology and his uneasy reconciliation with the imperfect union it represents. Combining both Anglo-American and French feminist perspectives, Restuccia attempts to bring together divergent readings of Forster's sexual politics. Her essay offers a means of examining the contradictory impulses the text displays while suggesting that feminists need to adopt equally contradictory modes of reading if they are to comprehend the radical potential of the text. The last essay, by Poll, concentrates on Forster's use of the ingenue figure in *A Passage to India*. In her reading, Poll suggests that Adela's status as ingenue enables Forster to dramatise the conflicts that beset the British imperialists.

In the final chapter, which deals with the implications of Forster's inscriptions of race and imperial discourse, the work of Jeffrey Meyers and Jenny Sharpe offers divergent ways of considering Forster's engagement with and inscriptions of history. While Meyers sets aside the question of sexual politics in his analysis of Forster's political and historical awareness, Jenny Sharpe's reading incorporates and critiques the work of feminists as she reads the complex significations of race and gender in the text. Sharpe's awareness of both feminist and post-colonial criticism brings this volume to a close with a double focus. This seems appropriate since, although an interest in Forster's imperialism characterises all of the critics included in this Guide, the question of gender is noticeably absent from earlier analyses of the text. Sharpe's essay, which brings recent post-colonial insights to bear on the text, also compensates for the lack of awareness of gender issues in the work of previous generations of critics. It is the feminist agenda, established in the 1970s, which marks out the distinction between earlier and later critics.

Forster's ability to convey the complex interplay between individuals and the cultural forces that operate on and through them continues to fascinate his readers. In the case of *A Passage to India* every exchange and failed exchange between individuals carries wider implications for the relationship between the subjugated and those who are empowered by virtue of race, class and gender. Between the Anglo-Indians and natives, between men and women, acclimatised colonisers and newcomers, the many differences between individuals, cultures, and political systems are dramatised. When Aziz is called to the house of Major Callendar and arrives too late to do his bidding – which he cannot, in any case, discover – the narrator comments that 'the coin which buys the exact truth has not yet been minted'.[10] This comment can equally serve as an introduction to the work of the critics whose essays are included in this Guide. Each one of them offers a different way of approaching *A Passage to India* but none can claim to offer a complete and exact means of interpreting the text, of reading its 'chains and clues' definitively. Taken together, however, they provide numerous points at which the reader can engage with Forster's work: from the ideology of the text to its narrative strategies and philosophical implications. While none of these essays may be held up as the 'exact truth' all of them nonetheless contribute to the 'understanding' that Forster found to be so elusive.

CHAPTER ONE

'A Delicious and Terrible Book':[1] The Reception of *A Passage to India*

FORSTER'S REPUTATION as 'the most attractive and the most exquisite of contemporary novelists'[2] was not diminished by the long silence that followed the publication of *Howards End*. In their reviews of *A Passage to India*, Forster's critics retain a clear sense of the previous literary accomplishments of an author still described as 'representative of his generation'.[3] For these critics, the emergence of Forster's novel represents a significant literary event and they frequently express, in their opening paragraphs, the sense of anticipation with which they greet its publication. This anticipation relates not only to Forster's previous achievements and silence but also to the fact that in *A Passage to India* he turns his attention to a topical political issue: the question of Britain's involvement in India and empire.

In his account of the importance of *A Passage to India*, Ralph Wright illustrates the intensity of the reaction, in 1924, to issues relating to racial politics and imperialism:

■ Race feeling, or the violent reaction from what seems the intolerable race feeling of our fellows, is strong in every one of us. It is almost impossible to start a conversation on India, at dinner or in a railway carriage, even in this country, without producing a heated quarrel. For in the case of India there is much more than even race feeling, which is strong enough, to disturb us. There is our behaviour to a conquered country. There is the ticklish question of conscience. There is great ignorance. There is a genuine hatred of muddling, and a suspicion that whatever we do, go or stay, we shall produce disaster. It is race feeling multiplied by the old Irish situation multiplied by money. There is hardly one man in a million who can keep his head when the subject turns up, or one man in a hundred thousand who will try to. And it is on this almost fratricidal subject that Mr. Forster has chosen to be fair.

11

At least we can be certain of one thing, that patriots on neither side
will bless him for it.[4] □

The overall critical reception of A Passage to India suggests that Forster's
Anglo-Indian novel more than confirmed his status and fulfilled those
expectations brought to the text by his readers. It was, in the words of
one reviewer, 'the most significant of the many Anglo-Indian novels
which have come to us in recent years'.[5] An impressive cross-section of
Forster's peers, including Katherine Mansfield, D.H. Lawrence, Rebecca
West and L.P. Hartley, wrote in praise of his novel. For them, the text
articulated what Leonard Woolf summarises as 'the real life and politics
of India, the intricacy of personal relations, the story itself, the muddle
and the mystery of life'.[6]

The majority of these early reviewers of A Passage to India measure its
success in terms of its realism and, in particular, Forster's ability to invent
convincing characters. Although the assumptions that underlie this kind
of criticism have been challenged by much contemporary theory, this
does not mean that these early reviews can be altogether discounted.
They reveal a great deal about the literary values of the 1920s and contribute to our understanding of the ways in which Forster himself was
constructed by his contemporaries. For it is significant that assessments
of A Passage to India relate not only to Forster's literary achievement but
also to the moral and political outlook the text is said to embody. One of
the striking things about the earliest responses to A Passage to India is the
extent to which both text and author are equally held up as objects of
critical scrutiny. A Passage to India is said to provide evidence of Forster's
humanity. Forster's truthfulness, fairness, wisdom and even, in the
words of J.B. Priestley, his 'exquisite sanity'[7] are all signalled by the text.
The judgements pronounced by the critics demonstrate their awareness
of the responsibility that attends any form of representation, but which is
especially pronounced when the representation in question relates to
racial and cultural difference. Underlying the often moralistic tone of the
critics as they view Forster's text is an understanding of the way in which
culture has the potential to transmit and sustain ideologies that enable
domination. The connection between culture and imperialism is of course
one of the principal concerns of Forster's novel. It is ironic, then, that
Forster's own contribution to literary culture becomes, in a curiously
circular fashion, the object that enables his critics to estimate the extent
to which he colludes with the ideology he otherwise appears to critique.

What additionally emerges from a reading of the early reviews is the
sense of critical continuity that exists between the first responses to A
Passage to India and more recent assessments of the text. More than seventy
years after the publication of Forster's novel, the debate about the
politics of the text remains intense. Although a history of decolonisation

separates today's reader of *A Passage to India* from those who first articulate their responses to it, issues relating to the construction of racial and cultural difference (which the text itself highlights) continue to be addressed with equal urgency.

The general praise that greeted the publication of *A Passage to India* should not obscure those points of critical contention that are also apparent in many of the reviews. Despite the evident focus on Forster's politics in the majority of the reviews, the following account of the text by Leonard Woolf notably skirts around the issue.

■ There are, first, certain obvious things which must be said about *A Passage to India*. It is superbly written. Mr. Forster seems now to have reached the point at which there is nothing too simple or too subtle for his pen; he is able to find words which exactly fit, which perfectly express, every thought which comes to him, and neither the thought nor the words are those which would come to anyone else in the world except Mr. Forster. If that is not one of the essential characteristics of a great writer or of great writing, then I have no knowledge or understanding of either. [. . .] In this book there are all the elements which made Mr. Forster's previous novels of such promise. There is the extraordinarily subtle and individual humour, the lifelikeness of the characters, the command of dialogue, the power of opening windows upon what is both queer and beautiful. The difference between *A Passage to India* and the former novels is that now Mr. Forster knows exactly how to use the elements of his genius. The promise of *Where Angels Fear to Tread* was renewed, but not fulfilled, in *Howards End*. None of these former books 'came off', and there were in them disconcerting lapses into 'silliness', if I dare say so – the silliness, not of a stupid, but of a clever man. But there is no silliness, no lapse, no wobbling in *A Passage to India*; it marches firmly, triumphantly, even grimly and sadly – the adverbs can only be explained by reading the book – through the real life and politics of India, the intricacy of personal relations, the story itself, the muddle and the mystery of life.

I have left my last paragraph for what I shall find most difficult to say. I ought, I know, to have said something about the plot, the story, the novel. They are extraordinarily interesting, but they are the superficies of the book. Even what I have been writing about in the previous paragraphs is on, or only just below, the surface. Nearly all great books, certainly nearly all great novels, have deep beneath their surface a theme or themes which are what give to the whole book its form, real meaning, greatness. Most writers are content with a single informing idea of this sort as the basis of their book, but what makes Mr. Forster's novel so remarkable is that he has a large number of such 'themes' which, interwoven with great imaginative subtlety, weave a strange and beautiful texture for the book itself. The old lady, Mrs. Moore, a superb character in the book, felt that '[o]utside the arch there seemed always an arch, beyond the remotest echo a silence' (p. 71). I feel the same about the book, when I look back on it, if one adds, perhaps, that beyond the remotest silence there is again an echo. There is the story itself with the two ladies who wanted to see India, the Anglo-Indian society of Chandrapore, and Aziz the only living Indian whom I have ever met in a book, and his friendship – which failed to be a friendship – with the Englishman Fielding. Behind that is an arch of politics, the politics of Anglo-India and the nationalist India. And beyond that is another arch, half mystery, half muddle, which permeates India and personal relations and life itself – '"[a]nd all the time"', as Mrs. Moore says, '"this to do and that to do and this to do in your way and that to do in her way, and everything sympathy and confusion and bearing one another's burdens. Why can't this be done and that be done in my way and they be done and I at peace? Why has anything to be done, I cannot see"' (p. 207). And beyond that the terrible arch of 'personal relations' – do 'we exist not in ourselves, but in terms of each other's minds?' – and, '[a] friendliness, as of dwarfs shaking hands'. And beyond that the still more terrible arch of disillusionment – 'the shadow of the shadow of a dream' (p. 262). So the book builds itself up, arch beyond arch, into something of great strength, beauty, and also of sadness. The themes are woven and interwoven into a most intricate pattern, against which, or in which, the men and women are shown to us pathetically, rather ridiculously, entangled. That is how the book presents itself to me immediately after having read it, and perhaps my description may be hardly intelligible to anyone who has not read it. If so, all I can do is to advise him to rush out to the nearest bookseller, buy a copy of the book, and read it.[8] □

Given Woolf's own background in the Colonial Civil Service and his fictional accounts of these experiences, his failure to comment in any detail on the politics of *A Passage to India* is noteworthy. The exceptional nature of this review is taken up by H. W. Massingham. His review singles out Woolf in order to advance a more general attack on 'this habit of our latter-day critics of writing on literature as if its form-pattern, or its spiritual rhythm, and not its meaning and content were the most important thing about it'.[9]

■ I read the other day a notice, in *The Nation*, of Mr. E. M. Forster's novel, *A Passage to India*. It was a very laudatory notice, written by a gentleman who expressed, with evident sincerity, his sense of the aesthetic and spiritual qualities of Mr. Forster's book, and gave an alluring picture of the delicacy and complexity of its structure, built up in 'arch beyond arch' of individual and personal and political relationships. At that point the criticism came to an end, with an asseveration [solemn declaration] of the extreme beauty of this production of Mr. Forster's. But on the actual subject of his work, beyond a general remark that it dealt with India, with the politics of Anglo-India, with Nationalist India, and with the visit of two English ladies to India, the article threw no light whatever. For all that one could tell, Mr. Forster might have written in a sketchy-spiritual way anything about India that had come into his head to write. The one palpable fact which was made clear to the reader was that he had strongly impressed Mr. Leonard Woolf with the beautiful way he had written it.[10] □

Massingham's desire to set aside Forster's aesthetics in favour of a discussion of his politics reinforces a conventional binarism that is particularly pronounced during the Modernist era and evident, for example, in the debates between Henry James and H. G. Wells. Although a distinction between aesthetics and politics is difficult to sustain, even given Forster's connection with Bloomsbury and 'the Woolves', it underpins much of the early writing on *A Passage to India*. Forster's alliance with either 'the preachers and teachers' on the one hand, or the 'pure artists' on the other is the subject of Virginia Woolf's speculations about him.[11] She resolves the issue for herself with the following comment:

■ Mr. Forster, it seems, has a strong impulse to belong to both camps at once. He has many of the instincts and aptitudes of the pure artist (to adopt the old classification) – an exquisite prose style, an acute sense of comedy, a power of creating characters in a few strokes which live in an atmosphere of their own; but he is at the same time highly conscious of a message. Behind the rainbow of wit and sensibility there is a vision which he is determined that we shall see. But his vision is of a peculiar kind and his message of an elusive nature.[12] □

Woolf's insistence that Forster inhabits both camps would appear to be shared by a number of other critics. Indeed, the fact that he manages to avoid overloading the text with partisan politics is often cited as evidence of his artistry:

■ The essence of propaganda, of blanket indictment of one race or another, is not in *A Passage to India*. Mr. Forster is too good a novelist, has too finely proportioned a reasoning faculty, to be concerned with 'issues' in his fiction. Only as an artist he is busy in aligning the forces that are within his ken.[13] □

Notwithstanding a general appreciation of Forster's combined effort, most of the discussion of *A Passage to India* relates to its value as a 'political document of the first importance'.[14] Unsurprisingly, among those many critics who choose to explore Forster's politics there is plenty of room for debate and disagreement. The points of unease or disaffection these reviews articulate frequently form the basis for the debates on Forster that engage his subsequent critics and are in turn the focus for the remaining chapters of this Guide.

A good deal of debate about the politics of *A Passage to India* centres on the question of characterisation (an aspect of the novel that then informs Forster's realism and his thematics). There would seem to be many possible explanations for this focus. Critics approaching his work often cite Forster's ability to portray 'with such precision and charm, what ordinary people are really like, the way they actually do think and talk',[15] as one reason for the esteem in which he is held. They bring this appreciation of Forster's characterisation, his 'surprising grasp of the modern character and the modern temperament',[16] to *A Passage to India*. However, an emphasis on character or, more specifically, the convincing portrayal of the individual in this text, would appear to be at odds with the political readings of character that are also a feature of these reviews. In *A Passage to India* Forster's characters are not simply individualised but also stand in as types. They are imbued with a representative status and significance depending on their race and culture, as well as their position within and attitudes towards a specific power structure. Surprisingly, there is little evidence in the reviews that the successful delineation of the individual for which Forster is renowned might be at odds with a reading of these characters as types. An appreciation of Forster's individual characters and a simultaneous analysis of their typicality is one paradoxical feature of the reviews.

An overview of the reception accorded *A Passage to India* reveals some common points of dissatisfaction and agreement among the critics. On the whole they have very little to say about the more contentious aspects of Forster's text – the alleged rape of Adela and its implications in terms of sexual and racial politics. J.B. Priestley, for example, describes Adela in language that is both telling and yet unselfconscious. She is, he says, 'so curiously barren like all her kind, who laboriously desire to do right without really spending themselves'.[17] Insofar as they address Forster's political engagement these critics choose to focus on the general anti-imperialist slant of the text. They acknowledge, for example, the ways in which Forster shows the iniquities of the imperialist administration and the shortcomings of those who uphold the system. Current criticism of *A Passage to India* demonstrates nothing short of a collective fixation with the Marabar Caves and the allegation of rape. Both the place and the event (or non-event) enable discussion of the construction of different

forms of otherness as well as analysis of Forster's deconstructive potential. The concept of indeterminacy that is so vital to contemporary critical
thought is clearly also pivotal to an understanding of Forster's text. It
exasperates a number of Forster's critics. A typical response to it comes
from Ralph Wright, who qualifies his praise of the text by highlighting
this aspect of the novel:

■ The book seems to me to be a real achievement. There are things in
it that I would have otherwise. There is a queer kind of mystery connected with the caves, where the terrible thing occurred, which is
never cleared up. This in itself would hardly matter. What does seem
to me to matter is a kind of mystical attitude to the caves, a suggestion
of nameless horror that it is *impossible* to explain. I do not believe in
nameless horrors, and I suspect Mr. Forster of doing so.[18] □

A more positive perspective comes from Elinor Wylie:

■ This particular passage, the passage to India, is rather a tunnel
driven through the dreadful solid obduracy of mortal confusion and
ignorance than any fair blue voyage of discovery. It arrives at a blank
wall, but its very frustration is more illuminating than the dazzling
successes of stupidity, which batters its head against this same blank
wall and sees the stars of empire. The portraits of individuals – and
these are brilliantly executed, beautiful in their precision and contrasted essences – are, I think, less important than the informing spirit
of the book, a humanity, an insight, a curious disturbing justice which
is beyond praise and certainly beyond my power to define.[19] □

Forster's indeterminacy baffles I. P. Fassett who, significantly, chooses to
associate it not with the Caves or rape but with Mrs Moore. He begins by
conceding that *A Passage to India* is a worthy, reasoned and well-crafted
text but this is not enough to distinguish it from other novels:

■ Why do we have to remind ourselves so incessantly that Mr.
Forster's work is admirable? In this book he responds to a call to write
about India. He has worked in the power of a clear-thinking, well-
informed mind; therefore he has produced a logical book. The
individual points of view of the various characters could only have
been determined by a man of great sensibility. The subject matter is
handled so competently that nothing is superfluous or out of place.
Mr. Forster is so very clever – what is it that his work lacks? What is it
that we miss in *A Passage to India*? Something that could lift it above the
level of Sound Contemporary Fiction where it must inevitably lie.[20] □

Having consigned *A Passage to India* to the category of 'Sound Contemporary Fiction', Fassett goes on to identify not, as one might suppose, what the text lacks, but what is 'superfluous' to it. Here, he alights upon the character of Mrs Moore, who is understood to be crucial to the novel but whose exact significance eludes the reader:

■ Is it possible that Mr. Forster has tried to supply this something in Mrs. Moore, that sinister, obscure, horrible woman whom he persists in twining so tightly into the thread of his story? I have said that there is nothing superfluous in *A Passage to India*, but I confess that it *would* be nice not to have to bother with Mrs. Moore. In her Mr. Forster has not given us one of his clear, cleancut figures. He has been very subtle. He throws out suggestions here and there as to the key to her nature. He surrounds her in mystery. Psychic influences play about her. It is all very vague.[21] □

Such a frustration with and hostility towards the enigmatic Mrs Moore is particularly significant as a response to a novel in which indeterminacy is the keynote. It seems to represent a form of displacement on the part of Fassett. His attempt to classify Forster's novel, to fit together the components that go to make up a whole narrative fails, because one elusive piece is missing or, when identified, simply does not fit. Mrs Moore, rather than the Caves or the crime, represents the obscure in this reading of the text. Fassett shares with many other critics an understanding of the political significance of the text and the 'sound' impulse that compels Forster to address the India question. Without denying the social significance of the text it is apparent that there are elements in *A Passage to India* that cannot readily be absorbed by a materialist analysis of its workings. Chief among these is the indeterminacy the text maintains. In many of the reviews the question of indeterminacy is ignored or neatly glossed as something that is superfluous to the politics of the text. Fassett himself chooses to fix his own sights on Mrs Moore and appears therefore to withdraw from the Caves and the implications of the alleged rape altogether. Once again, it is the character (or individual) rather than the place or the event that is privileged here.

The overwhelming significance of interpersonal relationships to *A Passage to India* drove D.H. Lawrence to comment, in one of his letters, that 'E.M. Forster does see people, people and nothing but people: *ad nauseam.*'[22] While Lawrence would appear to express a minority opinion about Forster's character-based fiction, other critics give voice to anxieties, not so much about the fact that Forster chooses this kind of representation, but that the context in which his characters operate diminishes their relevance. This tendency is illustrated by J.B. Priestley in the following extract:

■ While I enjoyed every moment of this book, however, I cannot help feeling sorry that Mr. Forster did not choose to mirror contemporary English society in that astonishingly just and sensitive mind of his. Anglo-India is caught here, I imagine, as it has never been caught before, and its sharp divisions, its crushing institutionalism and officialism, its racial and herd thought and emotion, provide an excellent background for Mr. Forster's somewhat elusive philosophy of personal relationships. But it is too much of a 'special case', and unless we too happen to be Anglo-Indians, Mr. Forster's little thrusts are too apt to give us the pleasant task of applauding the discovery of weaknesses outside ourselves instead of the less pleasant but more salutary and exciting business of acknowledging our own weaknesses.[23] □

These comments suggest a dissatisfaction with Forster's focus on the expatriate English community and stem from a sense of the 'otherness' of this community. The narcissistic desire to see oneself reflected in fiction is here thwarted by Anglo-Indian difference. Yet such a desire also encompasses, paradoxically, a wish to become the object of Forster's critique. The context or 'background' to *A Passage to India* acts as a barrier that prevents the process of identification and full appreciation of the text to begin. In this way, Forster's humanist appeal is limited or possibly even overtaken by the specificities of the Anglo-Indian situation. Other critics do not have any difficulty in absorbing the text, translating the specific context into a more general appreciation of humanist values. An unsigned review appearing in the *Times of India* illustrates this point. The review begins with the comment that it is 'not the studies of Anglo-Indian life which lend to the book its remarkable interest'[24] before going on to focus, once again, on character. This time, it is Forster's portrayal of Aziz as an individual and as simultaneous representative of 'Educated India' that draws praise:

■ The central figure of the story is a young Mahomedan doctor; and it is round his relation with Anglo-India that the theme revolves. We have never encountered a more finished study of the psychology of Educated India – deft, incisive, sympathetic, but disillusioned. The mental complexes and inhibitions; the mysticism; the modernism; the racial pride; the intellectual alertness; the supersensitiveness, are all there. [. . .] No one, we think, can pick it up without feeling compelled to turn its searchlight upon himself. It is a very genuine contribution, at once powerful, original, and thought-provoking, to the central problem in India to-day – that of relations between the races and creeds whom Fate has brought together in this distracted land.[25] □

Despite the initial focus on Aziz, Forster is said eventually to provide for his readers a 'poor little tragedy'[26] that engages their 'imagination' and compels them 'to turn [the] searchlight'[27] on themselves. In this way Aziz becomes the catalyst that enables Forster's readership to consider the ways in which they too are implicated in the politics of imperialism. The political importance of *A Passage to India* lies in the uncomfortable yet cathartic process of self-criticism that it enacts: '[i]f it is widely read as it deserves to be, it may exercise a salutary influence. For, like many of those drugs which relieve the ills of mankind, its bitterness in the mouth augments, rather than detracts from, its cathartic properties.'[28]

Although this criticism connects the fate of Aziz with the universal condition of 'mankind', this move does not entirely obscure the text's politics. The 'searchlight' illuminates the general weaknesses shown by human beings, along with their political attitudes. In this way, both the specificity of Forster's text and its wider implications are equally valued by the critic. Forster's ability to create a text that is of both particular and general significance is the basis of this assessment of *A Passage to India*.

In her account of *A Passage to India* Rose Macaulay makes the following remark:

■ Those who fear that [Forster's] peculiar gifts may be wasted in a novel about India can be reassured; they have full scope. He can make even these brown men live; they are as alive as his Cambridge undergraduates, his London ladies, his young Italians, his seaside aunts; they are drawn with an equal and a more amazing insight and vision.[29] □

Measuring Forster's skill as a novelist by his ability to embody the apparently lifeless 'other', Macaulay nonetheless refuses to be drawn into the politics of the text. She only goes so far as to acknowledge that Forster's representations of Anglo-Indians can be contested. She ends her review by inviting the participation of Anglo-Indians whose opinions she would 'like very much to know'.[30]

The Anglo-Indian response to Forster's text inevitably foregrounds the authority that supposedly comes with direct experience of British rule in India. The experience of India enables these critics to contest Forster's representations of Anglo-Indians and the British administration. From their perspective, Forster's 'realism' is evaluated according to the extent to which it coincides with their lived experience. These reviewers are far removed from the critical perspective offered by a more anonymous critic who, despite querying Forster's representation of Brahman India, concedes that the text shows 'a searching justice, and imaginative justice'.[31] What is paramount in the following extract is not simply the accuracy of Forster's depiction of the British judiciary in India but the responsibility that must go with any such representation. Here, Forster is found to be seriously wanting.

■ The account of the Mahomedan doctor's trial on the charge of having insulted an English lady is a serious blemish in the book, and as thousands of readers in England will doubtless take it as gospel, it is calculated to do grave mischief. All the codes appear to have been specially suspended for the occasion. An Indian of good social and official position is arrested summarily. It is a bailable offence, but bail is at first refused, then granted, and then again revoked. The superintendent of police conducts the prosecution before an Indian joint magistrate, and the European officials gather on chairs round the magistrate on the platform, interfering and interrupting. When they are made to leave the platform it is felt as a national humiliation, while all the Indians rejoice. Finally, when the prisoner is discharged without a stain on his character, 'the flimsy framework of the court broke up, the shouts of derision and rage culminated, people screamed and cursed, kissed one another, wept passionately' (p. 232). The account is so full of technical error – indeed, so preposterous, that it cannot even be called a travesty. It is much to be regretted that a writer with Mr. Forster's evident knowledge of the country should have thought fit to supplement his experience by so reckless a use of his imagination. If he did not himself know how an Indian trial is conducted, why did he not ask for information from someone who did?[32] □

Like Joseph Conrad, who drew explicitly upon his own colonial experiences for the writing of 'Heart of Darkness' (1902), Forster also had direct experience of his subject matter. This background appears to inform the critical perspective in a number of reviews. One critic, for example, comments that 'Dr. Aziz strikes one as less invented than overheard'.[33] Another suggests that the narrator doubles as a tour-guide in *A Passage to India*. Both roles are ascribed to Forster himself.

■ This novel gives us opportunity to make excursions into characteristic Indian scenes, accompanied by a skilful guide who refrains from making obvious comments. Without friction and with no apparent effort we are conducted from one place to another, from one group of Indians to another, each peculiar to itself, making no attempt to become like anything else.[34] □

Although Forster's travels through the Empire would seem to lend his work some kind of authority, claims to authenticity do not go unchallenged by the critics. The limits of his experience as well as how he chose to translate such experience into fiction are points debated, particularly by Forster's Anglo-Indian critics. A second dissatisfied view of Forster's verisimilitude comes from E. A. Horne in a letter to the *New Statesman*. Offering to 'convey to English readers how the book strikes an Anglo-Indian',[35]

Horne writes in some detail and, like the previous reviewer, focuses attention on the trial scene before going on to summarise his case against Forster:

■ Why are these people and these incidents so wildly improbable and unreal? The explanation is a singular but a simple one. Mr. Forster went out to India to see, and to study, and to make friends of Indians. He did not go out to see Anglo-Indians; and most of what he knows about them, their ways and their catchwords, and has put in his book, he has picked up from the stale gossip of Indians, just as the average Englishman who goes out to India picks up most of what he knows about Indians from other Englishmen. It is a curious revenge that the Indian enjoys in the pages of Mr. Forster's novel which profess to deal with Anglo-Indian life and manners; and some would say a just one. All the same, it is a thousand pities that Mr. Forster did not see the real Anglo-India, for he would have written an incomparably better and truer book; and we venture to suggest to him, next time he goes to India: '[t]ry seeing Anglo-Indians.'[36] □

Speaking on behalf of Anglo-Indians, Horne goes on to claim that Fielding is Forster's mouthpiece in the text. In the light of the comments cited above this association of the author with Fielding would appear to represent a case of mistaken identification, for it is the figure of Aziz who is called to mind in this passage. Indeed, the question of representation and counter-representation is central to *A Passage to India* and is a vital feature of the first exchange between Mrs Moore and Aziz. Their meeting will subsequently be reinterpreted by her son, Ronny Heaslop, from an Anglo-Indian perspective. While Mrs Moore concedes that this perspective can be validated by her own account of the meeting with Aziz, she finally refuses it:

■ In the light of her son's comment she reconsidered the scene at the mosque, to see whose impression was correct. Yes, it could be worked into quite an unpleasant scene. The doctor had begun by bullying her, had said Mrs Callendar was nice, and then – finding the ground safe – had changed; he had alternately whined over his grievances and patronized her, had run a dozen ways in a single sentence, had been unreliable, inquisitive, vain. Yes, it was all true, but how false as a summary of the man; the essential life of him had been slain. (p. 55) □

Forster's own emphasis on the differences that govern perception within the highly stratified and also polarised society he depicts in *A Passage to India* would seem to be confirmed by the first responses – from both Anglo-Indian and Indian readers – to his text. The following extract from a letter written by another Anglo-Indian takes up Horne's criticisms of Forster. While S.K. Ratcliffe concurs with the former correspondent on a number of points, including the 'farcical' court scene and 'unreality of the Anglo-Indian background',[37] he nonetheless recognises that Forster's Anglo-Indians 'are true in the essentials of character and attitude'.[38] He goes on to acknowledge the power of Forster's text as a contribution to the discourse surrounding the question of British imperialism:

■ The tremendous import of *A Passage to India* for our people is this: for all its mistakes and misreadings, it presents a society, a relation, and a system, which are in the long run impossible. Thirty years ago the station pictures of Rudyard Kipling flashed this truth for the first time over England. Mr. Forster's delicate pen is a far more deadly weapon.[39] □

While he is quick to acknowledge the impossibility of sustaining imperial power relations in India, Ratcliffe also speculates as to the response of educated Indians to their portrayal in Forster's text.

■ One reason suggested by Mr. Forster for the failure of the official garden party was that the Collector knew something to the discredit of every Indian present. Mr. Forster's Indians are all miserable creatures, feeble, fawning, dishonest, treacherous, or what not. True, they are shown usually, though not entirely, in relation to Anglo-Indians. But the fact is there, and here is the point: we knew enough of Mr. Forster's intellectual character and attitude to know that he must depict the representatives of the ruling race with severity; and we assumed that, of necessity, he would find examples of contrasted nobleness among the Indian people. He has not done so; and I suspect that to-day in the club of Anglo-India, the *Sahib-log* are asking derisively what need there can be of a defence for their own position and behaviour, if this is all that their merciless critic has to say for the educated Indians.[40] □

The following Indian response to Forster is worth quoting at length for two reasons. First, it details the various ways in which Indian culture has been absorbed and perhaps appropriated by 'sympathetic' Westerners. Secondly, it places *A Passage to India* firmly within the context of a whole history of literary representations of India. Central to this interrogation of Forster's position is the question of where the author is located in relation to his subject. Unlike the previous responses to Forster and his text, which emphasise direct experience of Anglo-Indian relations, this reader of *A Passage to India* chooses to value the 'detachment' that Forster displays. The review begins with a satirical look at the various ways in which 'sympathetic' Englishmen have responded to Indian culture and intervened in Indian life.

■ I have met the 'sympathetic' Englishman before, and I have always sympathized with him. For who would not sympathize with the Westerner who wears wooden sandals and yellow robes, takes to Gandhi's spinning-wheel and Tagore's hymn-singing and is given a seat of honour in the Indian National Congress as the only God-fearing Englishman alive? Or the ardent missionary who works for the uplift of the Indian peoples and after years of hard work (periodically described in an Evangelical paper) comes home to address Revivalist meetings, taking for his text: '[h]e maketh the sun to rise on the evil and on the good'? Or the eager Civil Servant who earnestly prays to the Almighty for strength and endurance to 'hold dominion over the palm and the pine' for the good of the palm and the pine? Or the fervent educationalist who is busy devising pedagogic methods in order to inculcate a taste for Milton and Shelley amongst a people who he is certain would be immensely the better for it? Or the robust-minded Englishman who is virtuously hurt at the incapacity of Eastern crowds to form a queue outside a theatre door?

One sympathizes with them, for it is impossible either to censure them or applaud them. Their diversity is evidence of the complexity and a tribute to the immensity of India. Their impatience and fanaticism is a tribute to their simplemindedness and evidence of their narrow vision.

And it is because India is used to this sympathy of the well-meaning propagandist kind, that there is a danger of *A Passage to India* being misunderstood by the majority of Indians. It is nothing to boast of that Mr. Forster has seen India 'from within', for every retired Anglo-Indian on the Isle of Wight who names his house 'The Shalimar' and arrays Khyber daggers and Benares brass-work on his mantle-piece has done the same. His great achievement is to have held India at arm's length, as it were, to have turned it round this way and that, and to have taken the lid off and looked within. He is a sympathizer who has retained his detachment. In a word, his is the sympathy of the artist. And if we in our turn sympathize with him, we do so in the sense of adequately responding to him and not in the sense of behaving kindly towards him. We do not see his point of view, we submit ourselves to a new orientation.[41] □

Interrogating the concept of sympathy, or the ability to share another's emotions, the reviewer clearly understands the ideological function of sentiment. Through a play on the words 'sympathy', 'sympathetic' and 'sympathise', he indicates a dialogue with those critics who evaluate Forster in terms of his affinity for his chosen subject. At the same time, this play on words also highlights the centrality of sympathy to Forster's own humanist exploration of Anglo-Indian relations. What makes

Forster stand out among his peers is not so much his own ability to sympathise but the element of 'detachment' he brings to his subject. In identifying this quality of 'detachment' with Forster the reviewer points out a subtle difference that sets him apart from other writers, an artistic perspective that enables him to break with past representations of the Indian in literature.

■ When I read *A Passage to India*, I was filled with a sense of great relief and of an almost personal gratitude to Mr. Forster. This was not because as an Indian I felt myself vindicated or flattered by the book. Indeed to know oneself is not to feel flattered, as many an Anglo-Indian reader of the book has discovered before me. It was because for the first time I saw myself reflected in the mind of an English author, without losing all semblance of a human face. Had I been a Jew living in the reign of Queen Elizabeth, I would have had a similar satisfaction at witnessing the first performance of *The Merchant of Venice*. Shylock is not exactly a deified Jew, but he is certainly a humanized Jew, which is far better. Mr. Forster in *A Passage to India* has created the Easterner in English literature, for he is the first to raise grotesque legendary creatures and terracotta figures to the dignity of human beings. [42] □

In another account, Bhupal Singh recommends *A Passage to India* as 'an oasis in the desert of Anglo-Indian fiction'.[43] He takes issue with the Anglo-Indian hostility towards Forster and his text and, crucially, attempts to distinguish between readings of character and type in the novel.

■ Mr. Forster's portraiture of Anglo-Indian life has called forth bitter protests from Anglo-India, and he has been accused of ignorance, if not of unfairness, in his delineation of the English colony at Chandrapore. It has to be admitted that most of the Anglo-Indians, from the Collector downwards, do not appear in a favourable light. Turton is a '"Burra Sahib"' (p.59), much too conscious of his position before whom other Europeans cringe. His hectoring manner to Fielding is specially offensive and typical of the attitude of the 'Heaven-born' towards the by-no-means unimportant officer of the Indian Educational Department. But Turton's behaviour is the result of Fielding's pro-Indian proclivities. Fielding is not 'pukka' (p.49). That is his main fault. His profession inspires distrust, his ideas are fatal to caste. Though the sahibs tolerated him for the sake of his good heart and strong body, it is their wives who decided that he was not a good sahib, and for that reason disliked him. He had to pay a heavy price for associating with Indians, and for his unconventionality and independence. Those critics who see in Turton's behaviour to Fielding something unreal, forget that it is not as types that Fielding and Turton have been delineated by Mr. Forster. They are individuals. All Collectors are not Turtons, as all College Principals are not Fieldings. Major Callendar, similarly, is not representative of Civil Surgeons. His treatment of Aziz is not typical of the treatment by Englishmen of their Indian subordinates. But Callendar's natural contempt and insolence are heightened by the knowledge that his subordinate is more efficient as a surgeon than himself. Mr. Forster is always careful to individualize his characters, even when he is painting them as representatives of a class. The traces of exaggeration, unreality, or unnaturalness that Anglo-Indians find in these characters are perhaps due to their habit of confounding the character with the type. The individual and class characteristics have been so cleverly combined in almost all the characters of Mr. Forster's novel, that even his minor characters have an exquisite sense of completeness. Mr. Forster is not so much a portrait painter as a psychologist. He observes human beings under certain conditions.[44] □

For Singh, a failure to recognise the individuality of Forster's types produces misreadings of the text and is likely to offend those parties who have a vested interest in Forster's representations. The kind of balance between the representation of the individual and type that Singh identifies with Forster's text suggests a movement from the particular to the general. This movement is also one that critics associate with other aspects of Forster's text. The last word goes to L. P. Hartley, who manages to summarise the impact of the text while also acknowledging the lack of completion that attends any such overview of so complex and layered a work.

■ *A Passage to India* is a disturbing, uncomfortable book. Its surface is so delicately and finely wrought that it pricks us at a thousand points. There is no emotional repose or security about it; it is forever puncturing our complacence, it is a bed of thorns. The humour, irony and satire that awake the attention and delight the mind on every page all leave their sting. We cannot escape to the past or the future, because Mr. Forster's method does not encourage the growth of these accretions in the mind; he pins us down to the present moment, the discontent and pain of which cannot be allayed by reference to what has been or what will be. The action of the book is not fused by a continuous impulse; it is a series of intense isolated moments. To overstate the case very much, the characters seem with each fresh sensation to begin their lives again. And that perhaps is why no general aspect or outline of Mr. Forster's is so satisfactory as its details.[45] □

CHAPTER TWO

'For Want of a Smile an Empire is to be Lost': Forster's Liberal Humanism

THE ESSAYS that comprise this chapter take as their starting point 'the values of a tradition and an ideology of which Forster has become a sort of secular saint: liberal humanism'.[1] Frequently used as a derogatory term, liberal humanism has been subject to a constant, necessary and often illuminating critique during the years following the Second World War.[2] The ideology and tradition out of which it emerges is said to be predicated upon what can at best be described as a naive understanding of power and subjectivity (and the relations between them) or, less generously, a deliberate refusal to take into account deterministic structures and forces. Along with its emphasis on the individual rather than social, political and cultural formations, the primary difficulty with liberal-humanist beliefs stems, for Marxist, feminist and post-colonial critics, not simply from its idealism but also its universalising impulse and apparent ahistoricism. Yet, as Tony Davies argues, '[t]he relationship between humanism and anti-humanism should not be seen as one of pure negation or hostility' since even those devoted to anti-humanist politics harbour a 'hidden affinity with what they deny: they generally serve openly humanist ends of intellectual clarity and emancipation, articulated around a recognisable ethic of human capacity and need'.[3] The essays included in this Guide would appear to bear out this point. The difference in outlook between the work of critics in this chapter and later accounts of Forster's work that are informed by feminist and post-colonial studies is not as great as one might assume.

Although Forster's early critics appear, in places, to echo the attitudes and sentiments they uncover in his work, they also demonstrate an awareness that Forster's liberal humanism is itself far from uncritical or unselfconscious.[4] F. R. Leavis, Lionel Trilling and Malcolm Bradbury all consider the various ways in which Forster himself interrogates and problematises the liberal-humanist agenda in *A Passage to India*. They

27

produce different readings of a text that, as John Colmer argues, 'makes no simple statements about friendship or political rule in India, but rather communicates a pattern of experience that bears a homologous relationship to the internal contradictions of liberalism and of British Imperialism, to the high promise of each and their disappointing failures'.[5] The identification and interpretation of such 'patterns' as they feature in *A Passage to India* and the ways in which they relate to Forster's own liberal humanism are central to this chapter.

As closely identified with the liberal humanist tradition as Forster, the work of F. R. Leavis provides a useful way into the debate about Forster's cultural allegiances and, indeed, his place within culture. Originally published in 1938, Leavis's essay on Forster was reprinted in *The Common Pursuit* in 1952. For Leavis, Forster's liberal humanism is extremely self-reflexive:

■ Pre-eminently a novelist of civilized personal relations, he has at the same time a radical dissatisfaction with civilization – with the finest civilization of personal intercourse that he knows; a radical dissatisfaction that prompts references to D. H. Lawrence rather than to Jane Austen.[6] □

This fleeting reference to Lawrence is supplanted at a later point when the attempt to identify 'the particular milieu and the phase of English culture with which Mr. Forster's work is associated'[7] leads Leavis to Bloomsbury. By seeking to place Forster within a specific literary and cultural tradition – a tradition that, in this instance, includes Jane Austen and George Meredith – Leavis hopes to discover 'the extent to which, highly individual as it is', Forster's work, 'in its virtues and limitations', can be said to be 'representative' of the culture to which it owes so much.[8] The degree to which Forster voices a collective sense of the failure of liberal humanism, then, is the main question Leavis addresses in his essay. Although he argues that both *Howards End* and *A Passage to India* stage versions of liberal-humanist crisis, Leavis disagrees with the solutions and resolutions to that crisis that the texts also promote. Acknowledging Forster's capacity to articulate doubts about the liberal-humanist project, Leavis maintains that, notwithstanding its problems, liberal humanism can adapt to contemporary reality. Since, for Leavis at least, the reality in question was the rise of Nazism and the possibility of a Second World War, such faith in liberal humanism can be understood as both optimistic and unrealistic.

Leavis begins his assessment of Forster by commenting on 'the oddly limited and uncertain quality of his distinction – his real and very fine distinction'.[9] He argues that Forster's work is marked by an extreme division between 'maturity and immaturity, the fine and the crude'.[10] When adopting the comic as his principal mode, Forster shows himself to be a 'born novelist', but his simultaneous attempts to make 'a poetic communication about life'[11] seriously undermine this achievement. Set beside Meredith and especially Henry James, Forster looks 'trivial' or 'unmistakably minor'.[12] This is not only because his 'radical dissatisfaction with civilization' leads him to stray beyond comedy but because it manifests itself in a 'preoccupation with sincerity', or 'preoccupation with emotional vitality, with the problem of living truly and freshly from a centre'.[13] Such dissatisfaction 'leads him, at any rate in intention, outside the limits of consciousness that his comedy, in so far as we can separate it off, might seem to involve – the limits, roughly, that it is Jane Austen's distinction to have kept'.[14]

Although Leavis praises Forster's 'characteristic comedy, with its light, sedate and rather spinsterly poise',[15] his equally 'spinsterly touch'[16] fails adequately to achieve the 'poetic communication about life' for which it also strives. Since it lacks the 'complex ironic pattern', 'startling psychological insight' and 'knowledge of passion' associated with James, Leavis concludes that 'Forster's art has to be recognized as only too unmistakably minor'.[17] Leavis does, however, concede that 'Forster's "poetic" intention is genuine and radical', even if his 'surprising immaturity'[18] (an immaturity that leads Leavis to identify Forster with Rickie, the central character in *The Longest Journey*), severely compromises and limits his art. Forster only begins to grow up, for Leavis, with the publication of *Howards End*. Following his accounts of Forster's early novels it is to this text and thence *A Passage to India* that Leavis turns his attention:

■ *Howards End* (1910), the latest of the pre-war novels and the most ambitious, is, while offering again a fulness and immediacy of experience, more mature in the sense that it is free of the auto-biographical (a matter, not of where the material comes from, but of its relation to the author as it stands in the novel) and is at any rate fairly obviously the work of an older man. Yet it exhibits crudity of a kind to shock and distress the reader as Mr Forster hasn't shocked or distressed him before.

The main theme of the novel concerns the contrasted Schlegels and Wilcoxes. The Schlegels represent the humane liberal culture, the fine civilization of cultivated personal intercourse, that Mr Forster himself represents; they are the people for whom and in whom English literature (shall we say? though the Schlegels are especially musical) exists. The Wilcoxes have built the Empire; they represent the 'short-haired executive type' – obtuse, egotistic, unscrupulous, cowards spiritually, self-deceiving, successful. They are shown – shown up, one might say – as having hardly a redeeming characteristic, except that they are successful. Yet Margaret, the elder of the Schlegel sisters and the more mature intelligence, marries Mr Wilcox, the head of the clan; does it coolly, with open eyes, and we are meant to sympathize and approve. The novelist's attitude is quite unambiguous: as a result of the marriage, which is Margaret's active choice, Helen, who in obeying flightily her generous impulses has come to disaster, is saved and the book closes serenely on the promise of a happy future. Nothing in the exhibition of Margaret's or Henry Wilcox's character makes the marriage credible or acceptable; even if we were to seize for motivation on the hint of a panicky flight from spinsterhood in the already old-maidish Margaret, it might go a little way to explain her marrying such a man, but it wouldn't in the least account for the view of the affair the novelist expects us to take. We are driven to protest, not so much against the unreality in itself, as against the perversity of intention it expresses: the effect is of a kind of *trahison des clercs* [the treason of intellectuals, the entry of academics into politics].[19] □

At the text's insistence, Leavis identifies the two families in *Howards End* – the Wilcoxes and the Schlegels – with the forces of capitalism and empire, art and culture respectively. He goes further, though, by aligning Forster himself with the Schlegels.[20] Both the author and his characters come, for Leavis, to stand as representatives of 'the humane liberal culture, the fine civilization of cultivated personal intercourse'. Revealing his own investment in the liberal tradition that is embodied in both Forster and his primary characters, Leavis suggests that the Schlegels are 'the people for whom and in whom English literature [. . .] exists'. They not only represent the cultured, educated and enlightened readership that Leavis imagines for Forster but also come, in the eyes of this critic, to embody literary value itself. Granted a privileged status by Leavis, the Schlegels are the chief source of his subsequent interest in the text. He proceeds with his analysis by tracing their progress and, by implication, the fate of the values they represent, throughout the course of the novel.

Given the claims he makes for the Schlegel sisters, it is not surprising that Leavis is somewhat perplexed by their fate. He has much less to say about the wayward Helen, who transgresses class and sexual barriers, than about Margaret's apparently compromising union with the family of empire-builders. Initially, he speculates that Margaret's motivation for marriage resides in 'her panicky flight from spinsterhood', but this proves to be an unsatisfactory explanation. Discounting Margaret's anxieties about spinsterhood as the grounds for her marriage, Leavis goes on to identify the crisis of *Howards End* with his other spinster figure – Forster himself: the marriage of Margaret and Henry, the coupling of the culture and capital, signals Forster's own sense of the inadequacy of the liberal-humanist position:

■ In Margaret the author expresses his sense of the inadequacy of the culture she stands for – its lack of relation to the forces shaping the world and its practical impotence. Its weaknesses, dependent as it is on an economic security it cannot provide, are embodied in the quixotic Helen, who, acting uncompromisingly on her standards, brings nothing but disaster on herself and the objects of her concern. The novelist's intention in making Margaret marry Mr Wilcox is not, after all, obscure. One can only comment that in letting his intention satisfy itself so, he unintentionally makes his cause look even more desperate than it need: intelligence and sensitiveness such as Howards End at its finest represents need not be so frustrated by innocence and inexperience as the unrealities of the book suggest. For 'unreality' is the word: the business of Margaret and Henry Wilcox is essentially as unrealized as the business of Helen and the insurance clerk, Leonard Bast – who, with his Jacky, is clearly a mere external grasping at something that lies outside the author's first-hand experience.[21] □

Although Leavis draws attention to the condition of economic dependency in which the Schlegels exist, he finds that the resolution to such a condition, as supplied by Forster, when he brings about the union of Margaret and Henry, represents an unnecessary compromise. In *Howards End* the marriage, along with the damaging effects of 'innocence and inexperience', suggest that liberal humanism is less able to adapt to reality than *in reality* it has proven to be. Leavis's criticism conveys the sense that the writer's novelistic resolutions to the problems that beset liberal humanism are inadequate. He does concede, however, that the very articulation of those problems, albeit in an exaggerated form, is crucial to the novel and the values it seeks to uphold.

In addition to questioning the representation of liberal humanism as it is embodied in Margaret, Leavis also highlights what he sees as Forster's unrealistic portrayal of the Wilcoxes. As representatives of 'action and practice' the Wilcoxes are unconvincing:

■ [W]ith merely Mr Forster's Wilcoxes to represent action and practice as against the culture and the inner life of the Schlegels there could hardly have been civilization. Of course, that an intellectual in the twentieth century should pick on the Wilcox type for the part is natural enough; writing half-a-century earlier Mr Forster would have picked on something different. But the fact remains that the Wilcoxes are not what he takes them to be, and he has not seen his problem rightly: his view of it is far too external and unsubtle. [. . .] Along with the concern about the practical insignificance of the Schlegels' culture goes a turning of the mind towards the question of ultimate sanctions. Where lie – or should lie – the real sources of strength, the springs of vitality, of this humane and liberal culture, which, the more it aspires to come to terms with 'civilization' in order to escape its sense of impotence, needs the more obviously to find its life, strength, and authority elsewhere?[22] □

If Leavis is unconvinced by Forster's portrayal of empire-builders and the liberal-humanist crisis in *Howards End*, he has fewer reservations about *A Passage to India*. Adopting the same critical approach to this novel as for *Howards End*, Leavis first seeks the author in the text and identifies him with Fielding. Yet, not only does Fielding, like Margaret, epitomise liberal-humanist values, he also supplies the reader with what she lacks. The very 'practical' qualities that Margaret's marriage to Henry provides are already present in Fielding. Unlike his female precursor, Fielding need not look to outside sources for support. Combining the values of Margaret and capabilities of Henry, Fielding is a more autonomous and also more convincing figure than Margaret:

■ Fielding, the central figure in the book, who is clearly very close to the author, represents in a maturer way what the Schlegels represented: what may still be called liberal culture – humanity, disinterestedness, tolerance and free intelligence, unassociated with dogma or religion or any very determinate set of traditional forms. He might indeed (if we leave out all that Howards End stood for) be said to represent what was intended by Margaret's marrying Henry Wilcox, for he is level-headed and practical and qualified in the ways of the world. His agnosticism is explicit. Asked '"Is it correct that most are atheists in England now?"' he replies: '"The educated thoughtful people? I should say so, though they don't like the name. The truth is that the West doesn't bother much over belief and disbelief in these days. Fifty years ago, or even when you and I were young, much more fuss was made"' (p. 124).
Nevertheless, though Fielding doesn't share it, the kind of pre-occupation he so easily passes by has its place in *A Passage to India* as in Mr Forster's other novels, and again (though there is no longer the early crudity) its appearances are accompanied by something unsatis-factory in the novelist's art, a curious lack of grasp. [. . .] Mrs Moore, as a matter of fact, is in the first part of the book an ordinary character, but she becomes, after her death, a vague pervasive suggestion of mystery. It is true that it is she who has the experience in the cave – the experience that concentrates the depressed ethos of the book – and the echo 'undermine[s] her hold on life', (p. 160) but the effect should be to associate her with the reverse of the kind of mysteriousness that after her death is made to invest her name. For she and the odd boy Ralph ('"[b]orn of too old a mother"' [p. 304]) are used as means of

recognizing possibilities that lie outside Fielding's philosophy – though he is open-minded. There is, too, Ralph's sister Stella, whom Fielding marries:

> 'She has ideas I don't share – indeed, when I'm away from her I think them ridiculous. When I'm with her, I suppose because I'm fond of her, I feel different, I feel half dead and half blind. My wife's after something. You and I and Miss Quested are, roughly speaking, not after anything. We jog on as decently as we can . . .'. (p.312)[23] □

Notwithstanding his appreciation of Fielding, Leavis is less than convinced by the mystical or spiritual element of *A Passage to India*. Here, it appears that the challenge to Fielding's secular world view comes in the less than adequate shape of Mrs Moore and her experiences in the Cave. Forster's indeterminacy, at this point, renders the religious challenge to liberal humanism too oblique for Leavis. Leavis, it appears, remains unconvinced by religious arguments because there are none:

■ Our objection is that it's all too easy. It amounts to little more than saying, 'There may be something in it', but it has the effect of taking itself for a good deal more. The very poise of Mr Forster's art has something equivocal about it – it seems to be conditioned by its not knowing what kind of poise it is. The account of the Krishna ceremony, for instance, which is a characteristic piece by the sensitive, sympathetic, and whimsically ironic Mr Forster, slides nevertheless into place in the general effect – there are more things in heaven and earth, Horatio – that claims a proper impersonality. [. . .][24] □

Following his analysis of *A Passage to India*, Leavis tries to locate the source of his general dissatisfaction with Forster. The element that enables him, at earlier points in his essay, to identify Forster with particular characters and in turn himself to identify with the values they represent, proves eventually to be the source of Leavis's difficulty. For it is Forster's personality that compromises his work. In the Modernist context the manifestation of such 'personality' is problematic, as indeed it is, for critics like Leavis, who elsewhere argues for 'detachment'. However, in this instance, the emergence of Forster's personality within his novels enables Leavis to reject his initial hypothesis that the writer's weaknesses might reflect those of the culture out of which he speaks:

■ Mr Forster's style is personal in the sense that it keeps us very much aware of the personality of the writer, so that even where actions, events and the experiences of characters are supposed to be speaking for themselves the turn of phrase and tone of voice bring the presenter and commentator into the foreground. Mr Forster's felicities and his charm, then, involve limitations. Even where he is not betrayed into lapses [. . .] his habit doesn't favour the impersonality, the presentment of themes and experiences as things standing there in themselves, that would be necessary for convincing success at the level of his highest intention. [. . .] When one has recognized the interest and value his work has as representing liberal culture in the early years of the twentieth century, there is perhaps a temptation to see the weaknesses too simply as representative. That that culture has of its very nature grave weaknesses Mr Forster's work itself constitutes an explicit recognition. But it seems worth while insisting at this point on the measure in which Mr Forster's weaknesses are personal ones, qualifying the gifts that have earned him (I believe) a lasting place in English literature. He seems then, for one so perceptive and sensitive, extraordinarily lacking in force, or robustness, of intelligence; it is, perhaps, a general lack of vitality. The deficiencies of his novels must be correlated with the weakness so apparent in his critical and journalistic writings – *Aspects of the Novel, Abinger Harvest* – the weakness that makes them representative in so disconcerting a way. They are disconcerting because they exhibit a lively critical mind accepting, it seems, uncritically the very inferior social-intellectual milieu in which it has developed.[25] □

As he shifts his attention away from personality and towards the culture (or, perhaps, for this critic, sub-culture) that shapes the writer, Leavis points the finger specifically at Bloomsbury. Forster's 'association' with this very loose and eclectic artistic and intellectual group leads Leavis to identify his work, and even its weaknesses, with the Bloomsbury aesthetic.

■ Forster, we know, has been associated with Bloomsbury – the Bloomsbury which (to confine ourselves to one name) produced Lytton Strachey and took him for a great writer. And these writings of Mr Forster's are, in their amiable way, Bloomsbury. They are Bloomsbury in the valuations they accept (in spite of the showings of real critical perception), in the assumptions they innocently express, and in prevailing ethos.

It might, of course, be said that it is just the weakness of liberal culture – 'bourgeois', the Marxist would say – that is manifested by Bloomsbury (which certainly had claims to some kind of representative status). But there seems no need to deal directly with such a proposition here, or to discuss at any length what significance shall be given to the terms 'liberal' and 'culture'. The necessary point is made by insisting that the weaknesses of Mr Forster's work and of Bloomsbury are placed as such by standards implicit in what is best in that work. That those standards are not complete in themselves or securely based or sufficiently guaranteed by contemporary civilization there is no need to dispute: the recognition has been an essential part of the creative impulse in Mr Forster. . . . [He] represent[s] . . . the finer consciousness of our time, the humane tradition as it emerges from a period of 'bourgeois' security, divorced from dogma and left by social change, the breakdown of traditional forms and the loss of sanctions embarrassingly 'in the air'; no longer serenely confident or self-sufficient, but conscious of being not less than before the custodian of something essential. . . . And it seems to me plain that this tradition really is, for all its weakness, the indispensable transmitter of something that humanity cannot afford to lose.

These rather commonplace observations seemed worth making because of the current fashion of using 'liberal' largely and loosely as a term of derogation: too much is too lightly dismissed with it. To enforce this remark it seems to me enough to point to *A Passage to India* – and it will be an occasion for ensuring that I shall not, in effect, have done Mr Forster a major critical injustice. For I have been assuming, tacitly, a general agreement that *A Passage to India*, all criticisms made, is a classic: not only a most significant document of our age, but a truly memorable work of literature. And that there is point in calling it a classic of the liberal spirit will, I suppose, be granted fairly readily, for the appropriateness of the adjective is obvious. In its touch upon racial and cultural problems, its treatment of personal relations, and in prevailing ethos the book is an expression, undeniably, of the liberal tradition; it has, as such, its fineness, its strength and its impressiveness; and it makes the achievement, the humane, decent and rational – the 'civilized' – habit, of that tradition appear the invaluable thing it is.[26] □

Despite his reservations about the value and status of Bloomsbury, Leavis finally embraces the liberal-humanist rhetoric at the close of his essay. In *E.M. Forster: A Study*, the American critic Lionel Trilling is no less convinced, in 1944, of the value of liberal humanism than Leavis had been before him.[27] Following Leavis, Trilling is quick to associate liberal humanism with Forster but while Leavis's commentary tends towards a somewhat general account of Forster's background, Trilling is more attuned to the specificities of the political context in which Forster worked. He begins his essay with a sketch of Forster's Indian travels and those early writings that 'depict the comic, sad confusion of a nation torn between two cultures'.[28] Alongside Forster's Indian experiences Trilling sets his wartime service in Egypt, which, as the critic notes, 'gave him not only the material for two books and many essays, but also a firm position on the Imperial question'.[29] Trilling continues his narrative of Forster's life and work by tracing his postwar journalism, his editorship of 'the *Daily Herald*, a Labour paper to whose literary page many well-known writers of liberal leanings contributed reviews'.[30] Trilling's account of Forster's experiences and his writings seems as much designed to highlight his first-hand experience of India and imperial rule (in Egypt) as to establish his liberal-humanist credentials. The latter, however, seem more cogently expressed in Forster's contributions to debates relating to British cultural life, rather than in his interventions into the history and politics of empire.

■ The political pieces are suffused with disillusionment about the war, a foreboding that a new war is imminent, a hatred of the stupidities of class rule. They pretend neither to originality of sentiment nor to practical perspicacity; they express, sometimes with anger, sometimes with bitterness, sometimes only with a kind of salutary irritation and disgust, the old emotions – the 19th century emotions, we almost feel, and we salute their directness – of a rational democrat confronting foolishness and pretence.[31] □

For Trilling, then, Forster's moral and ethical codes are the product of the Victorian era although no less admirable for being so. Yet, despite his apparent attention to the details of Forster's background, Trilling's assessment of his work eventually moves beyond such contexts to an appreciation of what is universal about *A Passage to India*. (Such a movement, from the specific cultural and political contexts in which Forster worked, to a general statement concerning the value of his writing, characterises all of the essays included in this chapter.)

In his analysis of *A Passage to India*, Trilling is first struck by the fact that, while it accounts for the book's popularity and its contentiousness, 'the public, political nature of the book is not extraneous; it inheres in the novel's very shape and texture'.[32] His analysis of the text itself begins with an assessment of this 'public, political quality'.[33] This Trilling relates to both Forster's control of his text and the reader's responses:

■ By many standards of criticism, this public, political quality works for good. *A Passage to India* is the most comfortable and even the most conventional of Forster's novels. It is under the control not only of the author's insight; a huge, hulking physical fact which he is not alone in seeing, requiring that the author submit to its veto-power. Consequently, this is the least surprising of Forster's novels, the least capricious and, indeed, the least personal. It quickly establishes the pattern for our emotions and keeps to it. We are at once taught to withhold our sympathies from the English officials, to give them to Mrs. Moore and to the 'renegade' Fielding, to regard Adela Quested with remote interest and Aziz and his Indian friends with affectionate understanding.

Within this pattern we have, to be sure, all the quick, subtle mod-ifications, the sudden strictnesses or relentings of judgment which are the best stuff of Forster's social imagination. But always the pattern remains public, simple and entirely easy to grasp. What distinguishes it from the patterns of similarly public and political novels is the rigor of its objectivity; it deals with unjust, hysterical emotion and it leads us, not to intense emotions about justice, but to cool poise and judg-ment – if we do not relent in our contempt for Ronny, we are at least forced to be aware that he is capable of noble, if stupid, feelings; the English girl who has the hallucination of an attempted rape by a native has engaged our sympathy by her rather dull decency; we are permitted no easy response to the benign Mrs. Moore, or to Fielding, who stands out against his own people, or to the native physician who is wrongly accused. This restraint of our emotions is an important element in the book's greatness.[34] □

Emphasising the value of objectivity and restraint, particularly in a text that deals with such a contentious subject, Trilling appears to congratu-late both Forster and his readership for their rational approach to the text. That the responses of the reader owe much to the manipulations of the author is one source of Trilling's admiration. Curiously, it appears that in this context Forster's lack of knowledge concerning Indian religion and culture can be turned to his advantage:

■ With the public nature of the story goes a chastened and somewhat more public style than is usual with Forster, and a less arbitrary manner. Forster does not abandon his right to intrude into the novel, but his manner of intrusion is more circumspect than ever before. Perhaps this is because here, far less than in the English and Italian stories, he is in possession of truth; the Indian gods are not his gods, they are not genial and comprehensible. So far as the old Mediterranean deities of wise impulse and loving intelligence can go in India, Forster is at home; he thinks they can go far but not all the way, and a certain retraction of the intimacy of his style reflects his uncertainty. The acts of imagination by which Forster conveys the sense of the Indian gods are truly wonderful; they are, nevertheless, the acts of imagination not of a master of the truth but of an intelligent neophyte, still baffled.[35] □

Although he sees the benefits that arise from the differences between Forster's background and the culture and country he seeks to represent, Trilling is still mindful of the politics of representation when it comes to the question of 'verisimilitude':

■ So the public nature of the novel cannot be said to work wholly for good. For the first time Forster has put himself to the test of verisimilitude. Is this the truth about India? Is this the way the English act? – always? sometimes? never? Are Indians like this? – all of them? some of them? Why so many Moslems and so few Hindus? Why so much Hindu religion and so little Moslem? And then, finally, the disintegrating question, What is to be done?[36] □

Instead of leading, as one might expect, into a direct exploration of the politics of representation in *A Passage to India*, or an analysis of the political impact of fiction, these questions are answered by a more limited discussion of character in the text. Here, Trilling's earlier praise of Forster's detachment seems to be called into question (at this juncture Trilling takes his cue from some of the reviewers who feature in the previous chapter). He resolves the apparent contradiction (between a detached and simultaneously partisan approach) by arguing that Forster's anger is productive and, quite probably, justified:

■ Forster's gallery of English officials has of course been disputed in England; there have been many to say that the English are not like that. Even without knowledge we must suppose that the Indian Civil Service has its quota of decent, devoted and humble officials. But if Forster's portraits are perhaps angry exaggerations, anger can be illuminating – the English of Forster's Chandrapore are the limits toward which the English in India must approach, for Lord Acton was right, power does corrupt, absolute power does corrupt absolutely.

As for the representation of the Indians, that too can be judged here only on *a priori* grounds. Although the Indians are conceived in sympathy and affection, they are conceived with these emotions alone, and although all of them have charm, none of them has dignity; they touch our hearts but they never impress us. Once, at his vindication feast, Aziz is represented as 'full of civilization . . . complete, dignified, rather hard' and, for the first time, Fielding treats him 'with diffidence' (p. 251), but this only serves to remind us how lacking in dignity Aziz usually is. Very possibly this is the effect that Indians make upon even sensitive Westerners; [. . .] generations of subjection can diminish the habit of dignity and teach grown men the strategy of the little child.

These are not matters that we can settle; that they should have arisen at all is no doubt a fault of the novel. Quite apart from the fact that questions of verisimilitude diminish illusion, they indicate a certain inadequacy in the conception of the story. To represent the official English as so unremittingly bad and the Indians as so unremittingly feeble is to prevent the story from being sufficiently worked out in terms of the characters; the characters, that is, are *in* the events, the events are not in them: we want a larger Englishman than Fielding, a weightier Indian than Aziz.[37] □

Touching reluctantly on the politics of Forster's text, Trilling speculates that the lack of 'dignity' that characterises the Indians in *A Passage to India* might well relate to the condition of subjection in which they find themselves. This possibility does not lessen Trilling's belief that Forster's characters – both English and Indian – are overwhelmed by the overall concerns of the text in which they feature. The brief speculations on the relationship between subjectivity and power, which the novel compels Trilling to make, seem to 'diminish illusion' and therefore compromise the text's realism. The possibility that such an engagement with the question of subjugated identities, which arises directly from Forster's depiction of particular characters, might constitute one of the text's more radical potentials is disregarded by Trilling. However, in this instance, as Trilling himself admits, the critic occupies a paradoxical position in relation to the text he scrutinises. Even though he insists upon 'realism' as the chief criterion by which to assess the text, he lacks first-hand experience of British rule in India and is therefore in no position to judge the accuracy of Forster's representations. Disregarding this difficulty, Trilling maintains that Forster's success depends upon the fact that the reader does not even question his representations: the aptly named 'illusion' of realism remains unbroken.

In his discussion of realism and character in *A Passage to India* Trilling suggests 'a severe imbalance in the relation of plot to story' in the text. Adopting Forster's own definitions of plot ('a narrative of events, the emphasis falling on causality') and story ('a narrative of events arranged in their time-sequence'),[38] he has the following to say:

■ The relation of the characters to the events [. . .] is the result of a severe imbalance in the relation of plot to story. Plot and story in this novel are not coextensive as they are in all Forster's other novels. The plot is precise, hard, crystallized and far simpler than any Forster has previously conceived. The story is beneath and above the plot and continues beyond it in time. It is, to be sure, created by the plot, it is the plot's manifold reverberation, but it is greater than the plot and contains it. The plot is as decisive as a judicial opinion; the story is an impulse, a tendency, a perception. The suspension of plot in the large circumambient sphere of story, the expansion of the story from the centre of plot, requires some of the subtlest manipulation that any novel has ever had. This relation of plot and story tells us that we are dealing with a political novel of an unusual kind. The characters are of sufficient size for the plot; they are not large enough for the story – and that indeed is the point of the story. [. . .][39] □

Although he draws upon *Aspects of the Novel* (1927) for his conceptualisations of plot and story, Trilling does not include in his analysis Forster's own critical comments on character:

■ The novelist [. . .] makes up a number of word-masses roughly describing himself [. . .] gives them names and sex, assigns them plausible gestures, and causes them to speak by the use of inverted commas, and perhaps to behave consistently. These word-masses are his characters.[40] □

In the following extract Trilling disregards his initial doubts and uncertainties concerning Forster's representations and his own ability to judge them. His analysis becomes more assured as he moves away from the specificity of the text and its politics. For Trilling, the text has more general implications and applications. These lead him away from his discussion of Anglo-Indians and on to what is older and more familiar ground, 'the theme of separateness, of fences and barriers'. This theme Trilling traces in turn to the Christian tradition.

■ Of the Anglo-Indian society it is perhaps enough to say that, 'more than it can hope to do in England', it lives by the beliefs of the English public school. It is arrogant, ignorant, insensitive – intelligent natives estimate that a year in India makes the pleasantest Englishman rude. And of all the English it is the women who insist most strongly on their superiority, who are the rawest and crudest in their manner. The men have a certain rough liking for the men of the subject race [. . .]. But the women, unchecked by any professional necessity or pride, think wholly in terms of the most elementary social prestige and Turton's wife lives for nothing else. [. . .] This is the result of the undeveloped heart. *A Passage to India* is not a radical novel; its data were gathered in 1912 and 1922, before the full spate of Indian nationalism; it is not concerned to show that the English should not be in India at all. Indeed, not until the end of the book is the question of the expulsion of the English mentioned, and the novel proceeds on an imperialistic premise – ironically, for it is not actually Forster's own – its chief point being that by reason of the undeveloped heart the English have thrown away the possibility of holding India. For want of a smile an Empire is to be lost. Not even justice is enough. '"Indians know whether they are liked or not"', Fielding says, '"they cannot be fooled here. Justice never satisfies them, and that is why the British Empire rests on sand"' (p.258). Mrs. Moore listens to Ronny defending the British attitude; 'his words without his voice might have impressed her, but when she heard the self-satisfied lilt of them, when she saw the mouth moving so complacently and competently beneath the little red nose, she felt, quite illogically, that this was not the last word on India. One touch of regret – not the canny substitute but the true regret from the heart – would have made him a different man, and the British Empire a different institution' (p.70).

Justice is not enough then, but in the end neither are liking and goodwill enough. For although Fielding and Aziz reach out to each other in friendship, a thousand little tricks of speech, a thousand different assumptions and different tempi keep them apart. They do not understand each other's *amounts* of emotion, let alone kinds of emotion. '"Your emotions never seem in proportion to their objects, Aziz"', Fielding says, and Aziz answers, '"Is emotion a sack of potatoes, so much the pound, to be measured out?"' (p.253).

The theme of separateness, of fences and barriers, the old theme of the Pauline epistles, which runs through all Forster's novels, is, in *A Passage to India*, hugely expanded and everywhere dominant. The separation of race from race, sex from sex, culture from culture, even of man from himself, is what underlies every relationship. The separation of the English from the Indians is merely the most dramatic of the chasms in this novel. Hindu and Moslem cannot really approach each other; Aziz, speaking in all friendliness to Mr. Das, the Magistrate, wishes that Hindus did not remind him of cow-dung and the Hindu Mr. Das thinks, '"Some Moslems are very violent"' – 'Between people of distant climes there is always the possibility of romance, but the various branches of Indians know too much about each other to surmount the unknowable easily' (pp.264–65). Adela and Ronny cannot meet in sexuality, and when, after the trial, Adela and Fielding meet in an idea, 'a friendliness, as of dwarfs shaking hands, was in the air' (p.262). Fielding, when he marries Mrs. Moore's daughter Stella, will soon find himself apart from his young wife. And Mrs. Moore is separated from her son, from all people, from God, from the universe.

This sense of separateness broods over the book, pervasive, symbolic – at the end the very earth requires, and the sky approves, the parting of Aziz and Fielding – and perhaps accounts for the remoteness of the characters: they are so far from each other that they cannot reach us. But the isolation is not merely adumbrated; in certain of its aspects it is very precisely analysed and some of the most brilliant and virtuoso parts of the novel are devoted to the delineation of Aziz and his friends, to the investigation of the cultural differences that keep Indian and Englishman apart.[41] □

Trilling confines his own investigation of 'the cultural differences that keep Indian and Englishman apart' to a restatement of an earlier point concerning the representation of Aziz. In his view, Forster's portrait of Aziz owes a great deal to a previous representation of 'unEnglishness', namely, the portrait of Italian masculinity one finds in *Where Angels Fear to Tread*.

■ The mould for Aziz is Gino Carella of the first novel. It is the mould of unEnglishness, that is to say, of volatility, tenderness, sensibility, a hint of cruelty, much warmth, a love of pathos, the desire to please even at the cost of insincerity. Like Gino's, Aziz's nature is in many ways childlike, in many ways mature: it is mature in its acceptance of child-like inconsistency. Although eager to measure up to English standards of puritan rectitude, Aziz lives closer to the literal facts of his emotions; for good or bad, he is more human. He, like his friends, is not prompt, not efficient, not neat, not really convinced of Western ideas even in science – when he retires to a native state he slips back to mix a little magic with his medicine – and he, like them, is aware of his faults. He is hyper-sensitive, imagining slights even when there are none because there have actually been so many; he is full of humility and full of contempt and desperately wants to be liked. He is not heroic but his heroes are the great chivalrous emperors, Babur and Alamgir. In short, Aziz is a member of a subject race. A rising nationalism in India may by now have thrust him aside in favour of a more militant type; but we can be sure that if the new type has repudiated Aziz's emotional contradictions it has not resolved them.[42] □

This suggests, perhaps unfairly, that Forster's notion of 'cultural difference' is unsophisticated or undelineated and that forms of otherness only signify for him in their relation to Englishness. Yet, Trilling's earlier allusion to Forster's 'Notes on the English Character' (1920), indicates the critic's awareness of the author's complex attitude towards Englishness itself. In Forster's view, the 'undeveloped heart' that is nurtured by the English middle classes and their public schools prevents comprehension of 'a world of whose richness and subtlety they [English males] have no conception' and is 'largely responsible for the difficulties, of Englishmen abroad'.[43]

Of greater significance to Trilling than Forster's depiction of a type of 'unEnglishness', is the question of Mrs Moore and Hinduism:

■ Aziz and his friends are Moslems, and with Moslems of the business and professional class the plot of the novel deals almost entirely. But the story is suffused with Hinduism. It is Mrs. Moore who carries the Hindu theme; it is Mrs. Moore, indeed, who is the story. The theme is first introduced by Mrs. Moore observing a wasp. [. . .] This wasp is to recur in Professor Godbole's consciousness when he has left Chandrapore and taken service as director of education in a Hindu native state. He stands, his school quite forgotten – turned into a granary, indeed – and celebrates the birth of Krishna in the great religious festival that dominates the third part of the novel. The wasp is mixed up in his mind – he does not know how it got there in the first place, nor do we – with a recollection of Mrs. Moore. [. . .] The presence of the wasp, first in Mrs. Moore's consciousness, then in Godbole's, Mrs. Moore's acceptance of the wasp, Godbole's acceptance of Mrs. Moore – in some symbolic fashion, this is the thread of the story of the novel as distinguished from its plot. For the story is essentially concerned with Mrs. Moore's discovery that Christianity is not adequate. In a quiet way, Mrs. Moore is a religious woman; at any rate, as she has grown older she has found it 'increasingly difficult to avoid' mentioning God's name 'as the greatest she knew'. Yet in India God's name becomes less and less efficacious – 'outside the arch there seemed always another arch, beyond the remotest echo a silence' (p. 71).

And so, unwittingly, Mrs. Moore has moved closer and closer to Indian ways of feeling. When Ronny and Adela go for an automobile ride with the Nawab Bahadur and the chauffeur swerves at something in the path and wrecks the car, Mrs. Moore, when she is told of the incident, remarks without thinking, '"A ghost!"' (p. 111). And a ghost it was, or so the Nawab believed, for he had run over and killed a drunken man at that spot nine years before. 'None of the English people knew of this, nor did the chauffeur; it was a racial secret communicable more by blood than by speech' (p. 113). This 'racial secret' has somehow been acquired by Mrs. Moore. And the movement away from European feeling continues: 'She felt increasingly (vision or nightmare?) that, though people are important, the relations between them are not, and that in particular too much fuss has been made over marriage; centuries of carnal embracement, yet man is no nearer to understanding man' (pp. 147–48). The occasion of her visit to the Marabar Caves is merely the climax of change, although a sufficiently terrible one.[44] □

Mrs Moore and her Indian experiences clearly carry a great deal of importance for Trilling and together make up the 'story' of *A Passage to India*. It is Mrs Moore's experience in the Marabar Caves that enables her to transcend her own systems of cultural and religious belief:

■ What so frightened Mrs. Moore in the cave was an echo. It is but one echo in a book which is contrived of echoes. Not merely does Adela Quested's delusion go in company with a disturbing echo in her head which only ceases when she masters her delusion, but the very texture of the story is a reticulation of echoes. Actions and speeches return, sometimes in a better, sometimes in a worse form, given back by the perplexing 'arch' (p. 71) of the Indian universe. [. . .] And of all the many echoes, the dominant one is the echo that booms through the Marabar cave.[45] □

The 'reticulation of echoes' in *A Passage to India* provides Trilling with a useful metaphor for the structure of Forster's text. While he derives some significance from Mrs Moore's echo, a sound whose reverberation signals the exhaustion of Christian beliefs, he feels less able to gauge the importance of Hinduism in the text. He states that, '[i]t is not easy to know what to make of the dominant Hinduism of the third section of the novel',[46] but is adamant that Forster cannot have meant Hinduism to represent a solution to the problem of imperialism. Like Leavis, Trilling sees the novel as articulating certain questions, rather than supplying answers. He understands these questions to relate to issues beyond the context in which they feature – that of imperial rule in India – and to assume universal significance.

■ Certainly it is not to be supposed that Forster finds in Hinduism an answer to the problem of India; and its dangers have been amply demonstrated in the case of Mrs. Moore herself. But here at least is the vision in which the arbitrary human barriers sink before the extinction of all things. [. . .] To such a pass has Christianity come, we can suppose Forster to be saying. We must suffer a vision even as dreadful as Mrs. Moore's if by it the separations can be wiped out. But meanwhile the separations exist and Aziz in an hysteria of affirmation declares to Fielding on their last ride that the British must go, even at the cost of internal strife, even if it means a Japanese conquest. Only with the British gone can he and Fielding be friends. Fielding offers friendship now: '"It's what I want. It's what you want"' (p. 316). But the horses, following the path the earth lays for them, swerve apart; earth and sky seem to say that the time for friendship has not come, and leave its possibility to events.

The disintegrating question, What, then, must be done? which many readers have raised is of course never answered or not answered in the language in which the question has been asked. The book simply involves the question in ultimates. This, obviously, is no answer; still, it defines the scope of a possible answer, and thus restates the question. For the answer can never again temporize, because the question, after it has been involved in the moods and visions of the story, turns out to be the most enormous question that has ever been asked, requiring an answer of enormous magnanimity. Great as the problem of India is, Forster's book is not about India alone; it is about all of human life.[47] □

Although Trilling's account of Forster's text initially promises a direct engagement with the politics of *A Passage to India* he, like Leavis, sidesteps this issue. For Leavis, the liberal-humanist crisis relates to its 'practical impotence' and its dependence upon capitalism. For Trilling, the imperial setting of *A Passage to India*, and the political context out of which it emerges, diminish in significance. As his account of the novel progresses, the specificity of the text gives way to a more general preoccupation with its thematics – at least, those that feed into more universal concerns. Thus, even the different kinds of division that operate in the text, between races, classes, genders, are subsumed under the less distinct heading of 'separateness'. Just how universal these concerns really are is obviously open to question, not least because of Trilling's emphasis on Mrs Moore's 'discovery that Christianity is not quite adequate', a point that is so vital to the 'story' of *A Passage to India*.

In her account of the way in which Western critics and readers have deciphered Forster's text, Sara Suleri draws attention to Trilling's work as an example of the 'liberal imagination'. This, she argues, enables critics like Trilling to 'legitimize a text like *A Passage to India* as a humanely liberal parable for imperialism'. It enables him 'to interpret the novel's depiction of Eastern action as a metaphor for the behaviour of the West. In other words, the only difference of India inheres in the fact that it is symbolic of something the western mind must learn about itself.'[48] Although this is a valid claim it should be noted that Trilling, like Leavis before him, does try to grapple with the specificity of Forster's text even if, in his final analysis, he retreats into a more familiar liberal mode.

In common with Leavis and Trilling, Malcolm Bradbury's contribution to the debate about Forster's liberal humanism – 'Two Passages to India: Forster as Victorian and Modern'[49] – begins with an attempt to place the writer within a particular political and cultural context. Writing in 1969, Bradbury maintains his distance from the dominant structuralist method of analysis through an invocation of Forster's liberal-humanist credentials. These are relayed in a language that owes much to Leavis and Trilling:

■ There are major writers whose work seems to us important as a contribution to the distinctive powers and dimensions of art; there are others whose work represents almost a personal appeal to value, and who therefore live – for certain of their readers, at least – with a singular force. There have not been many English novelists of our own time who have established with us the second function, but E. M. Forster is certainly one of them. He has served as an embodiment of the virtues he writes about; he has shown us their function and their destiny; he has left, for other writers and other men, a workable inheritance. Partly this is because he has always regarded art as a matter of intelligence as well as passion, honesty as well as imagination. In making such alliances he has given us a contemporary version of a once-familiar belief – that art can be a species of active virtue as well as a form of magic – and has thus sharply appealed to our sense of what man can be. Literary humanist qualities of this sort are not always easy to express today within the impersonal context of modern literary criticism – which tends, more and more, to ascribe virtue to structural performance within the text and to neglect what lies beyond. [. . .] Forster once told us that he belongs to 'the fag-end of Victorian liberalism' and the phrase is often taken with complete literalness and applied against him. As a result his intellectual and his literary destiny has been too readily linked with that strange death of liberal England which historians have dated around 1914, when the equation of economic individualism with social progress lost political force. Since it is easy to explain the exhaustion of political liberalism as a historical necessity, as the inevitable failure of a synthesis proven unworkable by the new social conditions of the second-stage industrial revolution, then it is also possible to see Forster's ideas and faith as historically superannuated, too. This view, indeed, has taken root – even though Forster recognises the ironies of the situation and works with them, even though he raises all the crucial questions about elevating social determinism above value; and we often overlook the fact that the liberalism he speaks for so obliquely has had a longer history as a moral conviction than as a political force, that it has as much to do with our idea of man and culture as with our political solutions, that it speaks for a recurrent need for the criticism of institutions and collectivities from the standpoint of the claims of human wholeness. But coupled with this there has been another distrust: distrust of the entire idea of art and culture as Forster suggests or expresses it.[50] □

Having suggested that Forster has been measured against his own yardstick, Bradbury places Forster's liberal-humanist ideology within the specific context of early twentieth-century political life but also points out that it predates the Modernist era. Existing before the specific manifestation of liberal humanism with which Forster is associated, the values to which Bradbury appeals also transcend the limited political use to which they have been put. Besides the political implications of Forster's liberal humanism, Bradbury goes on to locate another important source for a contemporary critical unease with Forster. This relates to the question of the redemptive value of art, a doctrine that arouses considerable suspicion. This doctrine, manifested in different ways, is the product not only of the Modernists but of the Victorians. Forster's own work, it seems, embodies both versions of this aesthetic appeal:

■ In this century critics have increasingly accepted modernist norms for the judgement of literature, even though, of course, many of our writers have not been modernists in the strict sense. Forster is a paradox here; he is, and he is not. There is in his work the appeal to art as transcendence, art as the one orderly product, a view that makes for modernism; and there is the view of art as a responsible power, a force for belief, a means of judgement, an impulse to spiritual control as well as spiritual curiosity. The point perhaps is that Forster is not, in the conventional sense, a modernist, but rather a central figure of the transition into modernism; and that is surely his interest, the force of his claim. He is, indeed, to a remarkable degree, the representative of two kinds of mind, two versions of literary possibility, and of the tensions of consciousness that exist between them. He stands at the beginning of the age of the new, speaking through it and against it. In this way his five novels – and particularly his last two – can be taken as reflecting the advantages of the humanist literary mind in an environment half hostile to it; they clearly and often painfully carry the stain of a direct encounter with new experience. Forster has been, by training and temperament, sufficiently the historian to see the irony: that culture itself is in history, that a humanist view of the arts as a way of sanely perceiving and evaluating is itself conditioned, for it has its own social environment and limits. So Forster is at once the spokesman for the transcendent symbol, the luminous wholeness of the work of art, out of time and in infinity, and for its obverse – the view that a proper part of art's responsibility is to know and live in the contingent world of history. [. . .] Of course, Forster's confession that he belongs to the 'fag-end of Victorian liberalism' does express a real inheritance; but that end is also the beginning of new forms of belief and of new literary postures and procedures. My point is that he emerges not as a conventionally modernist writer, but rather as a writer who has experienced, in a full way, the impact of what modernism means for us – a hope for transcendence, a sense of apocalypse, an *avant-garde* posture, a sense of detachment, a feeling that a new phase of history has emerged – while holding on (with tentative balance that turns often to the ironic mode) to much that modernism would affront.[51] □

For Bradbury, Forster's potential resides in his double or perhaps even multiple allegiance. He speaks through and against the Modernist age, and with traces of both the Victorian and Romantic heritage. As Bradbury argues, 'if Forster is indeed a Victorian liberal, as some of his critics charge, he is also deeply marked by the encounters that the moralised romantic inheritance must make with those environments which challenge it in matters of belief, technique, and aesthetics'.[52] Such challenges ensure that Forster's 'romantic inheritance'[53] can be traced to Wordsworth and Coleridge. It finds its expression in 'the claims on the one hand of the imagination and the poet's transcendent vision, and on the other of right reason and moral duty'.[54] Taken together, these claims go to create 'the personal connection between inner and outer world' that characterises Forster's work and enables him to take 'as his proper field the social realm of action as well as the life of the individuals in their personal relations'.[55] Like his fiction, the critical perspective Forster offers in his texts emanates from a number of sources, including 'right reason and culture [. . .] the heart, the passions, the power of visionary imagination that can testify, however inadequately, to the claims of the infinite'.[56]

Placing Forster's work within a specific political and cultural context, Bradbury goes on to elaborate its effects on Forster's aesthetic. Here he finds that Forster's complex and often ambivalent relation to modernism 'is matched by the curious aesthetic implications of his techniques in fiction', namely, 'its attempt to place the modes of symbolism and post-impressionism in the context of what might be considered the more "traditional" story-telling function; the novel *tells* (rather than *is*) a story, and it lives in the conditioned world of stuff, of event, of history'.[57] More than the other Modernist writers, Bradbury understands Forster's desire for transcendence to be conditioned by 'the world of men and things' and his distinctiveness to reside in 'the faint hope which he entertains on behalf of history: the hope that by understanding and right relationship men may win for it a limited redemption'.[58] Forster's 'need to synthesise an ever more eclectic experience' and articulate 'the chaotic welter of values, which has confounded the modern mind' does not, however, produce either unity or transcendence in his work. Instead, as Bradbury argues, 'his visions, though they may suggest an order or unity in the universe, are defined, increasingly from novel to novel, in terms of an anarchy that they must always comprehend'.[59]

For Bradbury, Forster's visionary aesthetic finds its fullest expression in *A Passage to India*. More specifically, Mrs Moore's comment, following her epiphany in the Cave, that '"[e]verything exists, nothing has value"' (p.160), announces the failure of Forster's own vision. What underlies Mrs Moore's comment is the sense that for Forster himself, his works 'are never fully redemptive, since the world of time persistently enlarges our feelings of intellectual, moral, social, and spiritual relativism, creating a world in which no one philosophy or cosmology accounts for the world order'.[60] This perception, which *A Passage to India* elaborates, might be said to represent 'the obverse of the unitary vision; and in [. . .] his fullest and most eclectic book, Forster gives us in full that possibility – and its sources in social relations, personal relations, and the realm of spirit'.[61]

Having outlined the forces that are played out within Forster's work as a whole and which find their ultimate expression in *A Passage to India*, Bradbury returns to the question of Forster's status as a writer. Like

Leavis and Trilling, he makes it clear that Forster is more complex than his reputation would allow:

■ Forster may have an ideal of unity, a will to a whole solution, but we mistake him if we see only that in him. For he is characteristically not a novelist of solutions, but rather of reservations, of the contingencies and powers which inhibit spirit. The power of sympathy, understanding, and community with all things is for him an overriding power; but its claim to wholeness is always conditioned, and mystery, to which we must yield, coexists with muddle, which we must try to redeem, or even accept in its nullity. Indeed, it is because Forster is so attentive to the forces in our culture and world-order which induce the vision of anarchy – and threaten through its very real powers not only the will to but the very insights of the whole vision – that he seems so central a writer; a novelist whom we in our turn have not always seen whole.[62] □

Like Leavis, Bradbury cites as a potential source of difficulty Forster's attempt in his work to combine the poetic mode, 'which goes with the view of art as a symbolist unity', with 'the comedy and the irony'.[63] Notwithstanding these structural and aesthetic tensions, Bradbury's subsequent overview of critical responses to *A Passage to India* leads him to consider 'contrasts of time and transcendence' in this text. In the reading of *A Passage to India* that follows Bradbury's discussion of Forster's complex significance, the focus remains firmly on 'time and transcendence'.[64] These two elements, for Bradbury at least, represent the novel's organising principles while also signalling the tensions within it.

■ To a considerable extent, the book deals in themes and matters we have learned to associate with Forster from his previous novels. Here again are those rival claims upon men and nature which dichotomise the universe – the claims of the seen and the unseen, the public and the private, the powers of human activities and institutions and of the ultimate mysteries for which the right institutions and activities have yet to be found. And here again Forster's own sympathies are relatively apparent. The book is focused upon the testing-field of human relationships, with their various possibilities and disasters; on the 'goodwill plus culture and intelligence' (p.80) which are the necessary conditions of honest intercourse; on the clashes of interest and custom which divide men but which the liberal mind must hope, as Fielding hopes, to transcend. Its modes of presentation are familiarly complex – moving between a 'poetic' evocation of the world of mystery and a 'comic' evocation of the world of muddle, which is in a sense its obverse and refers to the normal state of men.

But what is unmistakable, I think, is that in this book Forster reveals new powers and resources – of a kind not previously achieved in his fiction – and that this extension of resource is linked with an extension of his sensibility, and above all with a new sense of complexity. For instance, *A Passage to India* is not simply an international novel – in the Jamesian sense of attempting to resolve contrasting value-systems by means of a cosmopolitan scale of value – but a global novel. The contrast of England and India is not the end of the issue, since India is schismatic within itself; India's challenge is the challenge of the multiverse, a new version of the challenge that Henry Adams faced on looking at the dynamo. What the city is as metaphor in *Howards End*, India is in *Passage*; it is a metaphor of contingency. Forster is not simply interested in raising the social-comic irony of confronting one social world with the standards of another; he stretches through the social and political implications to religious and mystical ones, and finally to the most basic question of all – how, in the face of such contingency, one structures meaning.[65] □

While his own analysis oscillates between a focus on the temporal and the transcendent, Bradbury eventually leans towards the latter. Thus, the 'poetic' and 'comic' modes, representing mystery and muddle respectively, are superseded, in Bradbury's account, by a series of general points about the text's significance. India becomes 'a metaphor of contingency'. The social comedy of the text, which pitches different value systems and cultures against each other, belies the desire 'to call up, by a poetic irradiation, the ironies lying within the forces of mystery and muddle in the constituted universe of nature itself'.

In his account of *A Passage to India*, Bradbury draws a distinction between two interdependent movements in the text, between the 'human' and 'verbal' plots.[66] The former relates to Adela and the tensions and conflicts that arise from her Indian experience. It involves 'the world of personal relationships' and constitutes the 'social world'.[67] Out of this develops Forster's moral system and his engagement with liberal-humanist values:

■ The traditional repositories of Forsterian virtue – goodwill plus culture and intelligence – function only incompletely in this universe; and Forster's own liberal passion for social connection motivates a large section of the action, but does not contain its chief interest. In the deceptively guide-bookish opening chapter Forster establishes an appeal beyond the social world, to the overarching sky; it looks, at first, like a figure for the potential unity of man, the redemption that might come through breaking out of the social institutions and classifications that segregate them into their closed groupings, but the gesture has an ambiguous quality. The civil station 'shares nothing with the city except the overarching sky', but the sky itself is an infinite mystery, and reaching away into its 'further distance . . . beyond colour, last freed itself from blue' (p.32). Certainly, beyond the world of social organisation is that world of 'the secret understanding of the heart' (p.42) to which Aziz appeals; this is the world that is damaged when Ronny and Mrs Moore discuss Aziz and she finds: 'Yes, it was all true, but how false as a summary of the man; the essential life of him had been slain' (p.55).

Forster is, as usual, superb at creating that 'essential life' and showing what threatens it, and much of the book deals with its virtues and its triumphs. So at one level the social world *is* redeemed by those who resist its classifications – by Adela and Mrs Moore, Fielding, Aziz, Godbole. Forster does not belittle their victories directly except in so far as he sees their comedy. But he does place beyond them a world of infinitude which is not, here, to be won through the personal. For this is not the entire realm of moral victory in the novel; indeed, these acts of resistance, which provide the book's lineal structure, are usually marked by failure. Adela's is a conventional disaster; she makes the moral mistake of exposing the personal to the social. Fielding's is more complicated; he is an agent of liberal contact through goodwill plus culture and intelligence, but he, like Mrs Moore, meets an echo:

> 'In the old eighteenth century, when cruelty and injustice raged, an invisible power repaired their ravages. Everything echoes now; there's no stopping the echo. The original sound may be harmless but the echo is always evil.' This reflection about an echo lay at the verge of Fielding's mind. He could never develop it. It belonged to the universe that he had missed or rejected. And the mosque missed it too. Like himself, those shallow arcades provided but a limited asylum. (p.272)

As for Mrs Moore, who does touch it, she encounters another force still – the moral nihilism that comes when the boundary walls are down. Her disaster dominates the novel, for it places even moral and mystical virtue within the sphere of contingency; it, too, is subject to spiritual anarchy. Beyond the world of the plot, the lineal world of consequences and relationships, there lies a second universe of fictional structure, which links spiritual events, and then a third, which in turn places these in history and appeals to the infinite recession of the universe beyond any human structure that seeks to comprehend it. [68] □

Extending beyond the realm of the social and political, and the moral values to which they give rise, is the second plot. This second plot is much more difficult to define but is identified by Bradbury in the text's 'radiating expansiveness of language'. Highlighting the limited scope of the liberal-humanist response, the 'verbal plot' extends the scale of Forster's text so that it embodies the transcendent:

■ This we may see by noting that in this novel, as compared with the earlier ones, the world of men is clearly granted reduced powers. The universe of time and contingency is made smaller, by the nature that surrounds man, by the scale of the continent on which man's presence is a feeble invasion, by the sky which overarches him and his works. It is a world of dwarfs and of dwarfed relationships, in which the familiar forces of romantic redemption in Forster's work – personal relationships as mirrors to infinity, a willingness to confront the unseen – undertake their movements toward connection without the full support of the universe. The theme recurs, but Mrs Moore expresses it strongly in chapter xiv, when she reflects on her situation and grows towards her state of spiritual nullity in the cave:

She felt increasingly (vision or nightmare?) that, though people are important, the relations between them are not, and that in particular too much fuss has been made over marriage; centuries of carnal embracement, yet man is no nearer to understanding man. And today she felt this with such force that it seemed itself a relationship, itself a person, who was trying to take hold of her hand. (pp. 147–48)

The negative withdrawal is, of course, an aspect of that 'twilight of the double vision in which so many elderly people are involved' (p. 212), and it is not the only meaning in the book. But it is the dominant one. It is by seeking its obverse that Adela compounds her basic moral error:

It was Adela's faith that the whole stream of events is important and interesting, and if she grew bored she blamed herself severely and compelled her lips to utter enthusiasm. This was the only insincerity in a character otherwise sincere and it was indeed the intellectual protest of her youth. She was particularly vexed now because she was both in India and engaged to be married, which double event should have made every instant sublime. (pp. 145–46)

Human relationships are dwarfed not only by the scale of the historical and social world, which is potentially redeemable, but by the natural world, which is not.

Of course, intimations of transcendence are present throughout the novel. Structurally they run through the seasonal cycle, from decisive hot sun to the benedictive healing water at the end, and from Mosque to Caves to Temple. By taking that as his order, Forster is able poetically to sustain the hope of a spiritual possibility, a prefiguring of the world beyond in the world below. The climax of this theme is Godbole's attempt at '[c]ompleteness, not reconstruction' (p.283). But what happens here is that divine revelation is shifted to the level of the comic sublime. Forster's rhetoric now puts what has been spiritually perplexing – the webs, nets, and prisons that divide spirit as well as society – back into the comic universe of muddle. The Mau festival is the celebration of the formlessness of the Indian multiverse, seen for a moment inclusively. The poetic realm of the novel, in which above all Mrs Moore and Godbole have participated, and which has dominated the book's primary art, is reconciled with the muddle of the world of men, in an emotional cataract that momentarily repairs the divisions of the spiritual world (through Godbole's revelation) and the social world (through the festival itself). It satisfies much of the passion for inclusiveness that has been one thread in the novel, the desire that heaven should include all because India *is* all. Earlier the two Christian missionaries have disagreed: Mr Sorley, the more advanced, 'admitted that the mercy of God, being infinite, may well embrace all mammals. And the wasps? He became uneasy during the descent to wasps, and was apt to change the conversation. And oranges, cactuses, crystals and mud? And the bacteria inside Mr Sorley? No, no, this is going too far. We must exclude someone from our gathering, or we shall be left with nothing' (p.58). Godbole's universe of spirit is much more inclusive [. . .]. His doctrine – '[c]ompleteness, not reconstruction' – is, of course, a species of transcendence, a momentary vision of the whole, the invocation of a universe invested with spirit. It links up with the symbolist plot of the novel, its power as a radiant image, rather than with plot in the linear sense, with its world of 'and then . . . and then . . .' threading its way through the novel, to an old woman and a wasp, it takes these 'soliciting images' and puts them in new association – not with all things, but with each other and with what else comes almost unbidden into the world of spirit. But the stone is left, and equally spirit may or may not invest the universe in any of its day-to-day affairs: 'Perhaps all these things! Perhaps none!' (p.287). Things, in freeing themselves from their traditional associations, social and historical, form a new order, beyond dialogue, beyond human plot, in the realm where poetic figures function on their own order of consciousness. Yet here, too, irony is at work: mystery is sometimes muddle, completeness is sometimes the universe where '[e]verything exists, nothing has value'

(p. 160). If history ultimately obstructs, and does not give us a final, rounded structure in terms of human event, if the horses, the earth, the clutter of human institutions say, '"No, not yet"', then like obstructions dwell in the realm of spirit and symbol, too: the sky says, '"No, not there"' (p. 316).

The linear, social plot, then, has stretched a long way in search of a structure of its own that will provide coherence in the world, but if it finds one it is in the form of an oblique, doubtful, and ironic promise; personal relations only go so far to solve the muddle of history. As for the symbolist plot, it transcends but it does not redeem; it is there but 'neglects to come' (p. 96). The power of the novel lies, of course, in the Whitmanesque ambition to include multitudes, to find eternity in some order in the given world. But is this ambition realised? Intimations of eternity may have their symbols in the world of men (in love and relationship) and in the world of nature (in the force of mystery that resides in things); the social and the natural worlds have in them touches that promise wholeness. But they do not of themselves have unity; they are themselves afflicted by the double vision which is all that man can bring to them, grounded as he is in history and hope at once. The world stretches infinitely about us, and there is infinity beyond us. But questions bring us only to the unyielding hostility of the soil and the unyielding ambiguity of the sky.

The universe, then, is less intimation than cipher; a mask rather than a revelation in the romantic sense. Does love meet with love? Do we receive but what we give? The answer is surely a paradox, the paradox that there are Platonic universals beyond, but that the glass is too dark to see them. Is there a light beyond the glass, or is it a mirror only to the self? The Platonic cave is even darker than Plato made it, for it introduces the echo, and so leaves us back in the world of men, which does not carry total meaning, is just a story of events. The Platonic romantic gesture of the match in the cave is the dominating ambiguity of the book. Does it see *itself* in the polished wall of stone, or is the glimmer of radiance a promise?

> There is little to see, and no eye to see it, until the visitor arrives for his five minutes, and strikes a match. Immediately another flame rises in the depths of the rock and moves towards the surface like an imprisoned spirit: the walls of the circular chamber have been most marvellously polished. The two flames approach and strive to unite, but cannot, because one of them breathes air, the other stone. A mirror inlaid with lovely colours divides the lovers, delicate stars of pink and grey interpose, exquisite nebulae, shadings fainter than the tail of a comet or the midday moon, all the evanescent life of the granite, only here visible. Fists and fingers thrust above the

advancing soil – here at last is their skin, finer than any covering acquired by the animals, smoother than windless water, more voluptuous than love. The radiance increases, the flames touch one another, kiss, expire. The cave is dark again, like all the caves. (pp. 138–39)

Isn't it less the transcendence of a Whitman, uniting all things through the self and the ongoing lines of history, than the ambiguous and narcissistic transcendence of Melville, where the universe is a diabolical cipher, where the desire to penetrate meaning ends only in our being swallowed up in the meaning we have conferred? Isn't the novel not Forster's *Passage to India*, but rather, in the end, Forster's *Moby-Dick*?[69] □

CHAPTER THREE

'The Architecture of Question and Answer': Narration and Negation

CRITICS APPROACHING *A Passage to India* have often sought to impose a unity upon what is a complex and often elusive text. As the previous chapter demonstrates, Forster's liberal humanism has enabled critics who approach the text from a thematic perspective to emphasise the ways in which it apparently engages with the condition of humanity. Other critics have taken their cue, not from the ideology with which the text engages, but from the narrative itself. They have sought to place both Forster and *A Passage to India* within a specific literary tradition, looking back, for example, to the novels of Jane Austen or turning to the work of writers associated with the Modernist movement.[1] Still others have placed the structure of Forster's text at the forefront of their analyses and found within it a means of identifying the unities the novel promotes. The three sections of the text – 'Mosque', 'Caves' and 'Temple' – lead these critics to place their emphasis a little differently as they negotiate each of them in turn. Forster's textual divisions do not, however, prevent his critics from attempting to assign an overall meaning to the triadic structure of *A Passage to India*. The different interpretative possibilities suggested by the three sections of narrative are, in the final analysis, understood to contribute to an overall unity and balance by the close of the text.

In her overview of critical responses to the text, June Perry Levine points outs that 'virtually every scholar has agreed that the major structure of *A Passage to India* is a triad' but, as she also notes, the desire to uncover 'a complete set of parallels among the three sections has led to some ingenious readings' of Forster's text.[2] For E.K. Brown, Forster's titled sections supply the reader with a somewhat heavy-handed clue to interpretation. They 'warn of a meaning which goes behind story, people, even setting'.[3] Reuben A. Brower's interpretation of the triadic structure enables him to read each section in terms of different kinds of symbolism, even though these differences are set aside at the close of the novel when a unity asserts itself: '[t]o anyone familiar with the book the three title words are immediately and richly expressive. Each conveys a generalised impression of a salient object or event in the narrative, an impression that stands for and is inseparably connected with various large meanings.'[4] In *The Cave and the Mountain* (1966), Wilfred Stone turns his attention away from the three-part structure of Forster's text and towards the Marabar Caves. For Stone, the Caves can be seen as the source of textual unity since 'the book's fundamental structure consists of circle after circle echoing out from the caves at the centre to the outermost fringes of the cosmos. Although the book teems with variety, it is contained by this unity.'[5]

While the critics cited above have produced a range of stimulating readings of Forster's text, each of them assumes that a coherent critical narrative may be extracted from *A Passage to India*. This view runs counter to the readings of the novel that are included in this chapter and which all emphasise how *A Passage to India* challenges the drive for interpretative unity and coherence.

In *A Preface to Forster*, Christopher Gillie usefully points out that, '[t]he difference between "theme" and "technique" is often difficult to make', since 'what we see and understand has so much to do with the ways we see and understand'.[6] Although this is a valid claim, the critics whose work is addressed in this chapter all approach *A Passage to India* from what is predominantly a formal rather than thematic perspective. Providing detailed analyses of Forster's language and his narrative technique, the four essays considered here significantly overlap in terms of their emphasis on negation and indeterminacy in the text.

Influenced by Pierre Macherey's *A Theory of Literary Production*,[7] and Wolfgang Iser's *The Act of Reading*,[8] Gillian Beer's 'Negation in *A Passage to India*', published in 1980, strikes the keynote for the remaining essays in this chapter.[9] For Beer, as for the others, a consideration of 'the significance of gaps, fissures, absences and exclusions'[10] in Forster's text and readings of it, provides a means of understanding, not only the formal properties of the narrative, but also the wider signifying process in which it engages. Writing in 1990, Wendy Moffat, in '*A Passage to India* and the Limits of Certainty', considers the question of absence from an editorial perspective.[11] Not only does she focus her attention on the Marabar Caves and the indeterminate events that occur within them but looks, also, beyond Forster's published narrative to the earlier draft of the novel. The manuscript version of *A Passage to India*, published in 1978, provides for Moffat a means of uncovering, in the final version of Forster's text, traces of the revised and rejected original.[12] A comparison of the two versions illuminates Forster's writing process while also shedding light on the questions that have exercised so many critics of the text. In his deconstructive reading of *A Passage to India*, Robert Barratt elaborates, from a theoretically informed perspective, the significance of Forster's indeterminacy. Understanding the creative and conceptual potential of 'the ambiguity of absence',[13] Barratt attempts to bring contemporary critical insights to bear upon one of the central texts of Modernism. While showing an awareness of the interpretative power of ambiguity, Jo Ann Hoeppner Moran sets out to discover 'what really happened' in Forster's Caves.[14] Her conclusion offers a surprising way of reading the spirituality manifested in *A Passage to India*.

In her reading of *A Passage to India*, Beer begins by noting the crucial shift from 'character to language, to the text as process rather than the text as memory'.[15] Such a shift has marked out the transition from traditional ways of reading fiction to more contemporary approaches. She emphasises 'the text as process',[16] before going on to consider the challenges *A Passage to India* presents to its readers. Beer argues that Forster's text provides a useful way of understanding the interaction between text and reader that takes place during the interpretative process. In the case of *A Passage to India* this process is both complex and informative, not least because the text is concerned with:

■ gaps, fissures, absences, and exclusions: [it is] about bridge-parties that don't bridge, about caves broached by man-made entrances, about absent witnesses who do not witness and who are indeed already dead, about events which may or may not have occurred, about how society – how meaning itself – depends upon exclusion: 'We must exclude someone from our gathering, or we shall be left with nothing' (p. 58).[17] □

As Beer argues, negation is not simply a formal technique adopted by Forster but also represents one of the central concerns of the narrative. This relation between what the text says and how it says it is the focus of Beer's subsequent analysis of selected passages from the novel. When she considers the language and syntax Forster adopts, Beer is struck by the prevalence of the 'negative':

■ Negative sentence structures, together with the words 'no', 'not', 'never' and in particular 'nothing', predominate in the linguistic ordering of this novel. This is so to an extent that goes beyond the possibility of 'accident', far beyond the language of Forster's other novels. Nor can the insistent negativity be read simply as an unmediated representation of a particular class vernacular of the nineteen-tens and nineteen-twenties. Although it does draw upon habitual understatement and irony, it dislodges the assumptions embedded in such locutions. My first presumption on realising how frequent negative structures and vocabulary were in this text was that this would provide an inert and invariable medium of experience for the reader which would persistently controvert the book's topic: the will towards friendship and relationship. But as I moved further through the text I came to see that the uses of negation were themselves changing as the book went on. The function I had first noted is itself undermined before the book concludes. The shifting significance of negation in *A Passage to India* both challenges the older reading of the novel as essentially liberal-humanist, preoccupied with human personality, and raises questions concerning the Machereyan concept of the text as precipitated communal ideology [. . .]. So far as this text is ideological, it is an ideology which manifests itself as space – the space between cultures, the space beyond the human, the space which can never be sufficiently filled by aspiration or encounter. The presence of negative elements in the syntax of a sentence does not in itself necessarily enforce negation. However the nominalised form 'nothing' remains always significantly negative whether or not its force as negation is confirmed grammatically. The frequent use of the word 'nothing' in *A Passage to India* therefore supports my general argument that negation has ideological significance in this work. Negation and negativity in this novel are related in complex ways to place and space (inferiority and exteriority) and to the diverse shapes of inclusion and exclusion supposed by the different religious orderings of life.[18] □

While Beer understands that the negative undercuts the thematic concern of the liberal-humanist text, its function extends beyond this contrary linguistic drive. In the analysis that follows, Beer's attempt to map the changing function of the negative in *A Passage to India* is designed to lend support to her original thesis, that such negation 'has an ideological significance in this work'.[19]

■ The book opens with a description which negates even as it creates picturesque images. The whole opens with a phrase of exclusion – which is extended as absence:

Except for the Marabar Caves – and they are twenty miles off – the city of Chandrapore presents *nothing extraordinary*. Edged rather than washed by the river Ganges, it trails for a couple of miles along the bank, *scarcely distinguishable* from the rubbish it deposits so freely. There are *no* bathing steps on the river front, as the Ganges happens *not* to be holy here; indeed there is *no* river front, and the bazaars *shut out* the wide and shifting panorama of the stream . . . The zest for decoration stopped in the eighteenth century, *nor* was it ever democratic. In the bazaars there is *no* painting and *scarcely any* carving . . . Houses do fall, people are drowned and left rotting, but the general outline of the town persists, swelling here, shrinking there, like some low but indestructible form of life. (p. 31) [Beer's italics]

At the end of the paragraph the main clause of the sentence thrusts through to the positive ('Houses *do* fall, people *are* drowned') while the sense registers decadence and mortality.

The book closes in this way:

But the horses didn't want it – they swerved apart; the earth didn't want it, sending up rocks through which riders must pass single-file; the temples, the tank, the jail, the palace, the birds, the carrion, the Guest House, that came into view as they issued from the gap and saw Mau beneath: they didn't want it, they said in their hundred voices, 'No, not yet', and the sky said, 'No, not there'. (p. 316)

Negation persists, and though cast in abridged form ('didn't') it is re-iterated. The final negatives are localised in particular time and particular space: ('not yet', 'not there'). Since the book ends here, the negatives are given the authority of conclusion, but neither of them is absolute or universal. Other times, other places, are not entirely oblit-erated, but neither are they released into that which can be told within the book.

I am not claiming that negative forms are always significantly placed and used wherever they occur throughout the book – far from it. Indeed that is part of the point. For a good deal of our awkward and testing journey through the reading of this text negative sentence structures, and words like 'no', 'not', 'scarcely', 'barely', though omni-present are unemphatically there, hardly registered. They are *even* rather than cumulative in their effect, rarely releasing us into any kind of cri-sis. Negation is not used only at particularly significant moments: it is used everywhere. The factitious and the significant both find negative forms; and these forms occur both in dialogue and narrative. [. . .][20] ☐

Having focused the reader's attention on the opening and closing of the text, Beer goes on to select other passages from the novel that support her argument. These relate to the question of indeterminacy and its effects.[21]

■ The use of negative forms opens constantly towards indeterminacy. To say what something is *not* leaves open a very great area of what it might be. Such negatives are the most grudging form of identification and emphasize the extent of what is unsaid, or indescribable: take for example the first extended discussion of the Marabar caves, between Adela Quested and Dr. Godbole:

'Are they large caves?' she asked.

'No, not large.'

'Do describe them, Professor Godbole.'

'It will be a great honour.' . . . After an impressive pause he said: 'There is an entrance in the rock which you enter, and through the entrance is the cave.'

'Something like the caves at Elephanta?'

'Oh no, not at all; at Elephanta there are sculptures of Siva and Parvati. There are no sculptures at Marabar.'

'They are immensely holy, no doubt,' said Aziz, to help on the narrative.

'Oh no, oh no.'

'Still, they are ornamented in some way.'

'Oh no.'

'Well, why are they so famous? We all talk of the famous Marabar Caves. Perhaps that is our empty brag.'

'No, I should not quite say that.'

'Describe them to this lady, then.'

'It will be a great pleasure.' He forwent the pleasure, and Aziz realised that he was keeping back something about the caves. (pp. 91–92)

As the book goes on, we discover that Aziz was right only in broader sense – Godbole was not concealing *something*, but *nothing*.

'Nothing' is a word of power in this text. The theme of nothing is carried for a long time lexically, emerging only intermittently and later into action or character or landscape. It occurs in the first sentence of the book. [. . .] From that point on, the word occurs with increasing frequency. It is crucial in the scene where Adela first breaks off her engagement to Ronny and is there associated with all that resists identification. Adela, heavily feeling the absence of 'a profound and passionate speech' (p. 100), reiterates the words '"nothing else"' while absently watching a neat and brilliant bird. She asks Ronny to identify it:

'Bee-eater.'

'Oh no, Ronny, it has red bars on its wings.'

'Parrot,' he hazarded.

'Good gracious, no.'

The bird in question dived into the dome of the tree. It was of no importance, yet they would have liked to identify it, it would somehow have solaced their hearts. But nothing in India is identifiable, the mere asking of a question causes it to disappear or to merge into something else. (p. 101)

This escape from question and identification is repeated in the lies of the Indian characters, which open ways towards what might be, what may be wished, what might have been, routes out of determined. But that clause 'nothing in India is identifiable' also hints at a property of the word 'nothing' which becomes vital to the meaning of the book.[22] □

Although she argues that the multiple significations that emanate from Forster's particular use of the word 'nothing' contribute to the overall ambiguity of the text, one of the strengths of Beer's analysis is her attentiveness to the particular context in which the word appears.

■ 'Nothing' as a word has two natures. Set alone it expresses stasis, vacancy: Nothing. As soon as it becomes part of a sentence, though, it makes the whole organization of that sentence restless and unstable, expressive of contrary impulses. 'But nothing in India is identifiable' (p. 101). On first reading, and predominantly always, this means: 'it is not possible to identify anything in India'. But there is another organisation lurking as a shadow form in that sentence, the possibility that 'only in India is Nothing Identifiable'. The suggestion here is faint. Take, however, Aziz's description of Akbar's religion which sought to marry Hinduism and Mohammadanism and failed: '"Nothing embraces the whole of India, nothing, nothing"' (p. 156). The diagram of meaning is unstable, like an optical illusion. It alternates between 'There is nothing that embraces the whole of India' and – particularly with the force of the reiterated 'nothing': 'Nothingness embraces the whole of India.' When the caves are described before the characters visit them (and previous to that passage commenting on Akbar's religion) the reader is told:

> Having seen one such cave, having seen two, having seen three, four, fourteen, twenty-four, the visitor returns to Chandrapore uncertain whether he has had an interesting experience or a dull one or any experience at all. He finds it difficult to discuss the caves, or keep them apart in his mind, for the pattern never varies and no carving, not even a bees'-nest or a bat, distinguishes one from another. Nothing, nothing attaches to them, their reputation – for they have one – does not depend upon human speech. (p. 138)

We are entering the unsayable when we enter the caves: this is first expressed as alternation ('an interesting experience or a dull one') ending in negativity ('or any experience at all'). Identification and discrimination cannot be sustained ('it is difficult to discuss the caves, or to keep them apart in his mind'). 'Nothing, nothing attaches to them' (p.138). In this instance 'Nothingness' begins to predominate in the sense over 'There is nothing that attaches to them.' Nothing is a concept which is beyond human speech but which manifests itself as forceful. 'Nothing is inside them, they were sealed up before the creation of pestilence or treasure; if mankind grew curious and excavated, nothing, nothing would be added to the sum of good or evil' (p.139). 'Nothing' diminishes again but does not revert to absence.

Nothing is concave and convex: it retreats from us and emerges out and confronts us. It alternates. Linguistically it subverts fixed orders, and produces echoes and disturbances of received meaning. Mrs. Moore's experience in the cave is hideous because it challenges her values of individualism, discrimination and Christianity. The 'vile naked thing' which 'settled on her mouth like a pad' (p.158) proves to have been 'a poor little baby, astride its mother's hip' (p.159). That knowledge cannot restore to her the language of Christianity, 'poor little talkative Christianity' (p.161) because the echo has murmured: '"Everything exists, nothing has value"' (p.160). For her, and for us at this point in the book, that statement seems obliterative merely. But by the end of the book we are brought to see also that nothing *has* value.[23] □

Having provided a number of detailed examples of Forster's use of negation and 'nothing', Beer begins to see that notwithstanding the syntactic and semantic implications of these entities, meaning and value can be assigned to the terms. Bearing in mind the significance, following *Howards End*, of connection in Forster, Beer's emphasis on negation and rejection highlights the contradictory impulses that pervade his work. In *A Passage to India* separation and absence can be read in many ways: as the condition that defines the Modernist era; a way of dramatising cultural difference; a means of erasing the figure of the woman; or as a way of figuring spiritual exhaustion. Beer's own focus, in the latter half of her textual analysis, is dual for she divides her reading between the sacred and the profane, considering both the religious and sexual significance of absence:

■ Absence is a condition of God as it is of nothingness [. . .]. Absence is pure, complete. Presence is skeined out in time. Rarely, and then only in moments recognised as ravishing, can the totality of a person be present. In absence, the whole may be realised, though realised as gone. For this reason desire and absence are interlocked: absolutes capable of expression only in negative form. In this book both of them find a place – a location – in the caves [. . .].[24] □

Signifying both an extremely spiritual and also sexual experience, the notion of ravishment is crucial to the confusions that arise from the

Caves. In Beer's analysis, however, it seems that Forster's sexual symbolism is far more pronounced than the religious:

■ The entry into the caves and the descriptions of them have a sexual meaning which Forster recognises and develops. The caves which can be visited have been broached by man: 'elsewhere, deeper in the granite, are there certain chambers that have no entrances? Local report declares that these exceed in number those that can be visited.' When a match is struck in the cave

> [T]wo flames approach and strive to unite, but cannot, because one of them breathes air, the other stone. A mirror inlaid with lovely colours divides the lovers . . . Fists and fingers thrust above the advancing soil – here at last is their skin, finer than any covering acquired by the animals, smoother than windless water, more voluptuous than love. The radiance increases, the flames touch one another, kiss, expire. The cave is dark again, like all the caves. (pp. 138–39)

This language of desire and consummation is that of the flame and *its own reflection* – a reflexive place in which self divides into self and other or, for Mrs. Moore, the distinction between self and other can no longer be discriminatingly felt. These caves with their womb-like enclosure are not only representative of the female, but figure a dread of the female and a vengeance taken on her. It is the women who suffer in them, impacted within their own symbol. Women's psychosexual experience, Lacan suggests, forms the blind spot within Freud's symbolic system.[25] Forster, from his privileged sexually ambiguous place, images a blind spot in the caves.[26] □

Touching here upon the erasure of woman from the Symbolic order in Lacanian thought, Beer also refers fleetingly to Forster's homosexuality, as she muses on the significance of the 'blind spot' in the Caves. Since she does not develop these ideas the reader can only speculate as to their 'ideological significance'. At this juncture, Beer retreats from her analysis of 'the language of desire and consummation'. She moves abruptly to a brief discussion of the 'anthropomorphic or animistic'[27] in *A Passage to India* before turning her attention to Mrs Moore and Adela. Beer's movement, in her critical reading of Forster, between detailed textual and discursive analysis and the attempt to draw out the implications of her findings, creates an uneven essay. She proves to be much more incisive when dealing with the formal properties of Forster's text – his language and syntax – than when she tries to derive 'ideological significance' from her findings. Although she can be suggestive, Beer's analysis at these points is much less satisfactory than it is in the first half of her essay. It is unsurprising and not unwelcome when Beer returns to the question of negation as a linguistic feature of *A Passage to India*. This time, negation takes the form of a repeated 'either-or' formulation in Forster's sentences:

■ Alternation is neither dualism nor dialectic. In Hegelian dialectic two negations thrust through towards a positive outcome. In this book, there is rather a sense of prolongation, attenuation and loss connected with alternation and with the attempt to stabilise it by pairing. It is a way of using negativity which deprives it of its latent positive force and makes it function as that which mists, blurs, stains, tarnishes, spreads too thin. This form of negation permits no escape into energy. The wisest course in this text is to resist the obvious way out of alternation: that of pairing. Adela and Fielding shake hands like two dwarfs but eschew all other attempts to make arches. The two great props to marriage, we are later told, are religion and society. But neither of them is marriage. The crown to that arch is missing. The idea of pairing is absurdly, linguistically, reduced in the figure of the clergyman who accompanies Adela on an expedition from the ship on her way home. '"He turns to the East, he *re*-turns to the West"' (p.263). [. . .] After the defining negative of Adela's answer in the court-room, moving from '"I am not quite sure"', through shaking her head, to '"No"' (p.231), new possibilities of meaning begin to emerge. Indeterminacy is not abolished, however: we never know what happened in the caves, who followed her or whether anyone followed her – and to prove a man's innocence is to prove his non-involvement. Innocence moreover is there already and should need no proof. The act of proof creates nothing fresh.

The dreaming beauty and impassivity of the naked punkah wallah, his absolute *inattention* to the proceedings of the court as he pulls the fan, has released Adela. She has looked at what needs no interpretation or rationalisation. She is released from the need to identify. The detective story level of the plot has seemed to insist upon the importance of identification, but such efforts of the will and of the positive prove meagre. Only identification *with* has worth; identification *of* is paltry. That is why negation is the form that truth must take. So the holy and infuriating Godbole refuses directly to answer the question: '"Is Aziz innocent or guilty?"' put to him by Fielding, saying only that '"nothing can be performed in isolation. All perform a good action, when one is performed, and when an evil action is performed, all perform it"' (p.185).

At the beginning of Temple, alternation poises itself upon positive meaning. God 'is, was not, is not, was' (p.281). In this book attributes may be lost without loss of significance. The titles of all three books suggest enclosure: Mosque, Caves and Temple. But in this last book almost everything happens outdoors. There is a sense of free exteriority [. . .]. In this final book there is no need to exclude anyone or anything from the gathering. Not everyone understands the events, but they are all there, milling around. Discrimination is lost [. . .]. The whole festival is in honour of *the God without attributes*. [. . .][28] □

Beer's discussion of alternation as one form that negation takes in *A Passage to India* returns her to the opening of her essay and the close of Forster's text.

■ In the final paragraph, which I quoted at the beginning, separateness and equality are emphasised. The two riders swerve together and apart. They must ride single file, surrounded by the animate and inanimate other beings of India: horses, earth, rocks, temples, tank, jail, palace, birds, carrion, Guest House: 'they didn't want it, they said in their hundred voices, "No, not yet", and the sky said, "No, not there"' (p. 316).

'"In space things touch, in time they part"' (p. 199). Narrative always sets things in sequence. So throughout this work negation and 'nothing' are active rather than static, because they are energised by being involved in sentences, in paragraphs, in chapters. Their meaning is to some extent controlled by their being part of narration, rather than, say, of a lyric poem. But the uses of negation, alternation, and the indeterminate, make it possible for the text to register that which is not to be said, not to be written (as within the book Aziz never writes the poem he plans, whose topic constantly changes).

In the Bhagavad-gita it is said that God may be defined only by negatives. Forster's novel challenges through the habitual negativity of its language the beleaguered humanism of its characters. Forster's work presages the end of empire, not simply the end of the Raj in India (though it does that), but also the end of that struggle for dominion which is implicit in the struggle for language and meaning – the struggle to keep man at the centre of the universe. He sees what lies beyond the human need not be null or void. But it was not the nineteen twenties who saw it thus: it is we fifty years later who can recognise this [. . .]. And we can do so by studying not what is absent, but what is there: the language of the text.[29] □

Following Beer, Wendy Moffat begins her analysis of *A Passage to India* by drawing attention to the 'calculated ambiguities and deliberate omissions'[30] in the text. Her analysis of the novel sets out to uncover the motives behind Forster's ambiguities. She argues that '[b]y omitting as well as telling, he requires the reader to participate in what he conceives to be the puzzle of the novel's world, a process which displaces the reader in interesting ways'.[31] Moffat approaches the question of omission in Forster's text by focusing not only on what it does not say but also on what it once said. Her essay takes into account the original manuscript of the text, which, placed beside the published version, sheds light on the 'motives behind Forster's ambiguities'.[32]

■ Forster took pains to widen and deepen the enigmatic character of his novel, to make it a puzzle insoluble within its own terms, or without. Early drafts of *A Passage to India* reveal a number of false starts. Forster repeatedly revised drafts of chapters thirteen through sixteen, which comprise the crux of the novel, the visit to the Marabar Caves. When he began writing the novel, his intention was to make the cave scene central and significant, but he did not yet know how:

> When I began *A Passage to India*, I knew something important happened in the Malabar (sic) Caves, and that it would have a central place in the novel – but I didn't know what it would be . . . The Malabar Caves represented an area in which concentration can take place. They were to engender an event like an egg.[33]

The most radical turn from the manuscript to the finished version occurs in Forster's conception of the attack on Adela Quested. In the manuscript version, the 'event engendered' by the caves is an act of human violence:

> [Adela] stood for a moment in the cool, thinking about her plans and running a finger along the invisible wall. She thought what a pity it was . . . that she was not in love [with] Ronny . . . An extra darkness showed that someone was following her down the entrance tunnel. 'Dr. Aziz—' she began, glad to continue the conversation.
>
> At first she thought that he was taking her hand as before to help her, then she realised, and shrieked at the top of her voice. 'Boum' shrieked the echo. She struck out and he got hold of her other hand and forced her against the wall, he got both her hands in his and then felt at her breasts. 'Mrs. Moore', she yelled. 'Ronny – don't let him, save me.' The strap of the Field Glasses, tugged suddenly, was drawn across her throat. She understood – it was to be passed once round her neck, she was to be throttled as far as necessary, and then . . . [Forster's suspension points] Silent, though the echo still raged up and down she waited and when the breath was on her wrenched a hand free, got hold of the glasses and pushed them into her assailant's mouth. She could not push hard

but it was still enough to hurt him. He let go, and with both hands on her weapon, she smashed at him again. She was strong and had horrible joy in revenge. 'Not this time' she cried, and he answered – or the cave did. She gained the entrance of the tunnel, screamed like a maniac lest he pull her in when she stooped and regained the open air, her topi smashed, her fingers bleeding.[34] [Moffat's punctuation]

By contrast, in the published version, the only aspect of Adela's experience which remains 'solid and attractive' is her *doubt* about what happened in the caves. She tells Fielding after the trial that she may have been alone, and confesses that she may have been suffering from a delusion of being attacked – '"the sort of thing – though in awful form – that makes some women think they've had an offer of marriage when none was made"' (p. 240).

The episode in the early draft is organized around the watershed moment of the suspension points. Before the ellipsis Adela is passive, imagining the culmination of her attack in rape, calling out to her companions for help. Our sense of her helplessness is compounded by Forster's use of language here: the field glasses have more force of action than Adela (they are even capitalized), and the narration is cast in the passive voice. After the ellipsis, Adela rebuffs her attacker in a frenzy of revenge. There are two attempted rapes here, the first of Adela herself, the second Adela's figurative rape of her attacker. The violence on both sides of the ellipsis is figured in sexual terms: first Adela is forced against a wall and roughly molested; then 'when the breath was upon her' she uses the field glasses as a 'weapon' to push 'into her assailant's mouth. She could not push hard but it was enough to hurt him . . . She was strong . . .'.

June Levine has remarked that Adela's rage here is uncharacteristic of her personality in the final version.[35] Certainly Adela's motives are ambiguous. She seems to get joy from having a chance to victimize her attacker, but it is not the uncomplicated revenge of having the tables turned. Most curious of all is her retort '"not this time"'. The attack incites a kind of passion in her; her diction implies that she desires sexual fulfillment in the form of a power struggle – not '"not this way"' but '"not this time"'. The suggestion that Adela imagines Aziz as her rapist because she desires him, or because he desires sexual experience [. . .] seems more plausible and interesting here than in the final version.[36] □

In her reading of this original scene, Moffat's attention is drawn by the violence with which Adela legitimately resists her attacker. Despite the 'horrible joy in revenge' that also motivates Adela, Moffat argues that a more complex desire manifests itself in Adela's violence. It is Adela's sexual imagination, which positions Aziz as rapist either because she desires him or anticipates his desire, that attracts the critic's attention. Moffat's reading of the literal rape and her own identification of Aziz as the figurative victim of rape seem questionable here. They imply that Adela wishes for a sexual encounter that takes the form of a power struggle, but wishes it to occur at her own bidding. It is not so much the form the encounter takes but its timing and instigation that causes Adela's resistance. The words '"Not this time"' are, like so much of Forster's text, overdetermined. Jenny Sharpe, for example, reads in them Adela's historical memory of the Indian Mutiny. Alternatively, they might indicate Adela's own personal recollection of another molestation. Either of these readings, which emphasise different forms of history, national and individual, seem more plausible than the one offered by Moffat, which, although she concedes might be 'ungenerous', seems to represent something of a textual violation of its own. Her analysis of Forster's rejected draft of this section of the novel proceeds with an account of the ellipsis in this passage. The ellipsis stands as a figure for the eventual erasure of this draft version of Forster's text as well as the other absences that are integral to the final version:

■ The moments before and after the ellipsis are revealed to us, but what happens *during* the suspended moment? The ellipsis marks the termination of Adela's rapid train of thought: it is her substitution for saying the word 'raped', which she cannot articulate. 'She understood – it was to be passed once round her neck, she was to be throttled as far as necessary, and then . . .' The ellipsis also marks the temporal lull between the aggressive fury against Adela and her furious defense. Most importantly, it exists as a suspended moment, unseen by the reader. As such it is a type for the entire scene, which is excised in the final draft, and for Forster's method in creating this scene in the final version.[37] □

Inevitably, although it is excised from the final draft, the original version of the text leaves its traces. Once uncovered by the reader, these traces also raise a number of 'unsolved' questions about *A Passage to India*. Most troubling of all are not the questions that arise from the extract itself but from Moffat's own speculations:

■ Even here we do not know for certain who Adela's attacker is, though it is quite clear she is attacked. We make the unquestioned connection between the pronoun 'he' and Adela's assumption that Aziz is the 'extra darkness' which follows her into the cave. But the narrator neither confirms nor denies our suspicions, and Forster breaks off this draft too quickly for us to sense his intentions. The enigmatic reply '"not this time"' muddies our sense of what Adela fears and wants in this scene. She does not seem to be an entirely innocent victim; we might even (ungenerously) interpret these words to mean that she is asking to be raped at another time. At the least, Adela's statement shows she wants to fend off danger for the present; but the phrase reverberates in a weird way, and we cannot dismiss the sense that whatever the danger is, it remains both threatening and inviting.[38] □

Although the original manuscript passage has multiple significations, it is much less indeterminate than the final rendition. The substitution of one passage for another in the final version of the text provides a clue to Forster's own investment in the narrative and, specifically, his desire to leave the most crucial things unsaid.

■ But however troubling these questions, Forster rejects the early version because it solves too many tactical questions, and radically limits the interpretations of what happens to Adela in the cave. The draft offers the reader neither momentary nor permanent suspense. In contrast, the final version gives us both: the shift from Adela's point of view to Aziz's at this moment [. . .] affords Forster the momentary suspense of Adela's return to Chandrapore without informing Aziz or Fielding, or for that matter the reader, of her accusations against Aziz. And it produces a more lasting suspension of understanding.

The final version creates a strategy which gives Aziz's arrest at the railroad station more dramatic force, while assuring the reader of his innocence; after all, we provide his alibi, being in the cave with him at the moment of supposed attack. But the more abstract outcome of the change in draft is that the central event remains 'impermanent'. Unseen by Fielding and Aziz, not directly reported by Adela (who is spirited away until the trial scene, when she repudiates her accusation against Aziz), the moment is left obscure. Though we know Aziz does not rape Adela, we never know with certainty what happened to her.[39] □

At this point in her reading of the final version of *A Passage to India*, Moffat presumes a clarity and finality that the text does not uphold. Although Adela does retract her accusation, the *text* does not. Her comment, '"Let us say it was the guide"' (p. 261), suggests that an event, and perhaps a rape, did occur.

■ In abandoning the draft version of the attack, Forster empties his central scene of causality and point of view: what happens in the caves remains a cipher for all the characters. Our only witnesses are impaired – either close but not actually present (like Aziz), or incapable of articulation (like Adela). Thus Adela's experience in the cave in the final version, and its potential meaning, become a kind of metaphorical extension of Adela's strangled silence and the ellipsis in the earlier draft. It is open to us only through surmise, through Mrs. Moore's experience of the first cave (which may not be identical to Adela's) and Adela's strong but inexpressible sense of an 'echo' or 'living at half pressure' (p. 240) which persists in her mind. In the earlier draft Forster dubs his character Edith, a sensible if unglamorous Anglo-Saxon name. In the final version she has become Adela, from the Greek meaning 'unclear' or 'not manifest'. The change reflects Forster's systematic recasting of the manuscript so as to increase the enigmatic texture of the novel, and so of his moral world.[40] □

For Moffat, the enigmatic nature of the novel pertains not only to the central scene in the Caves but also to the generic identification of the text itself. According to Moffat, the text's apparent focus, in the opening chapters, on marital issues leads the reader to believe it will 'be a social comedy, a domestic novel of small entanglements'.[41] This assumption, which is developed by Elaine Showalter in her essay, omits the significance of the Indian location for Forster's text. The opening passage of the novel places the reader in a specifically imperial location but one in which the social order is marked by a spatial hierarchy. The apparent 'otherness' of the text is obscured by Moffat in her reading when, on turning her attention to the 'Moslem culture of Chandrapore', she argues that 'despite its characteristic details, it seems no more exotic or alien than, say, the situations of the Bennet family in *Pride and Prejudice*'.[42] As she elides historical and cultural differences, Moffat appears to domesticate the text. She goes on to argue that the 'social comedy' of the novel is undermined by a movement away from scenes of human exchange and interaction towards the more expansive natural world. The problem of identifying the generic properties of *A Passage to India* directly relates to 'our uncertainty about its moral world'.[43]

■ The genre of *A Passage to India* is disturbingly protean. Forster manipulates our expectations of genre in several ways, and if the novel were frozen at certain key scenes we would be convinced of its incontrovertible form as a melodrama, a detective story, a tale of the occult, a religious meditation, or a polemic against imperialism. [. . .] The questions which have evoked the most interest among scholars are grounded in the novel's protean genre and the difficult and often contradictory expectations it places on the reader. The political divisiveness of India and the compelling depiction of the Anglo-Indian occupation have led more than one reader, especially Forster's contemporaries, to a reading of *A Passage to India* as a political treatise, and indictment of the Raj and of imperialism generally. [. . .] But the behaviour of the British is a comparatively obvious target for satire, and the novel lacks the necessary didacticism to confirm this view. With the release of India from the British Empire, readings of *A Passage to India* as an attack on the British waned. More recent readings, and more compelling ones, centre on the politics of the novel in the word's widest sense [. . .].[44] □

Moffat's account, which sees the critical reception of *A Passage to India* as marked by the movement away from the politics of imperialism and towards a more general concern with politics in the 'widest sense', is obviously questionable. Moffat was writing in 1990, twelve years after Edward Said's groundbreaking *Orientalism* and the subsequent emergence of post-colonial critical discourse.[45] Curiously dated in her approach, Moffat cites Frederick Crews' *E.M. Forster: The Perils of Humanism* (1962), as an example of more recent readings of the text that engage with its wider politics.[46] As the title of his book indicates, Crews, in common with Forster's earliest critics, focuses his attentions on the problems that beset liberal-humanist ideology in the twentieth century.

Moffat's own analysis of *A Passage to India*, which has been so much concerned with Forster's editing of the novel, itself closes with her own imaginary cutting. Confronted with the third section of the text she suggests that '[p]erhaps the best way to see how the Temple section renews our uncertainty about genre is to ask what kind of novel *A Passage to India* would be if it ended after the Caves section'. She notes that '[l]ike the completed novel, it would end with Aziz and Fielding parting on terms of mixed sympathy and understanding [. . .]':[47]

■ But the 'Caves' section ends with Fielding's rational view uppermost. We are instilled with a sense of proper Anglo-Indian proportion as we follow him in his journey toward a more familiar landscape:

> In the old undergraduate days he had wrapped himself up in the many-coloured blanket of St. Marks, but something more precious than marbles and mosaics was offered to him now: the harmony between the works of man and the earth that upholds them, the civilization that has escaped muddle, the spirit in a reasonable form, with flesh and blood subsisting. Writing picture-postcards to his Indian friends, he felt that all of them would miss the joys he experienced now, the joys of form, and all this constituted a serious barrier . . . The Mediterranean is the human norm. (p. 278)

As he retreats from India toward the more 'harmonious' Venice, Fielding demonstrates a narrow ethnocentricism: he upholds a human norm which is Western in its orientation, and which is confused (perhaps shattered) by the alien and unrestrained ceremony of Gokol Ashnati in the Temple section.

Moreover, in this truncated version, the centerpiece of the novel would be Aziz's trial, with its elements of suspense, melodrama, and final resolution. After the trial, the novel contracts briefly. It seems to return to the world of the first chapters, where human institutions such as marriage and the law are capable of solving monstrous and untenable problems. Aziz's turning away from the experience of the trial, and his rejection of Western medicine, so essential to our sense of the untidiness of Forster's world, are introduced in the third section. Its inclusion denies us a sense of 'proportion' (p.253), which Fielding values and Aziz spurns; it also dwarfs Fielding's sense that '[t]he Mediterranean is the human norm.' Though to Western sensibilities justice prevails through Adela Quested's great personal courage and the staunch application of law in section two, the predictable resolution of melodrama evaporates in the final section.

What to make of Mrs. Moore's transcendent, almost occult knowledge of events she does not witness, which so irritated F.R. Leavis, among others, is also related to our unsettled sense of genre. The pattern of genre in *A Passage to India* is not presented as a dialectic – either comedy or tragedy, either fantastic or realistic, for example. Rather, we are turned back into a world which cannot be categorized, where intimations of interpretative wholeness are subverted once again.[48] □

In the concluding part of her essay Moffat relates 'a world which cannot be categorized' to Forster's desire to unsettle the 'Western sensibilities' of his audience with 'the echo of India's conflicting ways of seeing'.[49] Fielding's apparent capitulation to the European norm is refused by the text, which does not allow him to have 'the last word'.[50]

Moffat argues that Forster's interest lies in pitching different cultural systems against each other, not in order to make a point about cultural difference in an imperial setting but to undercut the Western reader's desire for 'permanence'. Forster's ambiguity 'is a protective stance [. . .] because he recognizes how much experience one person's certainty excludes'.[51] This recognition, for Moffat, somehow relates to Forster's sexuality:

As a closeted homosexual, Forster existed in public guise as a King's College novelist and genial spokesman for tolerance, and in private as a man whose sexuality, unrepressed and undisguised, might land him in prison. Like many of his not overtly homosexual fictions, *A Passage to India* figures Forster's unity in essentially androcentric terms: the desperate embrace between Aziz and Fielding at the end demonstrates their most passionate, and most unattainable, love. That the reader's comfortable experience of centrality be continually displaced is the object of his fiction: the method of *A Passage to India* embodies its moral message.[52] □

While Moffat argues that Forster's text works to undercut the reader's desire for unity, she nevertheless asserts, at the close of her account, a unity between the 'method' and 'message' of the text: between form and content.

In 'Marabar: The Caves of Deconstruction', published in 1993, Robert Barratt produces a reading of Forster's text that is informed by Jacques Derrida and Michael Ryan. Barratt begins his reading of the text by focusing on the Marabar Caves, which serve as a locus for the deconstructive analysis of *A Passage to India* he subsequently provides:

■ In an uncanny anticipation of the deconstructive approach, the Marabar Caves seem to function as a topographical model of deconstruction within the text. With the enigmatic presence of absence in the caves at the centre of the novel, Forster is able, through the decentring experiences of Mrs. Moore, Adela, and the Chandrapore Raj, to illustrate that:

> The exclusion of an outside in order to determine an inside already installs a differential relation between the inside and the outside, so that neither one exists apart from the other; it is itself only inasmuch as it is *different* from something other, as well as the other's *deferment*. The logic of priority and derivation can thus be reversed and displaced, as can the general axiomatic structure of inside and outside.[53]

In introducing the British Raj, Forster begins by revealing the silencing power of 'narrative imperialism' as the members of the Chandrapore Club define themselves with that arrogant certainty which inevitably reduces anything outside of its vision of itself. Consider, for example, Ronny's disturbance once he realizes not only that he has misapprehended his mother's nocturnal interlude at the mosque but also that this interlude proves to have been with a Mohammedan rather than 'young Muggins from over the Ganges'. Although he senses that 'his mother did not signify', he worries that she might infect Adela with a 'crooked' (p. 52) view of the native question and thus feels compelled to reimpose the fixed order of the prevailing view. Mrs. Moore herself challenges his interpretation of Aziz, but ultimately she surrenders to it and concludes, despite her own experience, that he was indeed 'unreliable, inquisitive, vain. Yes, it was all true, but how false as a summary of the man; the essential life of him had been slain' (p. 55).

Ronny's denial of his mother's experience of Aziz in favour of the superior certainty of the Raj version of Aziz is an enactment of the paradox articulated by the missionary, Mr Sorley; whether the line is drawn at Mohammedans or at bacteria, 'we must exclude someone from our gathering, or we shall be left with nothing' (p. 58).[54] □

As a 'topographical model of deconstruction' the Marabar Caves provide a means of figuring the central concerns of the text. These extend beyond questions of inside and outside to embrace models of self and other, along with the many forms of difference that are demarcated within conventional systems of classification. The interdependency of the apparently oppositional taxonomies that structure Western thought is scrutinised in Barratt's account of deconstruction, as in Forster's text. At the core of the novel and the theory that illuminates its operations is a critique of the liberal-humanist subject: the ego-centred, stable and coherent self:

■ The paradox is that so profound a notion of a central and enduring self presupposes difference from something else; 'the metaphysical reduction of the sign need[s] the oppositon it [is] reducing. The opposition is part of the system along with the reduction.'[55] Nowhere is this more clearly depicted by Forster than at the infamous Bridge Party. Mrs. Moore's innocent request to know who the visiting Indian women are is met with Mrs. Turton's unhelpful assertion that '"You're superior to them, anyway. Don't forget that. You're superior to everyone in India except one or two of the Ranis, and they're on an equality."' Able to speak Urdu only in 'the imperative mood' (p. 61), she finds, nevertheless, the haughtiness of her hierarchical security unsettled by the Indian women's mastery of English. She is forced to resume a more distant manner when she discovers that 'some of the group was westernized, and might apply her own standards to her' (p. 62). At least when dear Ronny dismisses this reductive relationship with the Indians as a mere '"side-issue"' (p. 68), his mother challenges him by claiming that his sentiments '"are those of a god"'. Unable to deny her challenge, Ronny seeks to validate the hierarchical opposition with the outrageous but comforting notion that '"India likes gods. And Englishmen like posing as gods"' (p. 69). As if in eager anticipation, Forster himself plays out this attempted inculcation of Adela and Mrs. Moore into the Raj worldview against the backdrop of 'the distant Marabar hills, which had crept near, as was their custom at sunset' (p. 65).

The Marabar hills are, from the outset, playfully depicted as a fist-like presence; monolithic but never fixed, always thrusting, rising, plunging or creeping. The extraordinary hollow centres within the fist's clutching grasp, moreover, defy articulation. Godbole, the one character who has been to the caves, is confounded by his own experience of them. In describing them he can only offer the tautologically empty definition of the word *cave*: '"there is an entrance in the rock which you enter, and through the entrance is the cave"' (p.91). Impatient with his strange imprecision, the other guests attempt to elicit clarity through comparison to other caves. They reduce Godbole's responses, however, to a series of inarticulate negations and ultimate silence. Like the reluctant immanence of Being that neglects to come in response to Godbole's imprecations, the essence of Marabar's Caves will not reveal itself in language. Situated always just beyond the reach of words it remains, like a Derridian *trace*, inaccessible to direct verbalization. As a result, all those seeking to know are left 'further than ever from discovering what, if anything, was extraordinary about the Marabar Caves' (p.69). All, that is, except Ronny, who, unperturbed by his own ignorance, professes with earnest British certainty that naturally he knows all about them.[56] □

Ronny's claim to a definitive knowledge where there is none not only represents an example of cultural imperialism but also demonstrates the inadequacy of his response to the indeterminacy and ambiguity that pervade Forster's text. Ronny's British arrogance is clearly reinforced by the power he is granted within the imperial system. Yet, beyond the realm of human interactions Forster's text also dramatises the 'resistance to the imagined fixity and precision of conventional language' through the Caves, and through another scene, to which Barratt draws the reader's attention:

■ Forster further presages the Marabar's disruptive indeterminacy in the wake of Adela's breach of her engagement to Ronny. Choosing not the Gangavati, but the Marabar road, the estranged pair motor off into the darkness. A jolt throws them into physical contact and a 'spurious unity' descends upon them, but Forster reminds us that even the darkness, 'absolute as it seemed, was itself only a spurious unity' (p.103). Almost immediately, moreover, an even greater bump disrupts the illusion of unity that the first jolt had engendered. The cause of the accident is as unknown as the road that gives rise to it, but the victims seem compelled to try to isolate and identify a causal connection. Determined to discover the animal involved by its tracks,

They traced back the writhing of the tyres to the source of their disturbance . . . Steady and smooth ran the marks of the car, ribbons neatly nicked with lozenges; then all went mad. Certainly some external force had impinged, but the road had been used by too many objects for any one track to be legible, and the torch had created such high lights and black shadows that they could not interpret what it revealed. (p. 104)[57] □

If Ronny stands in as an incompetent reader in Forster's text, the tyre tracks inscribe the multiple significations that his interpretative stance cannot negotiate. They serve as a graphic reminder that 'the permeation of any text by an indefinite and potentially infinite number of other texts implies that meaning is always already indeterminate'.[58] The 'indeterminate force' on the Marabar road interrupts the journey undertaken by Ronny and Adela and prefigures the expedition to the Caves where attempts to discover what happened also fail to bring about closure in the narrative.

In his own attempt to trace the significance of the Caves Barratt turns away from the articulations and non-articulations offered by Forster's characters and to the words of the narrator:

■ Though more forthcoming than Godbole, he concedes 'the unspeakable in these outposts' and finds himself similarly reduced to negative comparisons such as 'they are like nothing else in the world' and 'they bear no relation to anything dreamt or seen' (p. 137). Even his assertion that the caves 'are readily described', yields nothing more than a basic floor plan and an almost apologetic 'this is all, this is a Marabar cave'. [. . .] It is their discomforting lack of differentiation which accounts for the fact that 'nothing, nothing attaches to them, and their reputation . . . does not depend upon human speech' (p. 138). Rather than a knowable presence, the essence of a Marabar cave is ultimately an absence, a perfect mirror of 'its own darkness in every direction infinitely' (p. 139).[59] □

At this juncture Barratt perhaps justifies the anxiety, expressed at the close of his essay, that 'drawing parallels between modern post-structuralist theory and a Modernist narrative raises inevitable fears that one may be engaged in yet another form of narrative imperialism, or, at the very least, driving round pegs into square holes'. For though his own mirroring of theory and text is perceptive, the text also becomes an allegory of the critic's own reading process. Between theory and reader, Forster's text, and perhaps, more importantly, the way in which it might in turn resist deconstructive techniques, is obscured. At the same time, Barratt does not extend his critical perspective to call into question the theorists upon whom he relies. Theory and text reflect each other unproblematically:

■ As Forster's portrait of the Raj affirms, 'one cannot locate a proper ground of substance or subjectivity, ontology or theology, being or truth that is not caught up in a web of other-relations or a chain of differentiation'.[60] The Marabar cave, then, is a mirror waiting to disperse, divide and deconstruct the visitor's 'presence' not with a reflection of that 'presence', but rather 'that differential relation of alterity which breaks apart all "presence" of being or of conscious thought'.[61] Devoid of presence itself, the Marabar cave functions like Derrida's trace made manifest; 'it is not a presence but is rather the simulacrum of a presence that dislocates, displaces and refers beyond itself. The trace has, properly speaking, no place . . . for effacement belongs to the very structure of the trace'.[62]

Even as the elephant with its entourage moves towards the hills, 'a new quality occurred . . . Everything seemed cut off at the root, and therefore infected with illusion' (p. 152). The region surrounding the hills seems pervaded with the 'play of differences' which 'involves syntheses and referrals that prevent there from being at any moment or in any way a simple element that is present in and of itself and refers only to itself'.[63] 'What were these mounds – graves, breasts of the goddess Parvati? The villagers beneath gave both replies.' Even Adela is affected as she first cries out, '"a snake!"' and then, aided by the objective clarity of binoculars, concedes, '"it isn't a snake"' (p. 152) but a stump that looks like one. When Aziz looks through the binoculars, however, he, like the villagers, sees a snake that looks like a stump. 'Nothing was explained', confusion only increases as the stones of the Kawa Dol draw near, plunging 'straight into the earth, like cliffs into the sea' (p. 153).

Mrs. Moore, securely possessed of her metaphysical certainties that '"God . . . is . . . love"', and that He '"has put us on earth to love our neighbours and to show it, and He is omnipresent, even in India"' (p. 70), is swallowed up by the small 'black hole' (p. 158) of the first cave. It is in the claustrophobic confusion of the cave that she encounters the deconstructive force which 'reveals beneath the foundations of the metaphysics an indefinite root system that nowhere touches ground in a transcendental instance that would itself be without roots or ancestors'.[64] It manifests itself to her as a 'terrifying echo . . . entirely devoid of distinction'. Resistant to the constraints of the alphabet, it is '"bou-oum", or "ou-boum"'. No matter how different the original sounds, at once 'an overlapping howling noise begins, echoes generate echoes, and the cave is stuffed with a snake composed of small snakes which writhe independently' (p. 159). The echo works, like Derrida's *iteration*, 'to make visible the lack of ground for the alleged originary difference, thus rendering all subsequent distinctions indeterminate . . . It produces chaos because it magnifies and brings into view these initial uncertainties.'[65]

Almost immediately, it begins 'in some indescribable way to

undermine her hold on life' (p. 160). Her metaphysical certainties have been deconstructed, stripped of their 'presence' by the cave's 'absence'. '"Pathos, piety, courage – they exist, but are identical, and so is filth"' (p. 160). Suddenly, 'difference and identity relate to each other within each other, mutually supplementing each other in a way that precludes a rigorous hierarchical and oppositional division'.[66] The infinity and eternity of Mrs. Moore's *transcendental signifiers* have been robbed of their vastness. Into that vast emptiness now flows disillusion, and 'at the edge of her mind' the divine presence of her religion appears as 'poor little talkative Christianity' (p. 161), its divine words reduced to '"boum"' (p. 159). Unable, of course, to celebrate the absence of a centre or a ground, Mrs. Moore perceives it as loss of certainty and comes instead to what, for her, is that 'twilight of the double vision' where 'the horror of the universe and its smallness are both visible at the same time' (p. 212).

Adela, "from the Greek meaning 'unclear' or 'not manifest'",[67] purports, nonetheless, to be 'the logical girl' (p. 26), blessed with 'an abundance of common sense'. She wanders up the Kawa Dol preoccupied by a rationally detached self-analysis of her intended marriage. But the pattern of footholds on the rocks, identical to the pattern 'traced in the dust by the wheels of the Nawab Bahadur's car', somehow suggests to her that other question, 'what about love?' (p. 162). With her mind divided, albeit 'her emotions well under control' (p. 163), she enters her cave alone. But there, in the face of the irrational that inheres within it, her cool British rationalism fails. And when she flies headlong out of the cave, it is her very self that feels the threat of division. The struggle within her self against the disruption of her centre or ground takes on, in Adela's mind, the guise of an attempted rape by Aziz.

The illusion of attempted rape created by Adela in order to resist the division of her rational self is subsumed as reality by the Chandrapore Raj as readily as was the tree stump snake by the villagers. Indeed, once Adela is in their protective custody, the Club members fan the flickering flame of her delusion into a fine hatred and fear which borders on imperial madness. Invoking images of madonna figures of the Empire, helpless before attacking '"niggers"' (p. 188), the Raj appropriates Adela's imagined violation to raise its own hierarchical worldview to new extremes of certainty and presence. It is a certainty more than ripe for a deconstructive unravelling as Forster gives us the subaltern's unwittingly farcical pronouncement that '"any native who plays polo is all right. What you've got to stamp on is these educated classes, and, mind, I do know what I'm talking about this time"' (p. 192).

Vibrating between 'hard common sense and hysteria' (p. 199),

Adela finds the rational certainty of 'her own logic' still being challenged by the reversing, displacing force of the iterating echo of her own irrationality.[68] Unleashed by the 'absence' in Marabar it gives the 'presence' of her rational self no respite. Her newly awakened intuitive awareness recognizes that the incident 'was her crime, until the intellect, reawakening . . . set her again upon her sterile round' (p.200). Although Mrs. Moore refuses to offer Adela any insight into the persistence of her echo, her mere presence seems to add strength to the disruptive force of Adela's intuitive awareness. When she begins to profess Aziz's innocence, Ronny feels a 'shiver like impending death' (p.208) passing over him, and he quickly moves to reassert reason and certainty in the face of this disconcerting equivocation. In the face of her efforts to claim an intuitive perception of the truth of her experience, which now includes a belief in Aziz's innocence in 'the idea more than the words', Ronny assures her that her truth is 'complete illusion' (p.209). But the most revealing attempt to reestablish her previous conviction in the reality of Aziz's guilt is his reminder that '"the whole station knows it"' (p.210). Far too much has been invested by the Raj in her original version of what happened to let something like self-doubt and uncertainty disrupt it.[69] ☐

While Barratt brings the force of deconstructive criticism to bear upon the British in Chandrapore, and infuses the landscape they inhabit with unsettling tropes drawn from post-structuralist theory, it seems worthwhile adding, at this juncture, a supplement to his reading. This comes in the form of Paul B. Armstrong's 'Reading India: Forster and the Politics of Interpretation', published in 1992. Informed by Richard Rorty's notion of liberal irony, which Forster's work prefigures, Armstrong reads *A Passage to India* as a text that explores the difficulties of producing a 'non-reified' knowledge of otherness. In contrast to Barratt, Armstrong identifies the deconstructive potential of Forster's text with both Indian and British subjects:

■ Forster suggests the ubiquity of the obstacles to the ideal of knowledge he seeks by portraying the Indians as guilty of the same acts of misreading which he finds among the British, and for the same epistemological reasons. After the novel accuses the British of misconstruing Indian signs, it then shows the Indians committing the same mistakes.[70] ☐

Following Barratt's attention to the critique of British rationalism he uncovers in Forster's text, the supplement offered here balances and also extends the terms of Barratt's analysis. Crucially, it also calls into question the opposition between British and Indian systems of thought implied by Barratt.

Once he has dealt with various characters in the text, Barratt turns to the court scenes in *A Passage to India*, moving from individual to institutional examples of empiricism. Here, as at other key moments, Barratt lets Ryan explain:

■ Of course, since to focus or fix upon a single event or truth is itself 'necessarily to blur the edges or margins',[71] the court's very function has from the beginning rendered it susceptible to deconstruction.

> If an event or a thing is determined, if a decision is made to short-circuit the play of differential relations that mixes inside and outside at the margin and makes analysis potentially indeterminable, that determination is not a natural revelation of truth conceived as the presence of the thing itself, but an institution . . . that is, conventional and constructed.[72]

Such a constructed 'truth' is McBryde's general truth that, based upon the scientific principles of 'Oriental pathology', 'the darker races are physically attracted by the fairer, but not vice versa' (p. 222). Such a truth, in turn, reflects the degree to which the Raj's notion of critical inquiry and determination of truth coincides with the imposition of the monolithic institution of narrative imperialism. How fitting then that it is that other monolith, the Marabar Hills, which imposes its disruptive imprint upon the proceedings.

Although Adela takes the stand to present the critical element of a predetermined narrative, the blur of the margins is suddenly transmuted into the clarity of the centre:

> A new and unknown sensation protected her, like magnificent armour. She didn't think what had happened, or even remember in the ordinary way of memory, but she returned to the Marabar Hills, and spoke from them across a sort of darkness to Mr. McBryde. The fatal day recurred, in every detail, but now she was of it and not of it at the same time, and this double relation gave it indescribable splendour. (p. 230)

No longer terrified of this double vision, Adela retracts the truth upon which so much of the Chandrapore Raj's identity has come to be grounded. With the unwanted hollowness of truth and meaning finally penetrating the closed minds in the courtroom, that corner of the Raj begins to unravel. Major Callendar tries vainly to deny its very utterance through the futile intervention on '"medical grounds"' (p. 232). McBryde, dumbfounded, can only apprehend it in terms of broken machinery and madness. Mrs. Turton, fearing another Indian

Mutiny, takes on the tones of a shrieking harridan. 'To deconstruct the opposition', says Derrida, 'is above all, at a particular moment, to reverse the hierarchy.'[73] It must, 'through a double gesture . . . put into practice a *reversal* of the classical opposition *and* a general *displacement* of the system. It is on that condition alone that deconstruction will provide the means of *intervening* in the field of the oppositions it criticizes.'[74] The dynamic of deconstruction is both mirrored and elevated in Forster's exquisite summation of the court's collapse:

> And then the flimsy framework of the court broke up, and shouts of derision and rage culminated, people screamed and cursed, kissed one another, wept passionately. Here were the English, whom their servants protected, there Aziz fainted in Hamidullah's arms. Victory on this side, defeat on that – complete for one moment was the antithesis. Then life returned to its complexities, person after person struggled out of the room to their various purposes, and before long no one remained on the scene of the fantasy but the beautiful naked god. Unaware that anything unusual had occurred, he continued to pull the cord of his punkah, to gaze at the empty dais and the overturned special chairs, and rhythmically to agitate the clouds of descending dust. (pp. 232–33)[75] □

It is with this account of the courtroom drama, rather than the third section of the narrative, that Barratt's analysis closes. Notwithstanding his reservations about his own method of reading the text, Barratt reasserts the coincidence between Forster's understanding of truth, the work of the post-structuralists and, indeed, his own outlook. Curiously, like the two previous critics, he refers fleetingly at the close of his analysis to Forster's sexuality – a figure for otherness that is glossed in this account:

■ It seems to me, however, that the concerns of Forster's modernist text reveal a startlingly postmodern awareness of the imperfections inherent within a language that divides the world into the kinds of fundamental oppositions he portrays in *A Passage to India*. His text seems, moreover, a kind of working illustration of deconstruction in the way that the enigmatic indeterminacy of the Marabar caves at its centre works to destabilize the foundational truths of Mrs. Moore, Adela, and the Chandrapore Raj respectively. Perhaps born of the marginal vantage point dictated by his sexual 'otherness', Forster seems to have understood implicitly that the physical world is not a structure built out of independently existing transcendental truths, 'but rather a web of relationships between elements whose meaning arises from their relation to the whole'.[76] And instead of a well defined structure of determinate signifiers and signifieds, human language is much more like the sprawling, limitless interactive muddle or mystery that is India itself. Nothing is identifiable, 'the mere asking of a question causes it to disappear or to merge into something else' (p.101). Like Godbole's notion of acts of good and evil, meaning cannot be conceived of in definable isolation, but only in terms of the interconnectedness of everything.[77] □

The last essay in this chapter approaches Forster's indeterminacy from a completely different perspective to that of the three previous critics. Entitled 'E.M. Forster's *A Passage to India*: What Really Happened in the Caves', Jo Ann Hoeppner Moran's essay, published in 1988, takes what is perhaps the most frequently asked question about the text and claims to supply the answer. The question is turned into a statement and the promise of resolution. In order to solve the mystery of the Caves, Moran's detective work leads her firstly to consider the circumstantial evidence, Forster's own comments on his text:

■ Despite the centrality of the caves, it was E.M. Forster's intention in the final published version of *A Passage to India* that the reader come away from the cave sequence with an impression of muddle and a sense of inexplicable mystery. This failure to let the reader see clearly has struck some critics as unfair.[78] But when Goldsworthy Lowes Dickinson wrote to Forster in 1924 complaining that what happened in the caves was puzzling and that Forster should have been more explicit, Forster replied:

In the cave it is *either* a man, or the supernatural *or* an illusion. And even if I know! My writing mind therefore is a blur here – i.e. I will it to remain a blur, and to be uncertain, as I am of many facts in daily life. This isn't a philosophy of aesthetics. It's a particular trick I felt justified in trying because my theme was India. It sprang from my subject matter. I wouldn't have attempted it in other countries, which though they contain mysteries or muddles, manage to draw rings round them.[79]

Later, in 1934, in a review of a novel by William Plomer, Forster reflected that he had 'tried to show that India is an unexplainable muddle by introducing an unexplained muddle – Miss Quested's experience in the cave. When asked what happened there, *I don't know.*'[80] Because of Forster's unwillingness to tell what Adela experienced, we are still, as Louise Dauner puts it, 'literally and metaphorically, in the dark as to what really happened to Adela Quested in the cave; and yet this episode is the structural core of the novel'.[81]

The weight of critical opinion has concluded that Adela had a hallucinatory experience that she perceived as rape, prepared for by her ruminations on marriage with Ronny Heaslop and her sudden realization, as she toiled over a rock preparatory to entering the cave, that she did not love the man she planned to wed. That Adela was hallucinating is a solution suggested in the novel by Cyril Fielding but never quite agreed to by Adela, who responds, twice, '"perhaps it was the guide"' (p. 242) and '"Let us call it the guide"' (p. 261). Despite Adela's failure to embrace Fielding's suggestion, most commentators have built upon it, drawing, for example, parallels between the hallucinatory 'rape' and the rape that her union without love to Ronny Heaslop would have been.[82] Yet, there is something implausible about Adela's having forcefully torn the strap of her binoculars as the consequence of an illusion. And although it is not always convincing to conclude anything from an author's prior intentions, the earlier draft stages of the book make it clear that there *was* an assault of a definitely physical nature, even if that assault was by Aziz, an option no longer countenanced by the narrator in the final version, where Aziz's innocent actions are followed in great detail during the time Adela is in the cave.[83] ☐

Having dealt with the author of the mystery and considered the textual evidence, Moran turns to critical responses to the text, looking for a consensus:

■ Other commentators have responded to their reading of *A Passage to India* by concluding that Forster never satisfactorily explains what happened and probably did not know himself.[84] That the very center of such a carefully crafted novel as *A Passage to India* should remain unexplained seems inexplicable. That a novel where, as one critic puts it 'all details count, as they do in Hinduism itself', should not detail the crucial event in the novel seems, to some, like a failure.[85] That an author whose narrative voice is so omniscient and controlling should abandon his control at the critical moment seems inherently dishonest.[86] And yet, Forster, as narrator of *A Passage to India*, seems unlikely to have failed in such an obvious way in his greatest work or to have departed from his consistently honest and omniscient narrative stance even in the face of the mysteries and nihilism of the caves. In fact, Forster does tell us what happened in the caves, albeit in a typically subtle way, spacing out the clues to the solution through the text.[87] ☐

Moran then proceeds to make visible these clues and to deduce from them a theory about what occurs in the Caves:

■ Forster begins by telling the reader that the Marabar Caves are extraordinary. He says it twice in the first chapter and once again in the first chapter of Part Two. But what, the main characters ask (except Godbole who appears to know, and Ronny, who pretends to know), is extraordinary about them? Forster gives several answers. In the first place, they are not large, nor holy, nor ornamented, nor do they have sculptures, nor stalactites (pp. 91–92). The description is filled with negatives. Early in the novel Professor Godbole foregoes the pleasure of describing them in any positive way. In Part Two, it is noted that they are older than anything in the world, older than all spirit. Their pattern never varies; there are no carvings to distinguish them. Nothing attaches to them. Hinduism 'has scratched and plastered a few rocks' (p. 137), and Buddha 'left no legend of struggle or victory in the Marabar'. They are dark: 'there is little to see, and no eye to see it' (p. 138) without striking a match. The rocks absorb no sound, producing an echo that is 'entirely devoid of distinction' (pp. 158–59). There appears to be only one positive attribute – their highly polished stone surface, which takes a reflected light like an imprisoned spirit, yielding lovely colors and faint shadings that reveal the 'life of the granite' almost as though the stone were sensible, with 'fists' and 'fingers' and 'skin' (p. 138).[88] □

The anthropomorphic representations of the Caves provide Moran with an important clue to their significance. This she elaborates by considering the Jainist religion.[89] What is crucial here is the question of the stones and the way in which they might be read. As Moran points out, the stones appear to articulate themselves. As the Marabar expedition moves over them, 'the boulders say, "I am alive" and the small stones answer, "I am almost alive"' (p. 161). For Moran, the Caves and assorted stones form the bedrock upon which spirituality in *A Passage to India* rests. She argues that 'Forster is taking seriously the position advanced by some of the major religious and philosophical systems (for instance, Hinduism, Jainism, neo-Platonism) that caves and stones have life, and are of a deep spiritual nature'.[90] As she goes on to explain:

■ The jaina view is that there is a continuity of consciousness from the lowest to the highest stages, that every state has a soul, and that at no stage is any *jiva* [soul] to be despised or looked down upon. Life in all its forms is sacred and is not to be disturbed by any kind of violence. There is, in the jain religion, a profound reverence for life that extends even to stones and includes an ethical component, called *Ahimsa*, that insists on the strict observance of the principle of nonviolence. [. . .] Injury, for the Jains, involves positive interference, and so there is an exhortation to the religious to practice noninterference. Anyone violating that tenet, whether consciously or unconsciously, has left the world worse than she or he found it – has committed a crime that requires expiation.

Forster's treatment of the stones throughout *A Passage to India*, as well as his description of the Marabar caves, suggests his awareness of a Jain cosmology in which the human element is only part of a 'continuum of existence extending to oranges, cactuses, crystals, bacteria, mud and stones',[91] where stones, rocks and of course caves are not even necessarily the least of these elements.[92] □

Having outlined the philosophical, ethical and spiritual systems that coalesce in the Jainist religion, and which apparently inform *A Passage to India*, Moran turns her attention to Adela. How does an understanding of Jainism shed light on what happens in the Caves?

■ Two links are developed in the novel. In the first place, as the novel opens, Adela sees the caves and wants to touch them; following this, the narrator persistently links the caves to her marital concerns. At the very beginning, Adela, when she first sees the Marabar Hills in the distance, thinks, 'How lovely they suddenly were! But she couldn't touch them. In front, like a shutter, fell a vision of her married life . . . they would see the Lesleys and the Callendars . . . while the true India slid by, unnoticed. Colour would remain . . . and movement would remain . . . Perched up on the seat of a dogcart, she would see them. But the force that lies behind colour and movement would escape her even more effectively than it did now. She would see India always as a frieze, never as a spirit . . .' (p. 66).

During a conversation with Fielding in his Garden House, Adela's unpremeditated decision not to marry Ronny is linked to the Caves (pp. 90–91). This link is further confirmed, albeit negatively, when Adela, in following up her decision talks to Ronny, '"It's something very different, nothing to do with the caves, that I wanted to talk over with you . . . I've finally decided we are not going to be married, my dear boy"' (p. 99). Their subsequent reconciliation takes place on the Marabar Road, in the dark, (like the caves), and is related to their touching. As Adela gets closer to the caves, during the expedition, her mind becomes even more preoccupied with her upcoming marriage. Indeed, it is as she toils over a rock that the thought intrudes, '"What about love?"' (p. 162). The question was suggested by the rocks themselves, which traced a pattern similar to that of the car tracks on the Marabar road. She was vexed by the question, and her response is to stand with her eyes on the sparkling rock, feeling a lot 'like a mountaineer whose rope has broken' (p. 163). It is at this point, 'having no one else to speak to on that eternal rock' (pp. 163–64), that she asks Aziz her awkward questions about his marriage, concluding with the muddled and inappropriate question, '"Have you one wife or more than one?"' Aziz having lost his psychological poise, plunges into one of the Caves. Adela thinking simultaneously about her marriage and that 'sightseeing bores me' (p. 164), walks into another. It is at this point that the mysterious attack occurs, which Adela interprets as an attempted rape by Aziz. With her mind on marriage and the nature of love, any assault of her senses would naturally tend to be interpreted in a sexual framework, and it may be that Adela's later hysteria is related to her psychological realization that a loveless marriage with Ronny would be the equivalent to the rape she felt she had barely averted in the cave.

It is a full seven chapters after the alleged assault that Forster reintroduces Adela into the novel. In the internal dialogues and the externalized speech Adela engages in at this point, we have a commentary, widely spaced from the initial event, that enhances one's understanding of the earlier episode and helps unravel the mystery of it. Recuperating from the attack and her precipitous flight down a cactus-infested hill, Adela is acutely aware of the power of touch, for 'She had been touched by the sun, also hundreds of cactus spines had to be picked out of her flesh.' Previously she had not thought much about touch, as she tended to approach matters with her mind. Now everything was focused on the surface of her body. 'In space things touch, in time things part', she notes while the cactus thorns are being extracted painfully from her body. 'She would begin a speech as if nothing particular had happened' (p. 199).

> 'I went into this detestable cave', she would say dryly, 'and I remember scratching the wall with my finger-nail, to start the usual echo, and then as I was saying there was this shadow, or sort of shadow, down the entrance tunnel, bottling me up. It seemed like an age, but I suppose the whole thing can't have lasted thirty seconds really. I hit at him with the glasses, he pulled me round the cave by the strap, it broke, I escaped, that's all.' (p. 199)

As if to make sure that the reader does not miss this, Forster reiterates Adela's point on the next page. 'She had struck the polished wall – for no reason – and before the comment had died away he followed her, and the climax was the falling of her field-glasses' (p. 200). Forster is also careful to remind the reader of Adela's natural honesty of mind, a comment by the narrator that should alert the reader to take these passages at face value.[93] □

At this point, Moran moves towards her conclusion with the following conviction:

■ Adela's sense of having done evil ought also to be taken seriously. If the interpretation presented here is correct, it is not the caves that are evil but instead Adela's action in violating them. The echo, which stays with her, 'prolonged over the surface of her life' (p.200), is then the constant reminder of her violent act, despite her intellect's assurance that she committed no crime. If one takes to heart the Jain beliefs and the Jain nature of the caves, then one would have to agree with Chaman Sahni, that, 'from the Indian standpoint the caves cannot be conceived of as representing evil in the universe, as most western critics seem to believe'.[94]

By the time of the trial, Adela is no longer sure what happened. She now knows that Aziz did not follow her into the caves (p.231), but what did occur has become problematic. Fielding offers Adela the explanation that it was a hallucination. Only half-heartedly she thinks that perhaps it was the guide or someone else, an unknown person from another cave. Finally, just before her departure, she offers an explanation to Fielding, that arises out of a growing indifference. '"Let us call it the guide" . . . "It will never be known. It's as if I ran my finger along that polished wall in the dark, and cannot get further"' (p.261).[95] □

For Moran, these comments are misleading and Adela should not be taken at 'her word'. In a curious twist, it is the Caves that are victimised, albeit unintentionally, by Adela:

■ The most reasonable course of action for the reader and literary critic would seem to be to take Adela at her word and to assume that when she entered the cave she scratched or struck the polished walls to raise an echo. Although later she says she only ran her finger along the wall, Adela is not lying or trying to mislead, because, for her, there would be no fundamental differences between scratching, striking, or simply touching. For the caves, however, or for anyone who valued the caves (as did the local villagers, one of whom acted as a guide), there is a significant distinction between scratching and touching. The first implies a more violent action, a marking of the polished surface (where Forster has been at pains to note that no marks exist). Indeed, one might even go so far as to suggest a rape of the rock. Adela's action, taken in total innocence, may have had a more malevolent meaning to a devotee of the caves. The attack that then took place (probably by the guide although this too remains highly speculative) was never intended to be sexual but only to pull her away from the side of the cave. It took on sexual overtones only in Adela's mind, as a consequence of her preoccupation with her projected loveless marriage with Ronny. What may have been perceived by one person (an Indian) as an effort to stop a sacrilegious act was perceived by another (an Englishwoman) as a sexual assault. The muddle could not have been worse, nor the consequences more destructive. But as a metaphor for the book as a whole, concerned as Forster was with the uncomprehending manner in which the English had scratched (and hurt) the surface of India, it is perfect.[96] □

CHAPTER FOUR

'Centuries of Carnal Embracement': Forster's Sexual Politics

THE ESSAYS in this chapter all focus attention on the sexual politics of *A Passage to India*. Beginning with Elaine Showalter's 1977 essay on Forster's critique of marital ideology, the chapter goes on to consider Frances L. Restuccia's use of gynesis as a means of figuring the radically subversive potential of *A Passage to India*. In her attempt to synthesise both Anglo-American and French feminism, Restuccia engages with some of the assumptions made by Showalter, while elaborating and refining others. The final essay, by Eve Dawkins Poll, while informed by feminist discourse, focuses on the ideological and narrative function of the ingenue, the figure that enables Forster's representations of cultural difference to culminate in the calamity of the Caves. Although all three essays included here focus predominantly on issues relating to gender, none of the critics is unmindful of the imperial context in which Forster's sexual politics are dramatised.

Critics approaching the question of Forster's sexual politics are invariably drawn to Adela and Forster's representations of her experiences before, during and after the expedition to the Marabar Caves. Although the Caves are a fascinating source for speculation on the philosophical, intellectual and spiritual dimension to Forster's work, it is perhaps on a less cerebral plane that they exert the most critical interest.[1] For it is the body of the woman and, more specifically, the forces that operate within and upon that body that perplexes criticism of *A Passage to India*.[2] While early critics of the text have been prepared to accept Adela's naiveté, her foolishness, or even heatstroke as the source of calamity in the text, this picture of Adela has been made more complex by the emergence of psychoanalytic and feminist criticism.

Writing in 1962, Wilfred Stone offers the following 'diagnosis' of Adela's condition:

■ In clinical terms, Adela no doubt suffered a form of sexual hysteria. She had been tense all that day and, just before entering the cave, had suddenly noticed that Aziz was a very handsome man. She had just as suddenly realized that she and Ronny did not love each other. Moreover, she was in a near-panic about sex generally – virginal, frigid, afraid of being entered, afraid of that return downward and backward which is as illicitly tempting for women as for men.[3] □

While Stone's description of Adela is not altogether helpful as a means of clarifying Forster's sexual politics, Showalter's speculations on Forster's portrayal of both Adela and Aziz offer ways of interrogating the figure of the hysteric and the rapist respectively. In common with Poll, Showalter offers a number of possible answers to the crucial question posed by Restuccia: why does Forster 'invite[s] his reader to entertain the repulsive possibility that Aziz attempted to rape Adela'?[4]

The indeterminacy of *A Passage to India* when it comes to the question of what happens in the Caves opens up the text for feminist readers even as it thwarts the desire to know exactly what happened. The many possible readings of the Caves sequence not only inform the sexual and gender politics of Forster's text but also its inscriptions of cultural difference and power within the imperial context. It is impossible to review the Caves sequence without also taking into consideration Forster's depiction of Aziz, a figure who, like Adela, also comes under close critical scrutiny in any reading of the novel. The textual relationship between Adela and Aziz in *A Passage to India* represents a complex articulation of gendered and colonial power relations alike. As Vron Ware argues, '[g]ender played a crucial role in organising ideas of "race" and "civilization"' in Western discourse:

■ and women were involved in many different ways in the expansion and maintenance of the Empire. The presence of white women, for example, demanded that relations between the 'races' be highly regulated. The increasing number of white women who travelled out to join husbands and families in the colonies, or to work in their own right as missionaries, nurses and teachers, often had far-reaching effects on the social lives of male settlers, and consequently on the status and exploitation of black women.[5] □

In charting the journey undertaken by two such women, Forster's text leaves significant gaps in their narratives. Mrs Moore's spiritual journey and Adela's secular revelations eventually bring about the separation of the two women who travel to India together and have in common a relationship with the white, male imperial subject.

The sexual and racial politics of Forster's text cannot be approached solely by considering individual characters. Alongside Adela are placed the other Anglo-Indian women who, following the crisis in the Caves, and excepting Mrs Moore, form an uneasy sisterhood. For '[a]lthough Miss Quested had not made herself popular with the English, she brought out all that was fine in their character. For a few hours an exalted emotion gushed forth, which the women felt even more keenly than the men, if not for so long' (p.187). It is not simply the representation of Adela that attracts the attention of feminist critics but also the portrayal of these other women in the Anglo-Indian community. Along with the question of Adela, it is the politics of these other gendered representations that forms the basis of the arguments advanced in the following essays.

In 'A Passage to India as "Marriage Fiction": Forster's Sexual Politics',[6] Showalter begins by considering Forster's attitude towards the institution of marriage. In her assessment, she draws on biographical as well as fictional material, in order to show Forster's 'characteristic distrust of the marriage-code',[7] a distrust that aligns him with Fielding in A Passage to India:

■ 'Marriage is too absurd in any case. It begins and continues for such very slight reasons. The social business props it up on one side, and the theological business on the other, but neither of them are marriage, are they? I've friends who can't remember why they married, no more can their wives. I suspect that it mostly happens haphazard, though afterwards various noble reasons are invented. About marriage I am cynical.' (p.260) □

Having established an allegiance between Forster and Fielding, Showalter argues that their shared attitude towards marriage demonstrates a resistance to 'the desire for ownership'.[8] It represents a refusal of a domestic and gendered power structure and, beyond this, a critique of all other forms of ownership: '[l]ike John Stuart Mill, Forster saw the family as the primary socializing force; and like Mill, he suspected that the nuclear patriarchal family was the source of all other human power relations.'[9] By placing Forster and Fielding in relation to Mill's nineteenth-century liberalism, Showalter establishes the radical credentials of both the author and his fictional representative. Yet like Leavis, who invested Margaret Schlegel in Howards End with the full force of liberal-humanist ideals, Showalter is subsequently perplexed by the fate of her chosen character. Unlike Leavis, who was baffled by Margaret's marriage to Henry Wilcox, it is not so much the object of Fielding's desire that surprises Showalter, as the fact that he marries at all. In seeking the logic behind this turn of events Showalter speculates that Forster's homosexuality might have led him to 'yet another reluctant artistic surrender to bourgeois and heterosexual morality'.[10] Alternatively, she admits the possibility, advanced by George Steiner, that *A Passage to India* represents a subliminal reworking of *Maurice*.[11] If either of these readings is given credence, 'we would have to see the marriage of Fielding and Stella as hypocrisy, Forster's concession to the convention of "marriage fiction"'.[12] It is this somewhat judgemental conclusion that Showalter goes on to qualify. For she argues that Forster was not only critical of the institution of marriage but also attracted by the ideal of 'a marriage of true minds, a bond which could satisfy all of his needs for unity, fellowship, love, and continuance, without possessiveness or dominance. Beyond his cynicism, Forster dreamed of the potential of a permanent union.'[13] Such ambivalence towards marriage is further complicated, in Showalter's view, by the imperial setting of the novel:

■ Yet the Anglo-Indian setting, the structure which so liberated Forster's imagination, also reveals some shadows, some unilluminated corners where the author stands in ambiguous relation to the values of his novel. In this essay I wish to show how Forster's ambivalence towards women and marriage is a central quality of his book.

A Passage to India, which has as its central incident an alleged sexual assault, assumes in its narrative a correspondence between sexual and political relations. This aspect of the novel, which we would now call sexual politics, has not received much notice; Oliver Stallybrass is probably representative in regarding sex as a minor theme in *Passage*. Perhaps the oversight is due to the scale of the political and religious dramas in the book, which seem to dwarf its personal and sexual elements. Yet Forster sees connections between all these levels of experience. Demonstrating the links between the British family and imperialism, between purdah and Indian nationalism, Forster asks not only whether an Indian can be friends with an Englishman, but more profoundly, whether the institutions of marriage and the state are shaped to protect us from the threat of equality. The quality of 'asking' should be emphasized. Just as the ambiguous nature of the incident in the caves is central to his novel, ambiguous views on sexual relationships are at its peripheries.

An essential part of this demonstration is Forster's portrayal of his female characters. With the exception of Mrs. Moore, the English-women in the novel have been harshly treated by the critics. Forster, it is true, is hard on them; but not as hard as are critics, who notice the women only to condemn them. Wilfred Stone, for example, comments that 'Anglo-Indian women are even more obnoxious than their men'.[14]

At this juncture, Showalter does not attempt to refute the views of these critics nor, indeed, the way in which Forster depicts the women in *A Passage to India*. Instead, she assumes that Forster's women are accurate representations of a particular reality and seeks to rationalise them. Here, she looks outside the text to uncover the condition in which these fictional women lived. The social and cultural logic that supports the disempowered status of Forster's women provides Showalter with an explanation for their behaviour in the text. The Anglo-Indian women's deplorable attitude towards the natives originates in a denial of their own disempowered state:

■ Placed in a situation where they have no real identity, the recognition of others becomes their only guarantee of existence. Fielding is therefore a threat to them, because he ignores them. [. . .] The [women's] relationship to the Indian natives is even more threatening, because the women do not wish to confront the fact of their own subjection; to see themselves mirrored in this 'subject race', and to realize that they too are the objects of a 'contemptuous affection'. Maintaining status over the Indians gives them some reassurance.[15] □

Having accounted for the condition of the Anglo-Indian women, Showalter returns to the analogy between them and the Indian women that Forster's text asserts:

■ Yet Forster underlines the similarities between their positions and the natives. Like the Indians, the women are presented as intuitive, emotional, sensitive, inconsistent, and vain, living a precarious existence, dependent on the approval of the master race, and dimly aware that they always stand in danger of losing it. Like the 'uncertain, cowering, recovering, giggling' (p. 62) purdah women, to whom they feel a complacent superiority, the Englishwomen are infantilized. Narcissistic, weak, and helpless, they exert a childish tyranny over the men, for absolute powerlessness corrupts as well as absolute power. Collector Turton states, '"It's our women who make everything more difficult out here"', and he is not the only man in the novel who resents them. Perhaps as Forster notes, 'there is a grain of resentment in all chivalry' (p. 217).

Nonetheless, men and women together have managed to collaborate in the pretense that marriage brings them mutual contentment and fulfillment. Together, in the annual ritual of the Club play, they celebrate the marriage-ethic of England, tinned for belated export to the colonies like the peas and the salmon. Forster points up the irony of the occasion with particular care. First of all, in their isolation in the hot dark clubhouse, where the windows have been barred 'lest the servants should see their memsahibs acting' (p. 45), the Anglo-Indian women are in a kind of purdah themselves. Second, the play they have chosen, *Cousin Kate*, is a mildly anti-feminist comedy, a hit of the

London season of 1903 by H.H. Davies, in which the anonymous heroine, a successful novelist, yearns only for marriage. '"A woman's life is so meaningless by itself"', Kate insists. '"I have a profession, I'm successful, I'm invited and welcomed everywhere – but I'm lonely . . . I'd give it all up for a real home with a husband and children."'[16] As a final touch to this scene, the part of Kate is played by the adventurous Miss Derek, who, we later learn, is having an adulterous affair with Colonel McBryde. No irony, however, is perceived by the English-women, who have persuaded themselves that marriage and mother-hood should be the central realities of their lives.

The narrowness and specialization of their lives makes them espe-cially susceptible to moral atrophy, the occupational disease of the Anglo-Indian. Aziz points out at the beginning of the novel that while the British men, on the average, last about two years before surrender-ing their integrity, the women disintegrate in six months.

Forster's portrayal of the Englishwomen could be taken as an expansion of his friend G. L. Dickinson's hostile description in a letter: 'It's the women more than the men that are at fault. There they are, without their children, with no duties, with empty minds and hearts, trying to fill them by playing tennis and despising the natives.'[17] How much sympathy, then, does he feel for the women? I think we must accept the fact that Forster often saw women as part of the enemy camp. While not precisely antagonistic to them, he believed them to be allied with the forces and institutions of repression. As Quentin Bell puts it, Forster was 'happier with his own sex'.[18] And he was not very enthusiastic about feminism even as Virginia Woolf articulated it. Thus his attitude in this novel may simply be contemptuous, in the tradition of most male British travellers in India.

On the other hand, Forster tells us enough about the circumstances in which the women find themselves to make it clear that they are the victims and not the villains of their culture.[19] They too are exports from England, symbols of the distance between the rulers and the natives. It is not their fault that their presence is necessary to keep the men from sexual contact with the natives – male and female – as the food and tobacco shipments keep them from curry and *pan*. Forster resents the restraints – first external, and then absorbed – which keep the British from experiencing the mixture of the sensual and the holy which characterized India to him. In this sense, he sympathizes to a considerable degree with at least one Englishwoman, Adela Quested. In fact, there is much of Forster himself in Adela's struggle not to be pinned down by the codes of the compound.[20] □

This association of Forster with Adela significantly complicates Showalter's earlier comments on Forster's relationship to Fielding. Taken together, Fielding and Adela constitute an interesting interpretative coupling for Showalter. The fate of both figures becomes intimately bound up with Forster's resistance to and eventual reconciliation with a conventional marital ideology:

■ A significant subplot in *A Passage to India* is the struggle of Adela Quested to avoid this fate. A pilgrim, as her name suggests, Adela is in double jeopardy in India. Both British and female, she confronts forces in Chandrapore which work to make her smaller, duller, and weaker. In her painful quest, she succumbs temporarily to the marriage-ethic of Anglo-India, and to its corrupting and deadening influence; but ultimately she is able to cast it off, and to escape destruction, at the price of renouncing love.[21] □

As Showalter comments, 'Adela is one of the least class-bound characters in the book, except in the sense that she is limited by her sex [. . .]. In her rejection of the marriage-convention, she is yet unable to escape the cage of sex-roles.'[22]

At this point, Showalter's recognition of the textual parallels between disempowered women on both sides of the imperial divide moves her beyond the representations that feature in Forster's text. She takes her cue from Forster's novel, which, although 'chiefly interested in the claustrophobic codes of Western marriage' also 'touches on marriage-customs of India, which are much more sinister'.[23] In order further to explore these customs she turns to historical and sociological evidence. Her analysis of the text moves in this direction because despite the fact that 'critics have acknowledged that Indian society is not the ideal antithesis of British Imperialism, no one has pointed out the radical immorality of India's male supremacist culture, or even commented on the effects of purdah on Indian character'.[24] Here, Showalter's essay moves between textual analysis and an attempt to document socio-historical realities. Her reading of Aziz, the principal 'Indian character' in Forster's text is filtered through this documentation:

■ The institution of purdah, under which nearly 40 million women, mostly Moslem, were living as late as 1930, was a form of slavery responsible for widespread ignorance and disease. Among the poor, purdah was not strictly enforced, since the demands of survival often left no room for convention; and among the rich, adequate provision could be made to render a life of sequestration comfortable, healthy, and even luxurious. But among the middle classes (to which Aziz would belong) doctors found that women were coerced by 'conventional respectability [to adopt purdah] in its most rigid form without having the means to render the seclusion healthy or even tolerable'.[25]

The women's apartments were deliberately kept dark and airless; thus *purdahnashi* women were particularly prone to tuberculosis, and to many other diseases as well; in Calcutta in 1912, the death rate for women was 1.6 times that of men. Vitamin D deficiency produces disastrous effects; according to Dr. K. Vaughan, 'the present working of the purdah system, by depriving the girls and women of sunlight, is directly responsible for the production of osteomalacia [a condition especially frequent in pregnancy, characterized by softening of the bones, with subsequent deformity, weakness, and pain], gross pelvic deformity, and the deaths of thousands of mothers and children in childbirth annually'.[26] Aziz's wife, we should recall, is a purdah woman who dies in childbirth.

Reforms sought by the All-India Women's Educational and Social Conference in 1917 included abolition of purdah and child marriage, prevention of polygamy and enforced widowhood, and an end to commercial and religious prostitution. In a 1921 census, Calcutta (where Aziz plans to visit a brothel) was discovered to have 10,000 prostitutes, 1,000 under the age of thirteen; the practice of kidnapping lower-caste girls was widespread, as was their sale by parents. Marriage, moreover, resembled legalized rape. Fully half of the female population was married by the age of fifteen; their consent was not an issue, much less mutual love.[27] □

Showalter argues that these conditions are not the primary concern of Forster's text, which instead focuses on:

■ the corruption of the marital relationship when it is enforced on all; and on the effects of purdah on the moral and spiritual character of Indian men. In the character of Aziz particularly can be traced the egoism and limited vision which is the darker side of heroic and romantic nationalism.[28] □

In Showalter's subsequent reading, Aziz's performance in *A Passage to India* directly relates to his support of purdah, and its construction of woman as possession. His attitude towards his Indian wife, and towards Indian women has direct bearing on his responses to Adela. His cultural allegiances and his cross-cultural identification with 'all men' equally appear to compromise his integrity and eventually, in Showalter's account, come to inform his relationship with Adela:

■ As a doctor and a humanist, Aziz ought from the beginning to reject purdah, but his ego is deeply involved in it. '"I believe in the purdah"', he tells Fielding; he makes exceptions for his friends to see his wife: '"All men are my brothers, and as soon as one behaves as such he may see my wife"' (p. 128). For Aziz, women are possessions, albeit prized ones; that a woman is exhibited to her husband's friends is one more sign of her subjection; his convenience, and not her autonomy, is involved. Aziz's theory that the purdah can go when all men are brothers supposes humanity resides in men only; he does not see that the need to enslave women must be overcome before brotherhood can be achieved.

In all his sexual relations, Aziz consults his needs alone and reduces the woman to the level of an object. 'He begat his first child in mere animality' (p. 73), with a wife chosen by his parents and physically unattractive to him. The patient suffering and eventual death of this woman won his love, and he grieves for her. The experience, however, teaches him nothing about love; his attitudes toward women continue to be superficial and egotistical. For Adela he can feel no sympathy because he finds her ugly. Her 'angular body' and freckles are hideous to him (p. 85); furthermore, '"she has practically no breasts"' (p. 131). His reaction to the rape charge is largely one of out-raged sexual pride. Although Aziz is painfully aware of the racist myth believed by the British, that the darker races lust after the pinko-greys, he has his own sexual mythology; he believes that only physical beauty makes a woman desirable, and that plain women really yearn to be raped. Only an acknowledgement of this from Adela will pacify his outrage; he wants her to write an apology reading '"Dear Dr. Aziz, I wish you had come into the cave; I am an awful old hag, and it is my last chance"' (p. 252). Before the trip to the caves, he is planning an excursion to a Calcutta brothel, where he offers to find for Fielding a whore '"with breasts like mangoes"' (p. 131). His lust is 'hard and direct' (p. 116) in contrast to the English whom he perceives as either frigid or indiscriminating, willing to satisfy their needs in the Chandrapore bazaar. Even in prostitutes, Aziz's standards are high.

Aziz's inability to perceive women as other than objects alienates Fielding, who understands Adela's complexity and appreciates the nobility of her self-immolation. Fielding is puzzled by the crudity of Aziz's response to the trial:

> The underlying notion was, 'It disgraces me to have been men-tioned in connection with such a hag.' It enraged him that he had been accused by a woman who had no personal beauty; sexually, he was a snob. This had puzzled and worried Fielding. Sensuality, as long as it is straightforward, did not repel him, but this derived sensuality – the sort that classes a mistress among motor-cars if she is beautiful and among eye-flies if she isn't – was alien to his own emotions, and he felt a barrier between himself and Aziz when-ever it arose. It was in a new form, the old, old trouble that eats the

heart out of every civilization: snobbery, the desire for possessions, creditable appendages; and it is to escape this rather than the lusts of the flesh that saints retreat into the Himalayas. (p. 242)

After the trial, Aziz, who has become 'chief medicine man' (p. 289) to a Hindu court, takes up the cause of the emancipation of woman, but it is not at all clear that his theories are more than frivolous. 'His poems were all on one topic – oriental womanhood. "The purdah must go", was their burden, "otherwise we shall never be free!"' Yet he has a vague notion of hiding the women away from 'the foreigner' (p. 290); women are still possessions, to be released or held as nationalist feeling dictates. And as Fielding reminds him, his private life with his mistress contradicts his espoused doctrine: '"Free your own lady in the first place, and see who'll wash Ahmed, Karim, and Jamila's faces. A nice situation"' (p. 314).[29] □

At this point, Showalter clearly misses the opportunity to extend the terms of her own analysis. Previously, she argues that the behaviour of the Anglo-Indian women is conditioned by their relative disempowerment within a patriarchal system. Aziz's behaviour towards Adela is not apparently related to his status as a native within an imperial structure but to his Muslim inheritance. Even though Showalter is alert to the connection Aziz himself makes between sexual and racial politics, between the subjugation of women and the nationalist cause, she does not pursue this analysis. Her view seems to accord with that of Fielding, who sees that Aziz's position contradicts his politics. The possibility that Aziz's attitude towards Adela relates not so much to his Muslim cultural identity, but to his subjugated masculinity is here bypassed. Aziz is implicated in the oppression of Muslim women and, it is suggested, this must have some bearing on his attitude to the Anglo-Indian women, Adela included:

■ The central event of *A Passage to India* is a trial, and Forster uses it in the traditional literary way, as a spiritual test for all the characters in the book. The mysterious episode in the Marabar Cave is a screen upon which all the characters project their obsessions, personalities, and philosophies. It is important to see that the central male characters in the novel, Aziz and Fielding, undergo a trial as well as Adela; and that all three are guilty in some sense.
Freudian criticism has placed the blame for the incident in the Cave on Adela's projected sexual fantasies. [. . .] But the events in the Marabar Caves are too complicated, too closely connected to the moral experience of the main characters to be reduced to the hallucination of a repressed spinster, even if there were evidence for such a view in the

novel and in its early drafts. In fact, the evidence suggests the opposite – that Adela was not attracted physically to Aziz, and that she longed for emotion rather than sex. 'She did not admire him with personal warmth' (p. 163) according to the novel; in a manuscript Forster wrote emphatically that Aziz 'did not attract her in any sense'. Instead, Adela is undergoing a spiritual crisis; the deadly apathy of Anglo-India has infected her, and for a fortnight she has 'felt nothing acutely' (p. 145). Committed to a loveless marriage with Ronny, she confronts the evil meaning of the legalized rape such a marriage will entail.[30] □

Rejecting the psychoanalytic view, Showalter offers a description of 'loveless marriage' as 'legalized rape'.[31] This questionable association enables her to connect Forster's critique of conventional marriage to the incident in the Caves. It also leads to a somewhat confused language at this point, for the catalyst to Adela's 'spiritual crisis' is reached when she 'confronts the evil meaning of the legalized rape such a marriage [to Ronny] will entail'. The spiritual crisis would appear then to be grounded in a corporeal reality. Before turning to the Marabar Caves, Showalter suggests that the accident on the Marabar road following Adela's rejection of marriage to Ronny, prefigures the later 'assault':

■ In many details, besides location, the accident is like the assault, only more neutral because externalized. The car hits a mysterious animal which only Adela sees, and in her excitement she destroys all the evidence of its appearance (p. 104).[32] All the characters interpret the accident in terms of their personalities and cultural tradition; the Nawals and Mrs. Moore are sure the animal was a ghost; Ronny suspects a hyena, and uses the occasion to justify his views on the incapacities of Indians in an emergency. Adela is uncertain. Yet a fleeting sense of unity and sexual excitement brings Ronny and Adela together. On her way to the Caves, Adela recalls the accident twice, once on the train, once just before entering the Cave. Although she realizes that she and Ronny do not love each other, she determines to go through with the marriage: to break it off 'would cause so much trouble to others; besides, she wasn't convinced that love is necessary to a successful union' (p. 163). For this blackest of Forster's heresies, she will have to suffer.[33] □

From this perspective it appears that Adela is victimised in the text, not only by her unknown assailant but by Forster himself. Despite her earlier resistance of conventional sexual and cultural hierarchies, Adela's reconciliation to a loveless marriage indicates her rejection of a Forsterian ideal. In terms of Showalter's previous identification of Adela with Forster, it would appear that, at this point in the text, the two part company. However, Showalter does not resume the narrative of identification with which she commenced her discussion of Adela. She turns rather to Aziz:

■ Aziz's complicity in the collective evil which culminates in the cave has not been recognized, but it is as appropriate that he undergo a trial as Adela.[34] Generally, readers of the novel have accepted his defense: that rape is a compliment to the woman, and that he does not admire Adela, but finds her repulsive. Even Adela, in dreadful self-abasement, asks Fielding if he thinks she has had the sort of hallucination '"that makes some women think they've had an offer of marriage when none was made"' (p. 240). It is ironic that Forster here brackets marriage with sexual assault. He fails to make clear that rape is not a gesture of admiration but an expression of contempt or hatred. Aziz certainly does not love Adela, but he is contemptuous of her as he is of women generally.[35] □

In Forster's defence, it is Aziz's contempt towards Adela that suggests the motive for his attack.[36] Even though Aziz's response to Adela's lack of beauty is foregrounded it would seem as if Forster's irony operates here. Aziz's attitude towards Adela, as the narrator informs us, is apparently simplified by her lack of physical appeal.

■ How fortunate that it was an 'unconventional' party, where formalities are ruled out! On this basis Aziz found the English ladies easy to talk to, he treated them like men. Beauty would have troubled him, for it entails rules of its own, but Mrs Moore was so old and Miss Quested so plain that he was spared this anxiety. Adela's angular body and the freckles on her face were terrible defects in his eyes, and he wondered how God could have been so unkind to any female form. His attitude towards her remained entirely straightforward in consequence. (p.85) □

Passing over the minor spiritual crisis induced by Adela's lack of beauty, the narrator insists, too readily, that Aziz's attitude towards Adela is simplified in consequence of her appearance. Clearly constructing Adela as an inadequate female form, Aziz is later inspired to offer Fielding a more ample substitute for the flat-chested girl, with '"practically no breasts, if you come to think of it"', in the form of a prostitute with '"breasts like mangoes"'. That Aziz has clearly already '"come to think of it"' and that he speaks of it to Fielding, represents a sexual and cultural transgression on his part. Fielding's own response to Aziz's comments is relayed by the narrator, 'He smiled too, but found a touch of bad taste in the reference to a lady's breasts' (p.131). While uneasy with the sexual camaraderie

Aziz seeks to foster, Fielding does not appear to register the cultural transgression Aziz's comments entail. In his construction of Adela as both
sexual object and 'lack', Aziz's relation to her is far from 'straightforward'. If Forster's critics have failed to connect hatred and contempt
for women with sexual violence, his text does not.

The remainder of Showalter's analysis concentrates on the trial and
its aftermath. Yet though she argues that both Anglo-Indian and Indian
communities share the same 'cultural blindness', it is an assessment of
the former that dominates the last section of her essay.

■ Cultural blindness is apparent in the response of all participants in
the trial. Since both the British and the Indian cultures are permeated
by notions of hierarchy, exclusion, and dominance, they are unified
internally only in opposition to a common enemy; the trial provides a
temporary illusion of unity for both sides. Forster notes ironically and
at some length how sheer racism, and machismo – the imperialistic
duo so neatly connected in the work of an earlier passenger to India,
Rudyard Kipling – are the sources of 'all that was fine' (p. 187) in the
British character. Suddenly, faced with Adela-as-Victim, the women
feel like sisters, and resolve not to be snobs in the future. The men are
dizzy with the sense of patriarchal outrage: 'they had started speaking
of "women and children" – that phrase that exempts the male from
sanity when it has been repeated a few times' (pp. 190–91). Britannia
appears in the form of a Mrs. Blakeston – 'a brainless but most beautiful girl', who with her 'abundant figure' and 'masses of corngold hair',
symbolizes 'all that is worth fighting and dying for' (p. 188). The
intoxicating combination of sex and the possessive instinct stimulates
aggressive feelings and behaviour in the men whose irrational urges
to conquer and avenge are reawakened. In their metonymic system,
the attack on Adela is construed as an attack on male honor and British
authority; when Ronny enters the room, the men rise to their feet 'in
instinctive homage' (p. 195); his property rights have been challenged
as much as Adela's virtue.[37] □

Having detailed the collective response of the Anglo-Indians to the trial,
Showalter returns to Fielding and the question of his marriage:

■ For Fielding the trial poses a series of dilemmas and challenges. A
detached and dispassionate liberal, whose virtues have been 'equilib-
rium' (p. 129) and 'travelling light' (p. 121), he is forced to commit
himself to Aziz's party. In the long run, the trial changes his life, for he
meets Mrs. Moore's daughter Stella, and marries her. Fielding's independence and rootlessness protect him from the hysteria of the British
colony; yet, as Aziz perceives, there is something cold and inhuman in

his isolation. Working his way back into society presents Fielding with many problems. At first he is intimidated by the code of virile fellowship, even though he rejects the crude chauvinism of the British. Aziz makes him ashamed of his own predilections for privacy and sensual control, and he apologizes: "'It is on my mind that you think me a prude about women. I had rather you thought anything else of me'" (p.276).

Throughout the novel, Fielding is the most consistent critic of marriage; yet at the end he marries, and if we can trust Forster's hints (in Ronny's congratulations on his "'son and heir'" [p.303] and the comment that "'their union had been blessed'" [p.312]), will be a father. What has happened to the 'holy' (p.132) ideal of travelling light? In many ways, Fielding seems diminished by his marriage; in dwindling into a husband his values have changed, and he has become part of the community: 'he had thrown in his lot with Anglo-India by marrying a countrywoman, and he was acquiring some of its limitations, and already felt surprise at his own past heroism' (p.313). His marriage separates him from Aziz, and it is a sexual, as well as a political betrayal, for the idea of inter-racial love as a solution to international conflict is the underlying significance of their relationship.

Yet Fielding's commitment suggests that Forster recognized the sterility in his own ideal. Independence and singleness have personal but short-term satisfactions to offer. The other characters pay for their mistakes by exile and renunciation: Adela no longer wants love; Aziz returns to superstition, separation and the comic and suitable punishment of writing long and unpublishable poems on female liberation; he will no longer try to befriend an Englishman. Their decisions, while wholly understandable in terms of circumstances and psychology, are regressive. Fielding's marriage on the other hand is a role which holds out the promise of a new generation. [. . .] The hope of Fielding's marriage is that the negative aspects of the family – its possessiveness, its patterns of mastery and submission – will be cancelled by the mixture of the urban and rational Fielding strain with the sympathetic and mystical Moore strain. The descendants of the Fieldings and the Moores may evolve spiritually beyond their parents.

While it comes as a kind of comic reversal in the novel, Fielding's marriage is also the resolution of themes which Forster has carefully set out. In the Mosque section, a conversation between Fielding and Aziz has revealed the differences between their feelings about self-perpetuation. Aziz cannot understand a man who is indifferent to the immortality of paternity. Fielding insists that he would "'far rather leave a thought behind me than a child'" (p.130). Fielding echoes Bacon's adage when he suggests that "'any man can travel light until he has a wife or children'" (p.132); and Aziz sees the meaning of this at once: Fielding has nothing to lose. In fact, Fielding has nothing and in the aftermath of his encounter with Ronny at the club – his finest moment of public heroism – he experiences with sorrow the fact of his emptiness: 'he felt dubious and discontented suddenly, and wondered whether he was really and truly successful as a human being' (p. 197).

The marriage to Stella Moore resolves the question of Fielding's success by linking him both to the promise of new life and continuity, and to the regenerative cycles of Hinduism. It is to witness the rebirth festival of Shri Krishna that the Fieldings come to Mau; Stella and her brother Ralph are wordlessly responsive to what Fielding calls '"this Krishna business"'. There are hopeful signs that 'the Marabar is wiped out' (p. 313), that the participants have ended that cycle of pain and misunderstanding, and are ready to begin anew.

Yet Forster's uneasiness about this compromise is revealed in numerous details and omissions. The marriage to Stella takes place off stage, and is revealed in the Temple section to the astonishment of Aziz (who barely recalled that Stella existed). Although she actually meets Aziz, and is involved in the baptism-accident at the festival, Stella is never directly described; she is more shadowy and incorporeal than any character in Forster's fiction. In fact, she exists for the reader chiefly through her relationships as daughter, sister, and wife. Her brother Ralph is far more realized as a character. It seems as if Forster does not want to imagine her very fully. Furthermore, Fielding's attitudes toward his marriage are anxious ones. 'He was not quite happy about his marriage. He was passionate physically again – the final flare-up before the clinkers of middle age – and he knew that his wife did not love him as much as he loved her, and he was ashamed of pestering her.' Here Forster seems to be hinting that this is a December–May marriage, with Fielding driven by unreciprocated lust. A vaguer kind of sexual incompatibility is also suggested by this description; its disturbing implications for Fielding are reinforced by his statement that Stella's spiritual intensity makes him feel 'half dead and half blind' (p. 312). Despite all the symbolism of birth and rebirth in this section of the book, Fielding's marriage appears to have crippled and unmanned him.

Thus ultimately the view we have of Fielding's marriage is mixed, and undercut by Forster's own scepticism and mistrust. Even when it holds out the promise of the future, Fielding's marriage is a union of unequal partners: unequal in age, unequal in loving, and thus finally unequal in power. Although he worried much about continuance, Forster could not rejoice in the institutions which made it possible. Fielding's marriage is the most positive gesture towards spiritual evolution he can make; but at the same time, it is a surrender, and a microcosm of the failure of human relationships to solve human problems.[38] □

In '"A Cave of My Own": E.M. Forster and Sexual Politics', published in 1989, Frances L. Restuccia asks and provides a possible answer to the question of why Forster leads his reader to believe that Aziz is a rapist. Her reply to this question is related to the '"Oriental" lesson' of the novel, 'that one must preserve the indefinite nature of things, avoid fixing anything or seeking full clarity'.[39] In order to inculcate this particular lesson, Forster's text leads the reader to 'play [. . .] into the hands of racist Anglo-India' since 'if neither his innocence nor his guilt can be determined, Aziz becomes suspect. Adopting Eastern openness, in other words, requires paradoxically that one at least consider the imperialist position'.[40]

The way in which the character of Aziz is sacrificed to the textual inscription of Eastern indeterminacy is not, however, the prime focus of Restuccia's essay. Instead, it is the 'sexist implications' of such indeterminacy that concern the critic. Informed by the work of Edward Said[41] as well as Alice Jardine's notion of gynesis,[42] Restuccia also takes into account post-structuralist and French feminist notions of indeterminacy.[43] She argues that post-structuralist pronouncements on the indeterminacy of woman, especially when made by men, 'are apt to give one pause'.[44] The uneasiness with which the female reader greets 'Derrida's "French feminist" pronouncements is apt to resemble one's response to Forster's indulgence in Oriental indeterminacy'. Restuccia outlines her argument on the implications of Forster's indeterminacy in the following:

■ On the one hand, such indeterminacy holds open the shadow possibility (impossible to realize) that Aziz is guilty of attempting to rape Adela – no virtue there for the anti-imperialists. But it also prevents us from finding him, or anyone else, guilty of the book's offenses against women in general. Worse: not only does it keep a pervasive antifemale violence (verbal and mental) from crystallizing into a provable physical crime with a prosecutable criminal suspect, but it does so in the name of woman, woman-who-cannot-be-identified, since Forster (we will see) conceives of the unrepresentable Orient as female.[45] □

An inability to identify Adela's attacker coupled with the impossibility of defining woman herself makes Forster's text problematic for both postcolonial and feminist critics. Beyond the philosophical, linguistic and spiritual implications of Forster's indeterminacy are the political effects it entails. In order to uncover these effects and to show how Forster maintains the text's indeterminacy, Restuccia turns firstly to the figure of Aziz. Forster's evidence against him is considerable:

■ *A Passage to India* teases the scrupulous reader into realizing that Aziz is more than capable of assault – physically, temperamentally, even philosophically. 'He was an athletic little man, daintily put together, but really very strong' (p.40); mental willfullness complements Aziz's bodily strength. Offended and irritated by Dr. Panna Lal's 'ill breeding' (p.77) early in the story, Aziz makes his pony caper, spooking Dr. Lal's already spooked horse. As a result of this incident (as well as his fears that he had affronted the Collector by not attending the Bridge Party), 'The complexion of [Aziz's] mind turned from human to political. He thought no longer, "Can I get on with people?" but "Are they stronger than I?" breathing the prevalent miasma.' (The event fails to quell his aggressiveness: immediately thereafter, receiving Fielding's invitation to tea, Aziz's 'spirits revived with violence' [p.78].) If his own countryman's behaviour can trigger such excessive vengeance in Aziz, might not Adela's insults have piqued him to attack her? She has surely provoked him with her comment about all Englishwomen in India turning rude within a year and with her tactless question implying possible polygamy.

Aziz inflicts his temper not only on Dr. Panna Lal; this is no isolated case. For losing track of Adela at the Marabar Caves, the guide suffers Aziz's insidious wrath. And in the Guest House in the Temple chapter, annoyed by the picture of English unity that Aziz gets a glimpse of through surreptitiously reading Mr. and Mrs. Fielding's letters, 'in a spurt of temper he hit the piano' (p.303). (The term 'spurt' curiously constitutes part of an inconspicuous linguistic network that points to Aziz as a potential rapist. Forster's description of Aziz's talent as a medical doctor is charged with sexual overtones: 'His profession fascinated him at times, but he required it to be exciting, and it was his hand, not his mind, that was scientific. The knife he loved and used skilfully, and he also liked pumping in the latest serums' [p.71].) In taking a look at Ralph Moore's bee-stings, Aziz later raises his so-called scientific hands in a way that the intuitive boy perceives as '"unkind"' (p.304). Aziz seems nonplussed by Ralph's insight: he hides his allegedly sadistic hands behind his back as if they are appendages to be ashamed of. And so here too Aziz '"act[s] the criminal"' (p.172), to invoke Fielding's description of Aziz trying to flee after the visit to the Caves when Mr. Haq, the Inspector of Police, arrests him.[46] □

Forster's effective framing of Aziz does not necessarily lead the reader to a definite conviction about him. The evidence against Aziz, as summoned by Restuccia, underlines the position in which the text places its readers. Compelled to adopt an investigative stance ('like an Inspector of Police') or prosecutory role ('attorney'), the reader searches the evidence for proof of Aziz's guilt or Adela's culpability. The text's indeterminacy would seem then to give rise to a contrary impulse in its readers: the desire to fix the truth. Despite the 'disturbing details that would be of service to Western determinacy' the text nonetheless resists closure of the case against Aziz. He remains 'neither indictable nor exculpable'.

Aziz's attitude towards sex, manifested in his conversations with Fielding as well as the narrator's comments, serve to align him, curiously, with Mrs Moore:

■ While it is clear that Aziz is anxiously contemplating a visit to Calcutta, his attitude toward sex may at the same time be seen in general as akin to Mrs. Moore's own dismissive attitude toward the crisis in the Caves. 'Nothing had happened, "and if it had," she found herself thinking with the cynicism of a withered priestess, "if it had, there are worse evils than love." The unspeakable attempt presented itself to her as love: in a cave, in a church – boum, it amounts to the same' (pp.212–13). When it comes to views about sex, Mrs. Moore and Aziz seem to wonder: what is all the fuss? 'His mind here was hard and direct, though not brutal. He had learnt all he needed concerning his own constitution many years ago, thanks to the social order into which he had been born, and when he came to study medicine he was repelled by the pedantry and fuss with which Europe tabulates the facts of sex.' Aziz cautions himself practically about bringing 'disgrace on his children by some silly escapade' (further tempting us to imagine that he premeditates, at least unconsciously, making advances to Adela). But Aziz has no moral qualms about sex: he 'upheld the proprieties, though he did not invest them with any moral halo, and it was here that he chiefly differed from an Englishman. His conventions were social. There is no harm in deceiving society as long as she does not find you out' (p.116). In some fundamental way the novel suggests that if Aziz had tried to 'make love' to Adela or even if he had succeeded, it really is no big deal. It is as if the book wants its scapegoat Aziz to be just guilty enough to invite a challenge to the necessity of assigning guilt to anyone, and sufficiently innocent to obfuscate that challenge.

The case against Aziz exploits even apparently conflicting evidence. Aziz's lust for women compromises him; *and* his disparaging opinion of women, more specifically his 'unconquerable aversions' to British women – Adela in particular – [. . .] likewise works against him as it leads us to conjecture that he may have committed the assault out of hatred and/or revenge. No doubt motives behind attempted rape are rarely unalloyed; so I would not wish to preclude the possibility that it was one motive (revenge) and not the other (lust), or vice versa (lust and not revenge), the point being that in polymorphous ways the novel raises our suspicion of Aziz.

At the risk of sounding like Mrs. Turton (which is precisely the paradoxical position the novel's textuality and Oriental indeterminacy seem to put one in): Aziz *is* a slippery fellow. At times he appears to be an inveterate liar. During the morning of the caves incident, he tells 'a good many lies' out of various impulses, and even begins to swallow his own stories. Aziz relays to Fielding and Mrs. Moore, about himself and Adela, that they 'were having an interesting talk with [their] guide, then the car was seen, so she decided to go down to her friend'. The narrator spells out his own susceptibility to his own fabrications: '[i]ncurably inaccurate, he already thought that this was what had occurred' (p. 168).[47] □

Restuccia's analysis at this point takes in the manuscript version of *A Passage to India*. The 'repressed assault scene', she argues 'may be linked up with a general wave of misogyny. It even seems likely that the energy behind the attempted rape represented in the manuscript but unreleased in the novel's Cave scene spreads itself out subtly throughout the text'.[48]

Although Restuccia's argument has merit, it is unclear whether the text's misogynist impulse or Forster's misogyny is under scrutiny here. This is perhaps her point, for such is the indeterminacy of Forster's text that the sources of its misogyny are difficult to identify. Examples of anti-female invective emanate from both the conversations included in the text as well as the narrative commentary on the attitudes of the characters. The 'misogynist impulse' in *A Passage to India* is, as Restuccia argues, difficult to pin down. It is 'masked by an apparently respectable alliance of the modernist attention to the endlessness of interpretation and anti-Western indeterminacy'.[49] This aesthetic and philosophical agenda 'sustains the idea (the fantasy?) of (attempted) rape because the possibility cannot be unequivocally closed down'.[50] In addition, it also works to obscure both the events in the Caves and the fantasy that underlies the possibility of rape.

■ No one can be blamed for what I will show to be the book's hostility toward women – indeed it would be contrary to the novel's liberal, anti-imperialist charm to prolong the search for a criminal. Aziz seems to focus the sexism of *A Passage to India* in order to obscure it (there probably was no attempted rape), and only with the conviction that there was no attempted rape can we bear to hear it palliated (and if there were, what's the fuss?). No wonder Forster goes to the trouble of ventrilo-quizing a strange set of opinions about a nonexistent event: the event has to seem to occur for it to have such defusing efficacy. [. . .][51] □

In order to disentangle the politics of the rape or the rape fantasy, Restuccia provisionally adopts 'a rather conventional (for the most part, Anglo-American) feminist position'. She asks a number of questions, all of which are derived from the Anglo-American commitment 'to the ethical goals of humanism'.[52] How does Forster portray women in his text? How does the overall portrayal of women relate to the suggested rape? Is the text's misogyny concealed by indeterminacy? And finally, 'Why does Forster expose the racist impulses of the British through the suspected crime of rape? Why not robbery – of even a male character?':[53]

■ An Anglo-American feminist critique might begin by italicizing that a ganging up on women, especially British women, does take place. Indian men seem repulsed by British women, and vice versa. The book's inequitable logic is that women are condemned both for being repellent to Indian men and for finding Indian men repellent. [. . .] The novel's anti-imperialist theme, though it may justify the parody of the English in general, has little explanatory power regarding the distinctive loathsomeness of British women – unless Forster means to imply that imperialism is primarily a matter of female inhumanity and acquisitiveness.

Indian women hardly fare better than their British counterparts. They barely speak, nor, I suggest, does Forster want them to. Though the brothels are popular, Indian men in the novel show a lack of desire for their wives. [. . .] Indian women, most of them still under purdah, are useful principally to the extent that they foster male bonding. [. . .] Admittedly, there are a few moments in *A Passage to India* during which male characters object to the purdah. But it is because of their speciousness that such protests deserve attention. [. . .] Aziz opposes the unveiling of Indian women to the foreigner, as if he has the right to cloak or uncloak what he thinks of as his women at will. And those foreigners reading the novel may feel that they are being prohibited from meeting an Indian woman at this very point, since apparently Aziz has remarried [. . .]. Forster gives the last (dismal) word on the purdah to Fielding, and he is characteristically skeptical – skeptical that lifting the purdah will work, for who will '"wash Ahmed, Karim and Jamila's faces?"' (p. 314).

Forster is not merely diagnosing a fear. First of all, it is he who promotes the Eastern uncertainty of the book that, given this particular narrative construction, allows a woman to cry rape and then not know if it occurred. Whether or not there is a rape crime, there is a diffused antifemale sentiment – so that Oriental obscurity permits the antifemale sentiment to get expressed but not definitely to be assigned to someone who can be prosecuted for it. Second, misogyny is not only pervasive, located even in Fielding with whom one tends to identify Forster, but seems to be justified by a surplus of defective female characters. Except for Mrs. Moore, the British women are despicable (worse than the men). Third, instead of women, the novel celebrates men and love between men. *A Passage to India* culminates in a scene in which Aziz 'half-kissing' Fielding and Fielding 'holding him affectionately' (p. 316) pledge their friendship. With keen awareness of the resistance that will block progress for a long while, Forster envisions a future harmonious cohabitation of England and India, just as in *Maurice* he imagines another harmonious living arrangement between his hero, Maurice, and Scudder, a man of lower, servant rank.

This, then, is the sort of complaint that might be lodged against Forster. It has an Anglo-American sturdiness to it: misogynists are exposed, sexual battle lines are drawn, political issues are redescribed as sexual issues, large-scale social and cultural constructs are at stake. Indeterminacy *would* seem to be veiling something foul. And yet we must come to terms with Forster's Marabar caves. For the caves are female and seem to speak a language of their own.[54] □

Having gestured towards a 'conventional' Anglo-American reading of the text, Restuccia suggests that the indeterminacy of the Caves complicates this view. The reading of the Caves that follows is based upon what one might describe as an equally conventional rendition of French feminist theory:

■ The Marabar Caves, insofar as they are an emblem of India, house an abstract giant of a woman who feminizes India. Some nondescript mounds the travellers observe on their elephant journey to the caves serve as the upper torso of the huge earth-mother: 'What were these mounds – graves, breasts of the goddess Parvati?' (p. 152). The party moves on from breasts to vaginal entryway(s): 'The corridor narrowed, then widened into a sort of tray . . . Close above the mud was punched a black hole – the first of the caves' (p. 153). Then:

A tunnel eight feet long, five feet high, three feet wide, leads to a circular chamber about twenty feet in diameter. This arrangement occurs again and again throughout the group of hills . . . They are dark caves. Even when they open towards the sun, very little light penetrates down the entrance tunnel into the circular chamber . . . The walls of the circular chamber have been most marvellously polished . . . The sides of the tunnel are left rough, they impinge as an afterthought upon the internal perfection. An entrance was necessary, so mankind made one. (pp. 138–39)

The Caves are not only female morphologically but perhaps linguistically as well. Their echo identifies them as a maternal/female semiotic space in which the relationship between signifiers and signifieds – so vital in this novel to the English who desperately yoke them together –

gets ruptured. The Marabar Caves' echo will not preserve a long, solid sentence like those 'that voyage through the air at Mandu, and return unbroken to their creator' (p. 158). Instead of reiterating a speaker's words (clearly 'echo' is a misnomer), the walls of the cave return the 'same monotonous noise' (p. 159) to all speakers, a noise that is barely representable, so close is it to silence.

The monotonous 'echo' cuts off signifiers (the words visitors of the Caves call out) from signifieds (the meanings they seem to expect), leaving the signifiers to float meaninglessly. It does so by taking a sound that could have signified something and replacing it with a sound that cannot have any signified whatever. Reference is impossible because the sign itself has been rendered incomplete, there is only babble (the original signifier deprived of its potential signified and the '"boum"' without any conceivable signified), about to be sucked back into some sort of primal linguistic void. '"Boum" is the sound – as far as the human alphabet can express it, or "bou-oum", or "ou-boum", – utterly dull. Hope, politeness, the blowing of a nose, the squeak of a boot, all produce "boum"' (p. 159). The so-called echo breaks down the linguistic system that props up Western values. It 'began in some indescribable way to undermine [Mrs. Moore's] hold on life . . . It had managed to murmur, "Pathos, piety, courage – they exist, but are identical, and so is filth. Everything exists, nothing has value"' (p. 160). With the destruction of the sign comes the destruction of any possible hierarchy: 'If one had spoken vileness in that place, or quoted lofty poetry, the comment would have been the same – "ou-boum"' (p. 160). [. . .] Have we not, even more precisely in tune with Cixous, stumbled across a female wild zone, inhabited by Medusa? 'If several people talk at once, an overlapping howling noise begins, echoes generate echoes, and the cave is stuffed with a snake composed of small snakes, which writhe independently' (p. 159). The Caves turn Adela's single snake, real or illusory, into the multiple snakes of Medusa's swarming hair. But the key question is – is she laughing? Is she empowered? Would a feminist reader be wise to befriend her?[55] □

The 'linguistic activity of the Caves' is suggestive of the work of Alice Jardine and the notion of 'gynesis – the putting into discourse of "woman"'.[56] Although Jardine's own analysis of gynesis relates primarily to 'recent fiction and theoretical texts for the most part by men who are interested in its conceptual instability and destabilizing potential',[57] Restuccia extends this term to include Forster's Modernist text. The Caves, in particular, serve a 'gynetic' function: 'Their "boum" delegitimates master, linear linguistic structures that have provided the grounds for Western notions of legitimacy, leveling everything from marriage [. . .] to Christianity':[58]

■ *A Passage to India*, then, depicts as female that force which disrupts phallogocentric representation and Western patriarchal values. Forster seems to conceive of his assault on British imperialist certainties as a 'woman-in-effect', staging it in a cave with a womblike shape and a womblike sound [. . .]. Not only does Forster produce the gynetic Marabar Caves [. . .] but they also impel a bona fide female character to make these same shifts. However nonplussed by her experience at the Marabar Caves, Mrs. Moore carries their spirit with her – of space over time, otherness over sameness, hysteria over paranoia, the labyrinth over the city, nonmastery over mastery, and fiction over truth.[59] □

This potential for liberation is, however, significantly curtailed by the text:

■ Contrary to her plan [to retire to a cave of her own], Mrs Moore does die [. . .]. Likewise: babbling Medusa remains confined by the walls of the Marabar Caves, as if herself in Indian purdah, or British colonization. Although female instability and suppleness of identity can serve as ways of circumventing and maybe even abrogating Western patriarchal strictures, they can be liabilities as well. In *Gynesis* Jardine comments on the uncertainty and distrust the feminist reader is apt to feel 'especially when the faltering narrative in which (gynesis) is embedded has been articulated by a man from within a nonetheless still-existent discipline'.[60] (And certainly for the most part Forster clings to representational language and humanist values.) Critical of the British patriarchal, imperialist system, Forster offers a critique of many of the same facets of language and society that feminists themselves find oppressive. He goes so far as to put his novel's most powerful weapon against British absolutes in the form of a woman and, as I see it, gynesis. But the result for the very real historical woman turns out to be babble verging on silence and burial in '"a cave of [her] own"'. Jardine poses a vital question here: 'Is all of this another male fiction, or is it a larger process that can begin to free women – and men – from Man's truth?'[61]

Must we dismiss Forster and his brilliant book? It would seem a great loss to abandon the Caves, and their rebellious Medusa within, as well as Forster's gynetic '"boum"'. I would call instead for a primary and then a secondary oscillation in reading the novel. A feminist reader of *A Passage to India* might shuttle between an Anglo-American feminist critique that discovers in Forster's ingenious plot a misogyny that veils its anxiety about women with Eastern wisdom, and a more French feminist tactic that seizes on the subversiveness of the Marabar Caves. And this latter pole itself needs to be broken down into two equally crucial positions between which the feminist reader might again oscillate: on the one hand, appropriating the radical power of the Caves, and on the other, looking out for their danger for women – their incarcerating, marginalizing, and silencing of women.

Forster's plot allegorizes (no doubt unwittingly) the last point – that the very source of female empowerment can bring danger. In the role of Oriental goddess who emerges from the caves – locus of gynesis and synecdoche of Eastern wisdom – Mrs. Moore, now Indianized, effects the release of Aziz who, according to the text's Eastern logic of indeterminacy, theoretically may be guilty of attempted rape and at least stands in for the antifemale sentiment that ought to be punishable. That is: it is a woman-in-effect who/that causes for the search for a criminal – whether he be Aziz, another man, or a metaphor for all perpetrators of misogyny in the book – to be discontinued. A feminism that adopts the gynesis of Forster's text thus runs the risk of mystifying or occulting rape. Yet a feminism that either ignores or flees from the gynesis of Forster's text, reading it solely as politically objectionable, runs the risk of reducing a complicated work of genius and (more important for feminism) losing out on the subversive power that it has to offer, as feminism in general will lose out if it declines an alliance with modernity. In the case of many twentieth-century texts by male writers, it seems that unfortunately we cannot have one (subversive energy, gynesis) without the other (the politically objectionable, misogyny). Gynesis and misogyny, oddly enough, often turn up as strange bedfellows. But a double, oscillating feminist reading can disentangle them, exposing the one and warily embracing the other.[62] □

In 'The Colonization of the Ingenue in E. M. Forster's *A Passage to India*',[63] published in 1994, Eve Dawkins Poll considers the function of this familiar Forsterian figure as it relates to the politics of gender and imperialism in the text. Although Poll draws upon the theories of Homi Bhabha in her account of colonial stereotypes, this critical background to her reading remains firmly *in* the background rather than interrogated through her analysis of the text.[64] Poll's use of theory, then, is much less self-conscious than Restuccia's.

Poll's focus on the ingenue usefully shows how this figure enables Forster to explore both traditional notions of selfhood as well as alternative and more radical possible identities. The ingenue functions as a suitably transitional figure enabling Forster to illustrate the 'unique, unstable time'[65] between the Victorian and Modern eras. In contrast to Forster's other ingenue figures, Lucy Honeychurch in *A Room with a View* and Helen Schlegel in *Howards End*, Adela Quested is a much less 'clearcut' character. Her function in the text is multiple:

■ In this novel, Forster uses the figure of the ingenue to explore the tensions between the cultures that exist in colonized India. By using the body of a woman, not yet incorporated into the Anglo-Indian ideologies of attitude and lifestyle, he can test all of the boundaries of the structure of this society including imperial policy, economics, sexuality, and culture. The figure of Adela, who is already relegated to the margins by her biological category as a woman, provides a flexible representational point for him to explore both the English and Indian side of the colonial/imperial question. [. . .][66] □

As an ingenue figure, Adela's function relates also to that of Mrs Moore who 'serves as a vessel for exploring tensions that are not possible through Adela'.[67] In particular, 'Forster uses Mrs. Moore, carrying the wisdom of life experience, to deconstruct the imperial cant that her son conveniently uses to dismiss the situation in India'.[68] Taken together, Adela and Mrs Moore enable Forster to 'explode [. . .] the ideology and ethics of colonization'.[69] Through her reading of the ingenue, Poll demonstrates how Adela's transitional status allows Forster to dramatise the tensions and contradictions of imperial rule. This dramatisation is particularly acute when it relates to Ronny Heaslop, Adela's potential husband. His behaviour demonstrates not only his superior attitude towards the natives but also the status he assigns to women.

■ His self-complacency, his censoriousness, his lack of subtlety, all grew vivid beneath a tropic sky . . . When proved wrong, he was particularly exasperating; he always managed to suggest that she needn't have bothered to prove it. The point she made was never the relevant point, her arguments conclusive but barren, she was reminded that he had expert knowledge and she none. (p. 96)

Through Adela's analysis of the changes in Heaslop's character after he has become part of the imperial machinery, it becomes apparent that his Anglo-Indian indoctrination is emphasizing his treatment of her as a woman too. Where she was treated as an intellectual in England by him, she is now treated as a woman who does not understand in India. Before she is even officially part of their community, Heaslop is casting her in the role of an Anglo-Indian woman, who is 'protected' or rather colonized, albeit a little differently by the patriarchal construct of imperial rule. Adela's declaration that she wants to see the '"real India"' (p. 48) is the impetus for the cataclysmic chain of events which lie at the heart of Forster's novel. Forster describes Adela as highly rational but not very intuitive – a characteristic which her counterpart Mrs. Moore is rich in. At Fielding's tea party, Adela is enraptured by Aziz, who fictionalizes India and artistically embellishes his stories. However, Adela regards his descriptions as wholly factual:

> As for Miss Quested, she accepted everything that Aziz said as true
> verbally. In her ignorance, she regarded him as 'India', and never
> surmised that his outlook was limited and his method inaccurate,
> and that no one is India . . . She supposed him to be emancipated
> as well as reliable and placed him on a pinnacle which he could
> not retain. (pp. 88–89)

Forster's ingenue in her zeal to embrace India as *other* imbues Aziz
with virtues that surpass his role as individual. Rather than judge him
individually, he serves as her representative of 'India' the mystical
other with its ancient mysterious wisdom. While the other Anglo-
Indians devalue the natives, Adela overvalues them, seeing them as
separate and *other*, but simultaneously guaranteeing them a limited
individuality. Adela's desire to know India also is a struggle against
being assimilated into the Anglo-Indian attitude. After she becomes
officially engaged to Heaslop, she explains her fears to Aziz:

> 'Some women are so – well, ungenerous and snobby about
> Indians, and I should feel too ashamed for words if I turned like
> them, but – and here's my difficulty – there's nothing special about
> me, nothing specially good or strong, which will help me to resist
> my environment and avoid becoming like them.' (p. 157)

Adela struggles to maintain her own identity within the imperial
colony. Already she feels the yoke of becoming an Anglo-Indian
woman descending on her. She expresses this immediately after she
and Heaslop become engaged, knowing that she will now be known
as his fiancee: 'She was labelled now. She felt humiliated again, for
she deprecated labels' (p. 109). [. . .] Adela's discomfort at being
labelled reflects the pressure of the English community in India not
only that she adapt the Anglo-Indian attitudes, but that she become a
colonized female whose image is controlled by a patriarchal centre.
Her desire to know India is partially just a desire to revolt against
Anglo-India. By embracing India with all its qualities of instinct and
mystery, Adela is rejecting the cautious, predictable mold of the
Anglo-Indian woman.[70] □

This point concerning Adela's resistance to colonial ideology is supported
elsewhere by Alison Sainsbury who, like Poll, argues that Adela's fate
underscores Forster's critique of empire. She elaborates this point by
relating Forster's text to other Anglo-Indian domestic and romantic
fictions. When Forster's text is set beside these other novels it becomes

clear that it not only resists imperialist ideologies but also overturns the conventions of a particular literary genre:

■ *A Passage to India*, for its part, plays on the most conventional of stories told by Anglo-Indian domestic novels, a young girl journeying to India to acquire an imperial consciousness and a husband; in doing so, however, it exposes and overturns the assumptions that lie behind that plot. Unlike the heroines of countless Anglo-Indian domestic novels, its heroine, Adela, is emphatically not integrated into Anglo-Indian life; like her counterparts, she may acquire a new consciousness, but hers is one that demands that she leave India – and without a husband. Although one might surmise that Adela has simply failed the test that would grant her citizenship in the empire, Adela and Ronnie's [*sic*] engagement is treated in ways that reveal and then contest the imperialist ideology advanced by the Anglo-Indian romance [. . .].[71] □

The remainder of Poll's analysis concerns the development of Adela in relation to both Ronny and Aziz:

■ In allying herself with the land of the *other*, Adela emphasizes her separateness and independence from Anglo-India. One of the most pivotal relationships in *A Passage to India* is the one between Adela and Aziz. [. . .] But her very ambivalence between powerfulness (vis-a-vis Aziz) and powerlessness (vis-a-vis Heaslop) are [*sic*] worth exploring. Abdul JanMohamed in 'The Economy of the Manichean Allegory' discusses the unique relationship between the coloniser and the colonized:

> The colonialist's military superiority ensures a projection of his self on the *Other*: exercising his assumed superiority, he destroys without any significant qualms the effectiveness of indigenous economic, social, political, legal, and moral systems and imposes his own versions of these structures on the *Other*. By thus subjugating the native, the European settler is able to compel the *Other*'s recognition of him and, in the process, allow his own identity to become deeply dependent on his position as a master.[72]

Adela does not consciously acknowledge the fact that Aziz's grand hospitality, including his arrangements of an intricate and expensive expedition to the Marabar caves, springs largely from his recognition of the Anglo-Indian position as 'master' in India. In reality, Aziz only holds real affection for Mrs. Moore and Fielding. When he first meets Adela, he immediately judges her as an object, by her beauty alone.

[. . .] In spite of his ambivalence towards Adela, Aziz admits to himself that he does not like her as much as Mrs. Moore, and soon ingratiates himself to her. The power-based relationship that exists between Adela and Aziz is reminiscent of the relationship between Helen Schlegel and Leonard Bast in *Howards End*. Bast allows Helen to systematically take control of his life, inwardly acknowledging her to be a superior being to himself by virtue of her education and class. Although Aziz does place himself at the beck and call of Adela, he knows that it is only for political reasons. Even though Aziz does not view her as personally superior to him, especially since he still views her as a woman, he nonetheless views her as more powerful in a political sense. However, in both cases the women do not consciously acknowledge their influence and exploitation of these *othered* men. In reality, Adela is drawn to Aziz on a physical and symbolic level. While climbing the side of a hill leading to a Marabar cave with Aziz, she notes his appeal:

> What a handsome little Oriental he was, and no doubt his wife and children were beautiful too, for people usually get what they already possess. She did not admire him with any personal warmth, for there was nothing of the vagrant in her blood, but she guessed he might attract women of his own race and rank, and she regretted that neither she nor Ronny had physical charm. (p. 163)

Here, even though Adela is able to analyze and rationalize Aziz's physicality or her desire for him, she is able to stop herself from drawing cultural barriers between herself and him by saying that there was nothing of 'the vagrant in her blood'. On the symbolic level, Adela is drawn to the physical beauty of Aziz and the attributes that she embues him with as *other*. In effect she projects on Aziz the characteristics that she, her *self*, lacks. Ideologically, she can protest the unfair treatment of the colonisers toward the natives, but on a personal level she cannot even acknowledge that she is herself attracted to this native *other* primarily because he is so different. This dichotomy of being attracted to Aziz and mentally re-enforcing his status as a native pushes Adela to ask him if he has one wife or more than one. Aziz, although hiding it, is greatly offended. Adela's question vocally labels him as *other* and by the standards of the western world as uncivilized: 'The question shocked the young man very much. It challenged a new conviction of his community, and new convictions are more sensitive than old . . . but to ask an educated Indian Moslem how many wives he has – appalling, hideous!' (p. 164). It is this storm of emotions in both characters that catalyzes the most central and controversial event in Forster's novel.[73] □

Taking into account the various interpretations of the Caves scene, Poll argues that though Forster 'is obviously trying to expose and discredit colonial ideology [. . .] he is privileging knowable western culture and marginalizing the inscrutable eastern culture'.[74] When it comes to Adela, Forster allows her 'to be cast in the role of an objectified victim':[75]

■ Once Adela makes her charge against Dr. Aziz, she is embraced by the Anglo-Indian community [. . .]. The response of the Anglo-Indian women to Adela is one of compassion and sisterhood which evolves from their mutual fear of the natives. In 'On the Threshold of Woman's Era: Lynching, Empire, and Sexuality in Black Feminist Theory', Hazel Carby discusses the theories of Ida B. Wells and Anna Julia Cooper in clearly colonialist terms. She explained that 'as black women positioned outside the "protection" of the ideology of woman-hood, both Cooper and Wells felt that they could see clearly the compromised role of white women in the maintenance of a system of oppression.'[76] Carby further explains in saying that 'white women felt that their caste was their protection and that their interests lay with the power that ultimately confined them.'[77] Paralleling Forster's depic-tion of colonial India with Carby's discussion of the situation of Blacks in the United States, it becomes clear that in banding together out of fear against the natives the Anglo-Indian women are perpetuat-ing the patriarchal, imperial construct. The only white woman who does not take this stance is Mrs. Moore, who is still suffering from her experience in the cave. She offhandedly declares, '"Of course he is innocent"' (p. 209). She then insists on leaving before the trial, saying '"But I will not help you to torture him for what he never did. There are different ways of evil and I prefer mine to yours"' (p. 210). The one group that is virtually left out of the racial tension, and a large part of Forster's book, is the Indian women. Rarely giving them individual-ized status, Forster most often speaks of them in connection with the *purdah* veil or religious rule not allowing them to be viewed by those outside their family. In 'Recasting Women: An Introduction', Kumkum Sangari discusses the development of the private and public spheres in India:

> The process of formation of the private sphere as an indigenist alternative to Western materialism is, in a sense, instituted at the beginning of the nineteenth century and comes into its own in national discourse which sets out to establish . . . a series of oppo-sitions between male vs. female, inner vs. outer, public vs. private, material vs. spiritual.[78]

By concentrating on this aspect of Indian womanhood, Forster accentuates the stereotyping and objectification of these women and removes them from the arena of action by casting them as totally *other*. In banding against the natives, the Anglo-Indians simply enmesh the Indian women in that all-encompassing veil. Forster even comments that they are beyond consideration: '[a]nd a number of Mohammedan ladies had sworn to take no food until the prisoner was acquitted; their death would make little difference, indeed, being invisible, they seemed dead already, nevertheless it was disquieting' (p.218).

Adela, once she is under the protection of the British, now enters the realm of a symbol for the Anglo-Indian community devoid of her individuality: 'the issues Miss Quested had raised were so much more important than she was herself that people inevitably forgot her' (p.220). Even Adela's pain at her experience is minimized as Heaslop takes the center-stage of attention:

> At the name of Heaslop a fine and beautiful expression was renewed on every face. Miss Quested was only a victim, but young Heaslop was a martyr; he was the recipient of all the evil intended against them by the country they had tried to serve; he was bearing the sahib's cross. (p.192)

In casting Heaslop in the role of the martyr, it becomes clear that Adela's attack is viewed as a violation of him. In speaking to Fielding, the Collector articulates the attitude of the Anglo-Indian men:

> 'I have never known anything but disaster result when English people and Indians attempt to be intimate socially. Intercourse, yes. Courtesy, by all means. Intimacy – never, never . . . That a lady, that a young lady engaged to my most valued subordinate – that she – an English girl fresh from England – that I should have lived.' (pp.173–74)

In the Collector's response to Adela's charge, it becomes clear that the alleged attack/rape is viewed as a violation on many levels. The Anglo-Indian men view it as a violation of the boundary between races, as a violation of property (Heaslop's fiancee), and finally an affront to English power. [. . .] Once Aziz's trial begins, Adela begins to have doubts about her accusation. The chanting of the Indians outside the courtroom for the appearance of Mrs. Moore, who has died on the ship back to England, lifts the veil of confusion from Adela: 'she returned to the Marabar Hills, and spoke from them across a sort of darkness to Mr. McBryde. The fatal day recurred, in every detail, but now she was of it and not of it at the same time, and this double

119

relation gave it incredible splendour' (p.230). In this meditative state, Adela recalls that Aziz did not follow her into the cave and thus recants her testimony. Once Adela chooses to recant her testimony, she is rejected by both the Anglo-Indians, and the native population. As for the British 'Miss Quested had renounced her own people' (p.233). The Anglo-Indians see her as a traitor to their version of the truth; an English lady, violated by the brutish/evil native. The natives see her as a traitor to their version of the *truth*, an upstanding Indian man accused by a racist English woman:

> But while relieving the oriental mind she had chilled it, with the result that he could scarcely believe that she was sincere, and indeed from his standpoint she was not. For her behaviour rested on cold justice and honesty; she had felt, while she recanted, no passion of love for those whom she had wronged . . . And the girl's sacrifice – so creditable according to Western notions – was rightly rejected, because, though it came from her heart, it did not include her heart. (p.245)

Forster equivocates on the concept of *truth*, making it problematically relative between coloniser and colonized. In giving Adela the supreme courage that it took to resist the imperial influence and tell the truth, Forster leaves her ostracized by both the natives and the British in India. Even Heaslop, not surprisingly, breaks off their engagement: 'And Adela – she would have to depart too; he hoped she would have made the suggestion herself ere now. He really could not marry her – it would mean the end of his career. Poor lamentable Adela' (p.256). However, Forster does restore Adela's sense of self, which is now liberated from imperial hegemony but, at tremendous personal sacrifice. As with his other ingenue figures, Adela achieves identity at the cost of being permanently marginalized from the centre of society, which in this case is Anglo-Indian society. However, he does leave her with a concept of self which is no longer rigidly defined by Western rationality: 'Although her hard-school-mistressy manner remained, she was no longer examining life, but being examined by it; she had become a real person' (p.245). At this point, Forster returns his ingenue to England, leaving her future mysterious and somewhat un-resolved, in order to culminate the colonial question without her.[79] □

CHAPTER FIVE

'English Crime': Writing History and Empire

THE COMPLEX inscriptions of imperialist and/or anti-imperialist discourse in *A Passage to India* have drawn the attention of all the critics included in this Guide. Accorded an increasingly dominant place in the essays thus far discussed, the political implications of Forster's text and, in particular, its engagement with the history of subjugated India, are the central focus of the two essays included in this last chapter. Published in 1971, Jeffrey Meyers's 'The Politics of *A Passage to India*'[1] responds to critical misreadings of Forster's text that fail to see or misunderstand its politics. He sets out to redress this state of affairs by concentrating on three areas: the text's chronology and Forster's control of it; the events occurring in India between 1918 and 1924 and the textual traces left by these events. In contrast to Meyers, Jenny Sharpe's sense of history in relation to *A Passage to India* takes her back to 1857 and the Indian Mutiny or Sepoy Rebellion. Reading the text in terms of Indian resistance to imperial rule, both essays attend to the powerful historical and political resonances of Forster's text.

Writing prior to the emergence of a substantial body of theoretical and critical material on colonialism and imperialism, Meyers nonetheless prefigures many of the concerns of later critics. He begins his essay by pointing out the curious disjunction between the text's chronology and its ideology. Forster's own visits to India occurred in 1912 and 1921. As Meyers notes, although the events in the novel take place after the First World War, the 'ideas and attitudes of 1912' prevail in the reactionary imperialists Forster depicts. Critics have approached this aspect of the text by criticising Forster's lack of historical perspective or, alternatively, underplaying the changes that the text seems to ignore. Lionel Trilling suggests that Forster's text is historically inaccurate since 'its data were gathered in 1912 and 1922 *before* the full spate of Indian nationalism'.[2] K. W. Gransden goes further when he argues that pre- and postwar India are undifferentiated. As he asserts, 'the wartime gap would *not* have had much significance, for the World War had *little* effect on India, where the social and political pattern imposed by the British continued largely *unchanged* until almost the time of the final withdrawal'.[3] This point is challenged by Meyers, who argues that 'it is precisely during this period that the forces of Indian nationalism first began to operate with potent effect'.[4] From Meyers's perspective, Forster's text does engage with the changes that occurred between his first and second visit. While his reading of *A Passage to India* details this engagement, it also suggests that Forster deliberately shows the Anglo-Indians to be locked into past ways of thinking in order to heighten the ironic potential of the text. Whether the Anglo-Indians cling to redundant ideologies through an ignorance of anti-imperialist movements or because they cannot accept any challenge to their power is open to question. What is clear to Meyers is the way in which the Anglo-Indian attitude is also inadvertently reinforced by critics who fail to acknowledge the differences between India in 1912 and 1924.

In support of his argument that Forster was aware of more recent political and historical changes in India, Meyers turns to 'Reflections on India', a text published in 1922, in which Forster acknowledges the difference between his fictional representation of the Anglo-Indians and contemporary attitudes.[5] This text lends support to Meyers's argument, which he summarises in the following:

■ I believe that Forster's understanding of the overwhelmingly important events that occurred in India and in the entire world between 1917 and 1922 gives *A Passage to India* its political significance, and that in the novel Forster emphasizes the political implications of race relations, fear of riots, English justice and government, Hindu-Moslem unity, Indian Native States, nationalism and the independence movement.[6] □

The remainder of Meyers's essay sets out to substantiate this claim concerning Forster's engagement with history. The First World War, he argues, gave a great deal of impetus to liberation movements worldwide. In an Indian context, the significant events are 'Gandhi's rise to prominence, the Montagu Declaration (1917) and the First Government of India Act (1919), the Amritsar Massacre (1919), the Moplah Rebellion (1921), and the Khalifat Movements (1921–22)'.[7] Along with these significant historical events there is the first wave of Indian passive resistance, instigated by Gandhi in 1919 and supplemented by a campaign of civil disobedience commencing in 1920.

Meyers's subsequent reading of *A Passage to India* uses this historical and empirical data to show Forster's awareness of the often-violent power struggles that characterised British rule in India. He begins by pointing to Forster's oblique reference to the Amritsar Massacre.

■ At the height of the ugly British hatred, hysteria and fear, when the innocent Aziz is freed and the mob is rioting, just after Major Callendar boasts of his medical cruelties to the '"buck nigger"' (p.219) Nureddin and says '"there's not such a thing as cruelty after a thing like this"' (p.220), Mrs. Turton virulently responds '"Exactly, and remember it afterwards, you men. You're weak, weak, weak. Why, they ought to *crawl* from here to the caves on their hands and knees whenever an Englishwoman's in sight, they oughtn't to be spoken to, they ought to be spat at, they ought to be ground into the dust"' (p.220).[8] □

For those schooled in the history of British imperialism and Indian resistance to it, the text here alludes to the murder of more than three hundred and the wounding of more than a thousand people on the orders of General Dyer. More specifically, Mrs Turton's comments echo the infamous 'Crawling Order' that was instigated (also by Dyer) following the Massacre at Amritsar. At this point Meyers deploys Louis Snyder's account of the event:

■ The order was to the effect that no Indians should be allowed to pass through the street, but if they wanted to pass they must go on all fours, and pickets were placed at certain points in the streets to enforce obedience to this order . . . within a few minutes after [General Dyer] had passed the order and put the pickets, twelve persons had to be arrested for being insolent and he ordered them to be taken into custody, and the police took them through the street and the picket enforced the crawling order on them.[9] □

Moving on through his account of significant events, Meyers points out that two years after the Massacre, in 1921, '[s]everal thousand fanatical Moslems were killed by troops and violent crowds after they had skinned alive and slaughtered thousands of Hindus'.[10] Since the Moplah Rebellion occurred on the Malabar Coast, the naming of the Marabar Caves 'would remind everyone who knew India of the recent horrors'.[11]

In addition to these two historical resonances in the text, Meyers also highlights Forster's own support for the joint movement of Hindus and Moslems known as the Khalifat. Forster expresses his support for this movement in an article published in 1922.[12] Coupled with Forster's published criticisms of British rule in Egypt, this article provides evidence of his sympathetic attitude towards independence.[13]

In relation to *A Passage to India* Forster confirms Meyers's own reading

123

of the text when he says 'the political side of it was an aspect I wanted to express'.[14] In fact, as Meyers points out, the novel became a set text book for the Indian Civil Service. Its political influence is noted by Forster himself, who states that 'it caused people to think of the link between India and Britain and to doubt if that link was altogether of a healthy nature'.[15] This view is substantiated by Nirad Chaudhuri, who writes that 'it became a powerful weapon in the hands of the anti-imperialists, and was made to contribute its share to the disappearance of British rule in India'.[16]

In the remainder of his essay Meyers considers how Forster's political impulse is translated into his fiction. He suggests that although Forster is concerned with individuals, his text gestures towards the conflicts that beset nations. Thus, the Marabar Caves expedition 'suggests in miniature the difficulties of social life in all of India, and the multifarious differences that separate races and religions'.[17] The political impulse is further expressed in Forster's descriptions of Chandrapore, the social and philosophical ideas the text advances, and through the trial of Aziz, which functions as a 'political allegory':[18]

■ The opening description of Chandrapore emphasizes the physical opposition of the Indians in the squalid city near the river and the English in the civil station on the hill. In the next chapter, Aziz and his friends immediately introduce the social-political theme with which the novel is largely concerned: whether friendship with an Englishman is possible, and the contrapuntal chapters of the Mosque section reflect upon this question. The pleasant meeting in the mosque is followed by the frigidity of the club; the Indians discuss the 'Bridge Party' invitation, and the party fails. This disastrous party, Ronny's boorish and rude interruption of Fielding's tea party, the failure of the Bhattacharyas to fulfill their invitation, and the Nawab Bahadur's car accident, all indicate that friendship between a dominant and a subservient people is rarely possible. The final answer to the question of friendship is emphatically negative: English and Indians cannot be friends until Indians are politically independent. Aziz's vow to Fielding, '". . . India shall be a nation! . . . We may hate one another but we hate you most . . . we shall drive every blasted Englishman into the sea, and then . . . you and I shall be friends"' (pp. 315–16), echoes the belief of the Hindu nationalist Bankim Chatterjee: 'So long as the conqueror-conquered relationship will last between English and Indians, and so long as even in our present degraded condition we shall remember our former national glory, there cannot be any hope of lessening the racial hatred.'[19] *A Passage to India* embodies the truth that Orientals hate their European oppressors.

Forster's answer to such political hatred, which he again presents on the individual level is an ideal of personal behaviour and personal relations that is perhaps the major theme of the book, for it is echoed by three sympathetic characters, English and Indian, and embodied in the actions and fundamental goodwill of the hero, Fielding. Mrs. Moore expresses the beliefs of Aziz and Hamidullah when she appeals to her uncharitable son with a plea for '"Goodwill and more good will and more good will"', and begins to quote I Corinthians xiii.1, '"Though I speak with the tongues of men and of angels, and have not charity, I am become as sounding brass, or a tinkling cymbal"' (pp. 70–71). Forster also emphasizes the need for kindness in 'Reflections on India' and writes that

> The decent Anglo-Indian of today realizes that the great blunder of the past is neither political nor economic nor educational, but social . . . The mischief has been done, and though friendship between individuals will continue and courtesies between high officials increase, there is little hope now of spontaneous intercourse between two races . . . Never in history did ill-breeding contribute so much towards the dissolution of an Empire.[20]

The potent justification of the truth of Forster's social and political beliefs, which are fundamentally religious (though he is opposed to institutionalized and sectarian Christianity), comes from the Indians themselves. Forster's insistence on the need for kindness, charity and good will and his emphasis on the disastrous political effects of ill-breeding, are at the core of the charge made against the British by Gandhi: that they 'were "incompetent" to deal with the problems of India – which were not primarily administrative at all, but social and *religious'*.[21] And Vinoba Bhave, a contemporary Indian saint and Gandhi's adopted son, criticizes the West in purely Forsterian terms: 'You have developed the head; the heart did not keep pace. With us it was the opposite – it was with the development of the heart that we have been concerned in India.'[22] Adela's sacrifice was rightly rejected by Indians because it did not include her heart.[23] □

Produced before the most recent attempts to theorise imperial and post-imperial relations, Meyers's reading of Forster's text is both informative and at the same time limited. His insistence on 'the truth of Forster's social and political beliefs'[24] does not take into account the debate about Forster's highly ambivalent humanism nor, indeed, the indeterminacy of his text. In addition, the political vision Meyers promotes in his reading does not attend to the questions about Forster's sexual politics that the text raises and which are elsewhere contested by critics. The difference between Meyers's approach and that of Jenny Sharpe is essentially the difference between an unreflective understanding of the relation between text and history and a theoretically informed reading of this relation. For, extensively theorised in the 1980s and 1990s, post-colonial criticism has done much to challenge the assumptions that underlie Meyers's reading. At the same time, Meyers's comparative use of historical material prefigures, in a simplified form, the New Historicist methods of reading that emerged in the 1980s. Although more readily aligned with post-colonial critical interests, Sharpe's attention to the textuality of history and, by implication, the historicity of texts, shows the influence of New Historicist ways of reading. By way of contrast, and before moving on to consider a different use of and understanding of historicity, the conclusions drawn by Meyers in his essay must be considered:

■ In *A Passage to India* Forster also attacks the traditional (and mythical) justification of imperialism, that the natives are better off under English domination. Sir Alan Burns, former Governor-General of the Gold Coast, presents this argument as late as 1957: 'the subject peoples of the British Empire have greater liberty and better conditions of living than many of the inhabitants of independent countries'.[25] Fielding deliberately rejects this view, and in a discussion with Indians is too honest to give the conventional answer that England holds India for her good, which Ronny gives earlier in the novel. Aziz's assertion that there can be no self-respect without independence expresses Forster's understanding that Indians yearn for political freedom and do not care about economics, that they prefer to be ruled badly by themselves than well by others, and that no amount of progress can compensate for lack of liberty, and personal dignity, a lack that degrades every aspect of personal, cultural, social and moral life. This belief has always been held by Indian nationalists. Deshbandu Das, in his presidential address to the Indian National Congress in the 1920s, said, 'Morally, we are becoming a nation of slaves . . . Intellectually we have become willing victims to the imposition of a foreign culture upon us . . . there is inherent in subjection something which injures national life and hampers its growth and fulfilment'.[26]

The trial of Aziz is a political allegory on this theme. Adela's accusation of Aziz is also Britain's accusation of India, that she is poor, backward, dirty, disorganized, uncivilized, promiscuous, uncontrollable, violent – in short, that she needs imperialism.[27] His innocence is equivalent to India's right to freedom, which is symbolized by Aziz's transformation from subservient and passive before the trial to independent and nationalistic after it. Before his arrest he is not interested in kicking the British out of India; after his release he more formidably and proudly announces that he has become anti-British.

Adela's echo also has political implications, for it functions as a sonant conscience, sounding doubts about her charge against Aziz and expressing the guilt and fear of the English imperialists. When Mrs. Moore remains secluded, and Ronny supports Adela's charges, 'the echo flourished, raging up and down like a nerve in the faculty of her hearing, and the noise in the cave, so unimportant intellectually, was prolonged over the surface of her life' (p. 200). It resounds and haunts her periodically when she considers her accusation, diminishes when she thinks of retracting the false charges, and disappears only when she tears the veil of illusion and releases Aziz. After the trial when she tells Fielding she no longer has secrets, the evil echo leaves her and discharges itself into the Indian atmosphere of hatred, hostility, recrimination and animosity.

Finally, Forster's political ideas are prophetic. Aziz predicts not only the Hindu-Moslem unity against the British, but also that independence will be achieved in the next European war. He even prophesies a conference of Oriental statesmen such as that which took place thirty years later (1955) in Bandung, Indonesia. He deplores the policy of racial discrimination and declares colonialism an evil that should be eradicated.

Thus, political events and political ideas are closely related to Forster's moral ideas, which find their most profound expression in *A Passage to India*.[28] □

Of all the criticism on *A Passage to India* Jenny Sharpe's 'The Unspeakable Limits of Rape: Colonial Violence and Counter-Insurgency' represents perhaps the most complex response to the text.[29] In addition to her focus on imperial discourse – in the form of both historical and fictional texts – Sharpe also traces, from a feminist perspective, 'the signification of rape in Forster's novel to the historical production of a colonial discourse on the native assault of English women in India'.[30] Although the Indian Mutiny of 1857, or the First War of Independence, figures prominently in her analysis, Sharpe, in direct contrast to Meyers, asserts that she does 'not wish to suggest that literature and history are repetitions of each other'.[31] Instead, she takes the 'racial memory' of the Rebellion as 'a site of historical contestation'[32] during the years of decolonisation that Forster's fictional text encompasses. Through the rape or alleged rape, *A Passage to India* 'holds up for public scrutiny the racialization of imperial discourse'.[33] It enables Forster to re-enact, 'in the drama surrounding a rape, the fears and fantasies of an imperial nation over the intermingling of two races, the coloniser and the colonized'.[34] As such, it not only reveals the sexual politics of *A Passage to India* but also Forster's engagement with a powerful racial memory.

Post-colonial theory is a diverse field of study but Sharpe's work appears to operate within the spaces mapped by post-modern historiographers and post-structuralist theorists. As Patrick Williams and Laura Chrisman suggest, post-colonial theory engages with these other critical movements as it explores the following possibility:

■ If texts exist in what – to be deliberately unfashionable – one could call a dialectical relationship with their social and historical context – produced by, but also productive of, particular forms of knowledge, ideologies, power relations, institutions and practices – then an analysis of the texts of imperialism has a particular urgency, given their implication in far-reaching, and continuing, systems of domination and economic exploitation.[35] □

In order to bring together both feminist and post-colonial readings of the text Sharpe addresses the work of both Elaine Showalter and Brenda R. Silver.[36] She argues that although both critics 'situate the alleged rape within the larger frame of women's oppression' they fail to 'address the historical production of the category of rape within a system of *colonial* relations'.[37] In the case of Silver, a lack of awareness of cultural and racial difference leads her to align Adela with Aziz, placing them together under the category 'woman' and 'rapable'. As a means of dealing with different kinds of disempowerment, Silver's use of '"rape" as a master-trope for the objectification of English women and natives alike [. . .] produces a category of "Other" that keeps the colonized hidden from history'.[38] In order to bring this history to light, Sharpe adopts two related strategies. She identifies the 1857 uprisings 'as the beginnings of a racial discourse'[39] of sexual violence against white women and then sets about historicising the category of rape as it functions within an imperial context. In addition, Sharpe's account remains fully aware that historiography is 'subject to the rule of narrative discourse', and therefore requires close critical scrutiny. The last two sections of her essay are devoted, respectively, to detailed readings of what Sharpe calls '"The Reality Effect" of Historical Fictions' and '"The Ideological Effect" of Literary Plots'.

■ May 10, 1857, has been set down in colonial records as the infamous day in Anglo-Indian history. For the first time in their hundred-year stay in India, the British faced rebellions on a scale that threw the authority of their rule into crisis. A strange and horrifying tale took hold of the colonial imagination, spreading throughout Anglo-India and all the way back to England. Mutineers, the story went, are subjecting 'our countrywomen' to unspeakable torments. Natives, the story continued, are systematically raping English women and then dismembering their ravished bodies. Long before the British army regained control over its Indian territories, the tales of terror were discredited as having little or no historical basis. 'Fortunately the actual occurrence of these horrors was seldom proved', reports Pat Barr in her apologia for Anglo-Indian women, 'but they served to inflame public opinion in England and Anglo-India – particularly because the principal victims were said to have been women. The press in both countries waxed hysterical (sic) in demands for more severe punitive measures to be taken, and the rituals of revenge-killing were enacted even in the nurseries and schoolrooms of the homeland.'[40] Thus was the British reading public invited to share the terror of the white settlers, and their revenge, as letters, stories, and eyewitness reports slowly made their way back from India.

Our perception of 1857 has been colored by the years of myth-making that have gone into popularized narrations of the revolt. The accounts of white settlers in a state of exhaustion, terror, and confusion have since been sealed with the stamp of authenticity that guarantees all eyewitness reports. The rebellion was not quite the military insurrection that its designated name of 'Mutiny' suggests. Although initiated by Sepoy mutineers at Meerut, the uprisings included a heterogeneous cross-section of the North Indian population that extended far beyond the military ranks.[41] Nor was it simply a case of Sepoys suddenly turning against their colonial masters and slaughtering British officers and their families. The battles were far more protracted, involving maneuvers and countermaneuvers between the British and relatively autonomous native factions for control of disparate regions. Rebels (sometimes armed with heavy artillery) lay siege to colonial towns, while loyal soldiers were marched from one part of the country to another to reclaim fallen territories. Anglo-Indian communities trapped within towns were often cut off from food, water, medicine, and other necessary supplies. The East India Company, then entrusted with colonial administration, was unable to restore law and order for the good part of two years. Most Europeans, including women and children, suffered the 'mutilation' of bullet wounds or else 'fell victim' to diseases contracted during the long sieges. They did not, as was commonly believed, die at the sadistic hands of roving bands of *badmashes*. This latter belief, however, was reiterated and re-introduced in literature, paintings, and lithographs depicting leering Sepoys with their swords raised over the heads of kneeling women and children. The primary referent for the popular image of the Sepoy was the Cawnpore massacre.

Upon retreating from Cawnpore before an approaching British army, the Hindu rebel leader Nana Sahib ordered that his two hundred hostages, all of them women and children, be executed. The British army subsequently preserved Bibighar (the house in which the women were killed) with its dried blood and rotting remains as a kind of museum for passing troops to visit. Locks of hair from the dead women's heads were carried off as mementos and passed from hand to hand as the fetish objects of an erotic nightmare. Thus began the mythic invention of the dying women's torments, as soldiers covered the walls with bloody inscriptions in the hands of the 'ladies' directing their men to avenge their horrible deaths.[42] Nana Sahib has since been vilified in colonial historiography for having committed the unforgivable crime of desecrating English womanhood. Barr exhibits a predictable understanding of the Cawnpore massacre when she writes that there, 'one of the most revered of Victorian institutions, the English Lady, was slaughtered, defiled and brought low.'[43] The occurrence of even one massacre such as Cawnpore endowed all the tales of terror with their reality effect. British magistrates who were entrusted with investigating the stories, however, could find no evidence of systematic mutilation, rape, and torture at Cawnpore or anyplace else.

Anglo-Indian descriptions of the tortures drew on a stockpile of horrors culled from the great works of Western civilization. The Bible, Homer, Virgil, Dante, and Shakespeare all provided the Mutiny narratives with their charged plots of martyrdom, heroism, and revenge. The familiar and easily recognizable plots thus enabled the British to make sense of what was an incomprehensible event – impossible to comprehend because anticolonial insurgency had previously been unthinkable. Yet, it is the details concerning the crimes against English women that gave the familiar plots their historical efficacy. Although the British and Anglo-Indian presses claimed the stories to be 'too foul for publication',[44] they disclosed fragments of information in hints and innuendos that prompted their readers to search their imagination for the awful deaths. The following editorial, which appeared in a London newspaper during the early stages of the Mutiny, establishes the 'fact' that women and children were killed by first declaring little knowledge of events, then appealing to the imagination as a privileged source of information, before finally reporting what has only been heard: '[. . .] a large number of women and children, fell into the hands of the infuriate crew, thirsting for the blood of the infidel, and frenzied with bhang. We know little of the exact scenes which transpired, and imagination hesitates to lift the veil from them. We hear, however, that about 50 helpless women and children who had hid themselves in the palace on the outbreak were subsequently discovered, and the whole murdered in cold blood.'[45] As the mystery that imagination will reveal from behind the veil of ignorance, rumor has already been declared a truth.

The press tended to rely on the personal testimonies of people, many of whom were not present at the scenes they described. Attempts to establish the sources of stories proved that, as is the case with rumor, their origins were unknown.[46] Upon further questioning, so-called eyewitnesses admitted that what they 'saw' did not happen in their town but elsewhere, in the next town perhaps.[47] Some English readers did question the validity of the reports, while others, more sympathetic to the plight of the rebels, protested the brutal methods used for quelling the uprisings. The general tenor of the editorials and letters, however, exhibits a desire to transform rumor and hearsay into fact and information. The invented stories could be explained – and Barr does – as a terror-induced response to the discovery that rebels did not spare the lives of European women. Yet, the Victorian male's horror over anticolonial insurrection invading the sanctity of his home does not sufficiently account for the sexualization of the women's deaths.

The sensationalist accounts, which are to be found in private letters, news reports, and published narratives, all circulate around a single, unrepresentable center: the rape of English women. Upon declaring the crime 'unspeakable', the reports offer a range of signification that has the same effect as the missing details. In other words, they 'speak' a discourse of rape.[48] □

As Sharpe's reading of the fictionalisation of history shows, many of these texts share a 'common narrative structure':[49]

■ Variations on the basic structure of [. . .] an invented story – the humiliation, sexual assault, torture, and death of English women – recur again and again in Mutiny accounts. Its plotting belongs to a discourse of rape, a specifically sexual form of violence which has as its aim an appropriation of women as 'the sex'.[50] This appropriation takes place through the objectification of women as sexualized, eroticized, and ravaged bodies.

The narratives that stage the deaths of English women as a public spectacle constitute a violent appropriation of their bodies. As the following words of Sir Colin Campbell demonstrate, these stories bypass the mutilation of men to give a step-by-step account of the crimes perpetrated against women. What is noteworthy about this particular account is that the agent of torture is missing, it could be any native or every one. We will later see why no Indian – male, female, young, or old – escapes suspicion. The details concerning the disfiguration of English women have the effect of reducing them to their mutilated bodies. A construction of the women as 'the sex' is visible in the necessity to subject both their primary and secondary sexual organs to attack. In this narrator's hierarchy of tortures, the 'most horrible' mutilation is the loss of identity through an effacement of the facial features. By the time Campbell has finished with his account, there is nothing left to the English woman but her brutalized body:

> Tortures the most refined, outrages the most vile, were perpetrated upon men, women and children alike. Men were hacked to pieces in the presence of their wives and children. Wives were stripped in the presence of their husband's eyes, flogged naked through the city, violated there in the public streets, and then murdered. To cut off the breasts of the women was a favourite mode of dismissing them to death; and, most horrible, they were sometimes scalped – the skin being separated round the neck, and then drawn over the head of the poor creatures, who were then blinded with blood, driven out into the blazing streets. To cut off the nose, ears and lips of these unhappy women (in addition, of course, to the brutal usage to which they were almost invariably submitted), was merciful.[51]

The scene is staged in a manner that forces us to view the women's rape and mutilation through the 'husband's eyes'. We do not know what it means for the women to see their husbands killed, even though men are included among the victims. We are here reminded of the line from *A Passage to India* that depicts an Anglo-Indian response to news of Adela's assaults: '[the wife] was only a victim, but [the husband] was a martyr . . . he was the recipient of all the evil intended against them by the country they had tried to serve' (p. 192). Forster's words can be read as an indictment of narratives like Campbell's that formulate the assault of English women as an indirect attack on colonial men. The mutilations described, then, reenact a sexual nightmare that fixates on the bodies of not just women, but *women who belong to English men*.

The unacknowledged terror of the rape and mutilation stories is to be found in the element of doubt the uprisings introduced to the language of racial superiority. This terror can be read in the absence of narratives that objectify English men through descriptions of their mutilated bodies. The reports hold no elaborate details concerning the torture of men and certainly no mention of the male sexual organ being removed. Such a fragmentation of the male body would allocate English men to the objectified space of 'the class of women'[52] – a status denying British power at the precise moment that it needed reinforcing. Once an English man has been struck down, then anything is possible; in death his mortality is revealed and sovereign status brought low. A focus on the slaughter of defenseless women and children displaces attention away from the image of English men dying at the hands of native insurgents. Through an animation of 'women and children' (p. 190), the fiction of racial superiority could be upheld even as the seriousness of the revolt was recognized.

The Mutiny reports transform Anglo-Indian women into an institution, the 'English Lady', by selectively drawing on the Victorian
ideal of womanhood. This transformation permits a slippage between
the violation of English women as the object of rape and the violation
of colonialism as the object of rebellion. The value of the 'English Lady'
– her self-sacrifice, moral influence, and innocence – is thus extended
to the social mission of colonialism. Because of its close association
with her moral worth, the category of rape is reserved for English
women alone. The rape of Indian women is not directly revealed in the
information of the reports. It is revealed, however, in their repeated
disavowals that, unlike the treacherous Sepoys, English soldiers did
not rape enemy women. In even the most telling accounts, which are
to be found in private correspondences rather than published narratives, the rape of Indian women remains unacknowledged: 'We
advanced to the village and the general gave it up to the tender
mercies of the 84th, as he said, to do as they liked with. They did clear
it with a vengeance, for in 5 minutes there was not one live *nigger* in
the village.'[53] What happens to Indian women when subjected to the
'tender mercies' of British soldiers is predictably missing from this
report. In the place of that absent narrative, we have representations of
Indian women inciting the mutineers to rape and torture. [. . .][54] □

In direct contrast to the stereotypical passivity of Indian women, Mutiny
accounts see them as involved in the atrocities, orchestrating the actions
of the Sepoys. Such representations reinforce the notion that 'the native
woman is not rapable':[55]

■ Since it articulates the contradictions of gender and race *within the
signifying system of colonialism*, the sexual discourse of rape is overdetermined by colonial relations of force and exploitation. It is
helpful, when unpacking a colonial economy of signs, to consider
Elizabeth Cowie's important insight into the cultural production of
women as not only exchange objects but also as signs.[56] According to
Cowie, the exchange of women that reproduces their social roles of
wife, mother, etc. constitutes a transaction that also produces value for
a particular signifying system. In the case of the Mutiny reports, I
would argue that the display of the violated bodies of English women
produces the 'English Lady' as a sign for a colonial moral influence
under threat of native violation. The signifier may be 'woman' but its
signified is the value of colonialism that she represents. This might
explain why, despite the narrative energy going into a discourse on
the English woman, stories of the women themselves escape the narrations. Since the signifying function of woman-as-victim in the
Mutiny reports depends on her social role of wife and her restriction

133

to the 'innocent' space of the domestic sphere, the English woman's access to colonial power is denied. There exists, as a consequence, a fracture between the colonial woman's positioning within the Mutiny reports as passive victim or violated body and her own sense of 'self'.

What is striking about the English women who narrate their Mutiny experiences is their reliance upon a language of colonial authority. As they express their horror and fears in personal diaries, journals, and letters, they do not always respond to the threat of rape and torture from within their socially constructed gender role. In other words, they do not necessarily turn to their husbands for protection. There are, of course, the Harriet Tytlers who write of keeping poison nearby and instructing their husbands to avenge their deaths.[57] But there are also the wives of officers and civil servants who claim to have scared off hostile villagers by speaking to them authoritatively. These women were not always successful and some of them were killed for attempting to intimidate the rebels with commanding voices. By appealing to their own sense of authority under conditions that did not always guarantee its success, however, these women demonstrate a modicum of faith in their ability to command the natives. An official history negates the Anglo-Indian woman's access to colonial power, for her value to colonialism resides in her status of 'defenseless victim' alone. In this regard, as feminists, we should not similarly efface European women's agency by constructing them as the victims of colonial relations that are patriarchal alone.[58]

We see, in the invented stories of rape and mutilation, colonial power relations being written on the bodies of women. Their savaged remains display a fantasy of the native's savagery that screens the 'barbarism' of colonialism. Presupposing their women to inhabit a domestic sphere that was safe from colonial conflict, Anglo-Indian men responded as good soldiers, fathers, and husbands to the stories of rebels executing their women and children. They reasserted claim over what was rightfully theirs by protecting the victims and punishing the offenders. And the honor of the victim was often defended by making the punishment fit or (as was more often the case) exceed the crime. After the British gained control over Cawnpore, they forced captured rebels to lick floors clean of dried blood before hanging them. It was also common practice to tie mutineers to the front of cannons and explode their bodies into minuscule pieces. The roads down which an avenging army marched were lined with the dead bodies of Indian men, women, and children dangling from the trees as a message to the populace about the consequences of rebellion. Upon recapturing Delhi, the British army was reported to have massacred anywhere from twenty-five thousand to thirty thousand of its inhabitants. The response of revenge for the dishonor of English women thus not only reestablished a claim of lawful (sexual) ownership but also enforced violent strategies of counterinsurgency.

Mutiny historiography understands the brutality with which the uprisings were suppressed as the uncontrollable rage of Victorian men responding to the desecration of their women. When posited as a cause, the rape and mutilation of English women explains British reprisals as the aberrant response of otherwise civilized men driven mad at the thought of their tormented women. Thus adhering to the logic of colonialism as a civilizing influence, this explanation reconfirms the morality of the civilizers. By reading the sexualization of insurgency in the reports *as the effect of a violence already sanctioned by the structures of colonialism*, we see that the discourse of rape in fact normalizes repressive measures against anticolonial insurgency. Almost immediately after the outbreak of the Mutiny in May, an act giving summary powers to officers was passed. It was superseded by a more extreme Act of June 6th. 'Under that last Act', records Sir George Campbell in his memoirs, 'such powers were given to all and sundry, and barbarities were committed with a flimsy pretext of legality'.[59] The campaign of terror was thus already under way long before the news of Cawnpore (the massacre occurred on July 15) reached the ears of British soldiers.[60] What confirmed the atrocities against English women were the punishments that supposedly reflected them. Conducted as highly ritualized and publicized spectacles designed to maximize native terror, British retribution against rebels served as its own model for the torture and mutilation the army was ordered to quell.[61] 'My object', Brigadier-General Neill, one of the more infamous avenging officers, admits, 'is to inflict a fearful punishment for a revolting, cowardly, barbarous deed, and to strike terror into these rebels.'[62] The narratives of sexual violence cleared a space for what Neill, alluding to the punishment he administered, calls a 'strange law'.[63] His words reveal a discourse of power that violently enforced colonial law in the name of English women. What I am suggesting is that the sexual signification of the Mutiny reports sanctioned the use of colonial force and violence *in the name* of moral influence. During the course of the nineteenth century the 'English Lady' came to be invested increasingly with the self-sacrifice of colonialism, its ideological mission that was silently underpinned by apparatuses of force.

The sexual nightmare of rape and mutilation remained fixed within the British imagination throughout the nineteenth century, forming an historical memory of 1857 as the savage attack of brown-skinned fiends on defenseless women and children. It was possible, by the end of the nineteenth century, to relive the 'heroic myth' of British martyrdom by making a pilgrimage to all the major sites where

Europeans had been killed.[64] One site of particular mythic proportion was Cawnpore, where a plaque was placed on the well into which Nana Sahib threw the dead bodies of his hostages. Its inscription appropriately captures the racial memory produced about the Mutiny: '[s]acred to the perpetual memory of a great company of Christian people, chiefly women and children.'[65] This inscription, like the imaginary ones on the English women's bodies, was a spectacular sign of Indian savagery to be read by future generations. The tales of sexual violence consequently screened the even more savage methods used to ensure that natives knew their proper place as well as the vulnerability of colonial authority. It is here, in the memory of 1857 as the violent attack of natives on English women, that we are to find a historical explanation for the plotting of rape in *A Passage to India*.[66] □

Turning from the extremely contested accounts of the Mutiny, Sharpe goes on to consider ways in which these narratives both haunt and constitute Anglo-Indian fiction, Forster's text included. She identifies, in the Mutiny, a challenge not only to British authority but to the stereotypical view of the Hindu as 'licentious, but effeminate; cruel, yet physically weak; duplicitous rather than savage'.[67] Rewriting this script in the wake of the Mutiny, the British identify the insurrection with the attempt to restore the Mogul king to power. Since the uprising is understood in terms of Muslim barbarism it is, as Sharpe notes, significant that Aziz 'is a Muslim, and one who indulges in orientalist fantasies about his Mogul ancestors at that'.[68]

In the final section of her essay, Sharpe suggests a continuity between the 1857 Mutiny and the Amritsar Massacre of 1919. The violent response of the British to a public gathering of 1919 was legitimised as a means of avoiding the calamity of 1857. Forster's text, begun in 1913 (and completed in 1924) and alluding to the events of both 1857 and 1919, is, as Sharpe asserts, 'critical of a community obsessed with the racial memory of 1857'.[69]

■ The Anglo-Indians of Chandrapore turn to the Mutiny as a convenient proper name for characterizing the events surrounding Adela's accusation of rape and Aziz's subsequent arrest. The district superintendent of Police, Mr. McBryde, advises Fielding to '"[R]ead any of the Mutiny records"' (p.178) for understanding the psychology of the Indian criminal mind. As the court case draws nearer, the explosive atmosphere of 1857 is recreated in the club members who debate what they should do about the hostile Indian mobs demanding that Aziz be released. Their discussion centers on defending their 'women and children' (p.190), a particularly charged phrase for eliciting cries of revenge. One young, golden-haired woman whose husband is away is afraid to go home 'in case the "niggers attacked"'. Her fellow Anglo-Indians invest the image of 'her abundant figure and masses of corngold hair' with the full value of colonialism; for them, 'she symbolized all that is worth fighting and dying for' (p. 188). Parodies of this sort can be read as sobering reminders of colonial retributions against a rebellious Indian population committed in the name of English women.

A Passage to India recreates in the drama surrounding Aziz's arrest the precariousness of the imperialist mission under threat of insurrection. It is a vulnerability that necessitates the positing of a native desire for white women as the 'chief cause' for interracial conflict. In all those scenes that allude to Dyer's command at Amritsar and the racial memory of the Mutiny, the novel also shows the fear of a native assault on English women to be a screen for imperialist strategies of counterinsurgency. In other words, it draws attention to a discourse of rape deployed in the management of anticolonial rebellion. Such stagings, however, do not disrupt the dominant Mutiny narrative but simply question its premises. What does reveal the fictionality of colonial truth-claims is the element of doubt Adela introduces into the certainty of a crime confirming the native's depravity.

During the trial, Adela delivers a verdict that throws the place of imperial law into chaos. '"Dr Aziz never followed me into the cave"' (p. 231), she declares, '"I withdraw everything"' (p. 232). When situated within the racial memory of the Mutiny, her extension and withdrawal of her charge drives a wedge of doubt between a colonial discourse of rape and its object. In other words, Adela's declaration of Aziz's innocence undermines the racist assumptions underpinning an official discourse that represents anticolonial insurgency as the savage attack of barbarians on innocent women and children. Yet, Forster does not replace the certainty of an attack with its negation but rather with a narrative suspension that opens up the space for a mystery. After the trial, Fielding explores with Adela four possible explanations for what happened: either Aziz did molest her, she claimed he did out of malice, she hallucinated the attack, or someone else followed her into the cave (the guide and a Pathan are offered as two likely assailants). Although Fielding rules out the first two possibilities, Adela gives no indication to him (or the reader, for that matter) whether she reacted to a real or imaginary assault. She finally admits that the only one who knows for sure is Mrs. Moore, whom she claims to have acquired her knowledge through a telepathic communication. As he keeps forcing Adela to return to the question of what happened in the caves, Fielding soon realizes that the very multiplicity of explanations offer [*sic*] no easy resolution to the mystery:

> Telepathy? What an explanation! Better withdraw it, and Adela
> did so . . . Were there worlds beyond which they could never
> touch, or did all that is possible enter their consciousness? They
> could not tell . . . Perhaps life is a mystery, not a muddle; they
> could not tell. (p.261)

As readers, we are perhaps less satisfied than Fielding with the 'life is
a mystery' (p.261) response, for critics have, and still do, search their
imagination for an explanation [. . .].[70] □

Forster's edited version of the Caves scene, to which Sharpe refers, represents one possible rendition of what happened. Although deleted from
the final draft, it has been read, as Sharpe notes and the essays in this
Guide demonstrate, as evidence of the silencing of women in the text. In
the deleted scene, it is Adela's resistance to her attacker that attracts
Sharpe's attention. Following Sharpe's account of the Mutiny, it is clear
that Adela's eventual recanting of her rape narrative also, paradoxically,
represents a form of self-defence. Refracted through the discourse of the
Mutiny, Adela's resistance to the myth of the native as rapist might be
said to represent a refusal of the 'script' allotted to the 'English Lady'. By
retracting her accusation, Adela radically deviates from that script and
the racial and sexual hierarchies it bespeaks:

■ Like the Anglo-Indian women who survived the 1857 attacks,
Adela's act of self-defense is at odds with a dominant discourse that
constructs the 'English Lady' as a passive victim. As a consequence,
one cannot help but notice a resemblance between the absent text of
her struggle and an official discourse which erases colonial women's
agency. In fact, feminist critics have submitted Forster's deletion of
this scene as the sign of a more pervasive silencing of women, the
repression of a misogyny that returns in subtler forms throughout the
novel.[71] What these readings cannot account for, however, is that the
'passive victim' is recorded in the deleted script as 'feminist England',
but only at the risk of confirming the attempted rape. A clearing up of
the mystery in favor of Adela's guilt or innocence consequently
adheres to the terms of a discourse that displaces racial signification
away from colonial relations onto narratives of sexual violence. We see
that a restoration of the silenced stories of English women alone cannot disrupt a colonial plotting on interracial rape.

The racial and sexual significance of rape in *A Passage to India* does
not issue from Adela's experience in the cave; the answer is not to be
found there. To clear up the mystery of what happened in the caves by
searching our imagination for the missing details involves reading
Forster's novel according to the narrative demands of the Mutiny

reports. To read the mystery itself as an effect of that colonial history, however, is to see in its indeterminacies the imprint of a racial memory and 'to trace the path which leads from the haunted work to that which haunts it'.[72] In the place of 'what happened in the caves', I offer a different kind of question, one suggested by Adela's cry in the deleted assault scene. Managing to free herself from the grip of her attacker, Adela screams – '"Not this time."' What are the other times, the other assaults to which her triumphant cry alludes? I think that I have already answered that question.

If we are to study literature for its disruptions of an ideological production that prevents social change, we can no longer afford to restrict our readings to the limits of the literary text. Rather, we should regard the literature as working within, and sometimes against, the historicist limits of representation. *A Passage to India* contends with a discourse of power capable of reducing anticolonial struggle to the pathological lust of dark-skinned men for white women. Adela serves the narrative function of undermining such racial assumptions but then, having served her purpose, she is no longer of interest to the concerns of the novel. The 'girl's sacrifice' (p.245) remains just that, a sacrifice for advancing a plot centered on the impossibility of a friendship between men across the colonial divide. As feminists, we should not reverse the terms of the 'sacrifice' but, rather, negotiate between the sexual and racial constructions of the colonial female and native male without reducing one to the other. Like Fielding and Adela who confront the mystery in the multiplicity of explanations, we should recognize that there are no easy resolutions.[73] □

NOTES

INTRODUCTION

1 E.M. Forster, 'Prefatory Note to the Everyman Edition' (1957), reprinted in *A Passage to India*, ed. Oliver Stallybrass (London and New York: Penguin, 1989), pp. 317–18.

2 E.M. Forster, 'E.M. Forster on his Life and Books: An Interview Recorded for Television', *Listener*, 1 January 1959, pp. 11–12.

3 It is perhaps surprising, then, that Forster's work should be invested with such nostalgia, as for example when it has been adapted for film by the Merchant Ivory team, or appropriated as an integral part of the 'Raj revival' of the 1980s. For accounts of David Lean's 1984 adaptation of *A Passage to India* see Laura Kipnis, '"The Phantom Twitchings of an Amputated Limb": Sexual Spectacle in the Post-Colonial Epic', *Wide Angle: A Film Quarterly of Theory, Criticism and Practice*, 11.4 (1989), pp. 42–51; Khani Begum, 'E.M. Forster's and David Lean's (Re) Presentations and (Re) Productions of Empire', *West Virginia University Philological Papers*, 40 (1994), pp. 20–29; and Salman Rushdie, 'Outside the Whale', *American Film*, January–February 1985, pp. 16–18.

4 Peter Burra, 'Introduction to the Everyman Edition' (1934), reprinted in Appendix 2 of *A Passage to India*, pp. 319–33.

5 Burra, p. 319.

6 Burra, p. 327.

7 Burra, p. 327.

8 Burra, p. 327.

9 Burra, p. 324.

10 E.M. Forster, *A Passage to India* (London and New York: Penguin, 1989), p. 40. All subsequent references to *A Passage to India* are from this edition and included in parenthesis in the text.

CHAPTER ONE

1 Sylvia Lynd, 'A great novel at last', *Time and Tide*, 5 (1924), pp. 592–93 and *E.M. Forster: The Critical Heritage*, ed. Philip Gardner (London and Boston: Routledge and Kegan Paul, 1973), p. 216. All of the reviews incorporated in this chapter are reprinted in *E.M. Forster: The Critical Heritage* (hereafter *CH*). Original publication details for the articles along with references to this text are given in the notes.

2 Rose Macaulay, 'Women in the East', *Daily News*, 4 June 1924, p. 8 and *CH*, p. 196.

3 Ralph Wright, *New Statesman*, 21 June 1924, pp. 317–18 and *CH*, p. 221.

4 Wright, pp. 317–18 and *CH*, pp. 221–22.

5 D.L.M., *Boston Evening Transcript*, 3 September 1924, p. 6 and *CH*, p. 261.

6 Leonard Woolf, 'Arch beyond Arch', *Nation and Athenaeum*, 14 June 1924, p. 354 and *CH*, p. 205.

7 J.B. Priestley, *London Mercury*, July 1924, pp. 319–20 and *CH*, p. 228.

8 Leonard Woolf, 'Arch beyond Arch', *Nation and Athenaeum*, 14 June 1924, p. 354 and *CH*, pp. 204–05.

9 H.W. Massingham, 'The price of India's friendship', *New Leader*, 27 June 1924, p. 10 and *CH*, p. 207.

10 Massingham, p. 10 and *CH*, p. 207.

11 Virginia Woolf, 'The novels of E.M. Forster', *Atlantic Monthly*, November 1927, pp. 642–48 and *CH*, p. 322.

12 Woolf, pp. 642–48 and *CH*, p. 322.

13 Laurence Stallings, 'When Rudyards cease their Kiplings and Haggards Ride no more', *World*, 13 August 1924, p. 9 and *CH*, pp. 241–42.

14 Rebecca West, 'Interpreters of their Age', *Saturday Review of Literature*, 16 August 1924, p. 42 and *CH*, p. 254.

15 Macaulay, p. 8 and *CH*, p. 196.

16 R. Ellis Roberts, *Bookman*, July 1924, pp. 220–21 and *CH*, p. 231. An exception to this praise of Forster comes in the form of a review by Gerald Gould, *Saturday Review*, 21 June 1924, p. 642 and *CH*, pp. 218–20. He argues that Forster is not a novelist since 'his medium is really the

fairy-story; for in a fairy-story the characters may be as thin and faint and fantastic as you please'. When he turns his attention to *A Passage to India*, Gould elaborates this view by stating that 'Forster cannot lodge his spirits in human bodies. He can give them every finest shade of feeling and perception; he can mercilessly record their language, their thoughts, even the hinterland of their thoughts, but he cannot make them come alive.' Gould's review of *A Passage to India* is consistently hostile to the novel and its author and stands out for this reason.

17 Priestley, pp. 319–20 and *CH*, p. 229.

18 Wright, pp. 317–18 and *CH*, p. 224.

19 Elinor Wylie, 'Passage to more than India', *New York Herald Tribune*, 5 October 1924, p. i and *CH*, p. 277.

20 I. P. Fassett, *Criterion*, 3.9 (1924), pp. 137–39 and *CH*, p. 273.

21 I. P. Fassett, pp. 137–39 and *CH*, pp. 273-74.

22 *The Collected Letters of D. H. Lawrence*, ed. Henry T. Moore (Heinemann, 1962), II, p. 799 and *CH*, p. 275.

23 Priestley, pp. 319–20 and *CH*, pp. 228–29.

24 Unsigned notice, *Times of India*, 23 July 1924, p. 13 and *CH*, p. 239.

25 *Times of India*, p. 13 and *CH*, p. 239.

26 *Times of India*, p. 13 and *CH*, p. 239.

27 *Times of India*, p. 13 and *CH*, p. 239.

28 *Times of India*, p. 13 and *CH*, pp. 239–40.

29 Macaulay, p. 8 and *CH*, p. 197.

30 Macaulay, p. 8 and *CH*, p. 198.

31 *Observer*, 15 June 1924, p. 5 and *CH*, p. 211.

32 'A striking novel', *Statesman* (Calcutta), 15 August 1924, p. 6 and *CH*, pp. 245–46.

33 'C. M', *Manchester Guardian*, 20 June 1924, p. 7 and *CH*, p. 213.

34 'S. A', *Springfield Sunday Republican*, 19 October 1924, p. 5a and *CH*, p. 282.

35 E. A. Horne, letter to the editor, *New Statesman*, 23 (1924), pp. 543–44 and *CH*, pp. 246–47.

36 Horne, pp. 543–44 and *CH*, p. 250.

37 S. K. Ratcliffe, letter to the editor, *New Statesman*, 23 (1924), pp. 567–68 and *CH*, p. 252.

38 Ratcliffe, pp. 567–68 and *CH*, p. 252.

39 Ratcliffe, pp. 567–68 and *CH*, pp. 252–53.

40 Ratcliffe, pp. 567–68 and *CH*, p. 253.

41 'Hommage à M. Forster by "An Indian"', *Nation and Athenaeum*, 4 August 1928, pp. 589-91 and *CH*, pp. 289-90.

42 'Hommage à M. Forster', pp. 589–91 and *CH*, p. 290.

43 Bhupal Singh, *A Survey of Anglo-Indian Fiction* (Oxford: Oxford University Press, 1934), pp. 221–32 and *CH*, p. 293.

44 Singh, pp. 221–32 and *CH*, p. 294.

45 L. P. Hartley, *Spectator*, 28 June 1924, pp. 1048–50 and *CH*, p. 227.

CHAPTER TWO

1 *A Passage to India*, ed. Tony Davies and Nigel Wood, Theory in Practice Series (Buckingham: Open University Press, 1994), p. 5.

2 In the context of Forster studies a key text is Frederick C. Crews' *E. M. Forster: The Perils of Humanism* (Princeton, New Jersey: Princeton University Press, 1962). In his chapter on *A Passage to India* Crews follows closely the line taken by Lionel Trilling but suggests that Forster's attempt to approach the incomprehensible 'seems to announce the end of the traditional novel as he found it; between pathetic futility and absolute mystery no middle ground remains for significant action' (p. 163).

3 Tony Davies, *Humanism* (London and New York: Routledge, 1997), p. 35.

4 This is in marked contrast to more contemporary views of Forster's humanism. As Paul B. Armstrong notes, 'When Forster is invoked by politically minded contemporary critics, it is usually to attack or dismiss him. His name has become a token for error or lamentable naïveté, whether he is presented as an illustration of the fallacies of liberal humanism, or as a last remnant of British imperialism, or as a practitioner of traditional narrative methods who lacks self-consciousness about the epistemological ambiguities of language.' Paul B. Armstrong, 'Reading

India: E.M. Forster and the Politics of Interpretation', *Twentieth Century Literature: A Scholarly and Critical Journal*, 38 (1992), p.365. The contemporary critical views of Forster that Armstrong addresses in his essay include Benita Parry's 'The Politics of Representation in *A Passage to India*', in *A Passage to India: Essays in Interpretation*, ed. John Beer (London: Macmillan, 1985), pp.27–43 and Sara Suleri's 'The Geography of *A Passage to India*', in *E.M. Forster: Modern Critical Views*, ed. Harold Bloom (New York: Chelsea House, 1987), pp.169–75.

5 John Colmer, 'Promise and Withdrawal in *A Passage to India*', in *E.M. Forster: A Human Exploration, Centenary Essays*, ed. G.K. Das and John Beer (London and Basingstoke: The Macmillan Press, 1979), p.127.

6 F.R. Leavis, *The Common Pursuit* (London: Penguin, 1963), p.262.

7 Leavis, p.261.

8 Leavis, p.261.

9 Leavis, p.261.

10 Leavis, p.261.

11 Leavis, p.261.

12 Leavis, p.264.

13 Leavis, p.262.

14 Leavis, p.262.

15 Leavis, p.262.

16 Leavis, p.262.

17 Leavis, p.264.

18 Leavis, p.264.

19 Leavis, pp.268–69.

20 See also Daniel Born's 'Private Gardens, Public Swamps: *Howards End* and the Revaluation of Liberal Guilt', *Novel*, 25 (1992), pp.141–59.

21 Leavis, pp.269–70.

22 Leavis, p.270.

23 Leavis, pp.272–73.

24 Leavis, pp.273–74.

25 Leavis, pp.275–76.

26 Leavis, pp.275–77.

27 Lionel Trilling, *E.M. Forster: A Study* (London: The Hogarth Press, 1969), pp.117–38.

28 Trilling, p.118.

29 Trilling, p.118.

30 Trilling, p.120.

31 Trilling, pp.120–21.

32 Trilling, p.123.

33 Trilling, p.123.

34 Trilling, pp.123–24.

35 Trilling, pp.124–25.

36 Trilling, p.125.

37 Trilling, pp.125–26.

38 E.M. Forster, *Aspects of the Novel* [1927] (London and New York: Penguin, 1990). Forster's definitions of plot and story appear on pages 87 and 42 respectively.

39 Trilling, p.126.

40 Forster, *Aspects of the Novel*, pp.54–55.

41 Trilling, pp.128–30.

42 Trilling, p.131.

43 E.M. Forster, 'Notes on the English Character', in *Abinger Harvest* (London: Edward Arnold, 1936), p.5.

44 Trilling, pp.131–33.

45 Trilling, pp.133–34.

46 Trilling, p.136.

47 Trilling, pp.137–38.

48 Suleri, pp.107–08.

49 Malcolm Bradbury, 'Two Passages to India: Forster as Victorian and Modern', in *E.M. Forster: A Casebook*, ed. Malcolm Bradbury (London: Macmillan, 1979), pp.224–43.

50 Bradbury, pp.224–25.

51 Bradbury, pp.225–27.

52 Bradbury, p.226.

53 Bradbury, p.226.

54 Bradbury, p.227.

55 Bradbury, p.227.

56 Bradbury, pp.227–28.

57 Bradbury, p.229.

58 Bradbury, p.230.

59 Bradbury, p.230.

60 Bradbury, p.230.

61 Bradbury, pp.230–31.

62 Bradbury, p.231.

63 Bradbury, p.231.

64 Bradbury, p.232.

65 Bradbury, pp.232–33.

66 Bradbury states that '[o]ne way of putting the situation is to say that the human plot of the novel is set into singular relation to the verbal plot, with its radiating expansiveness of language' (p.234).

67 Bradbury, p. 235.
68 Bradbury, pp. 236–38.
69 Bradbury, pp. 238–42.

CHAPTER THREE

1 I have already discussed F. R. Leavis's attempt to place Forster in relation to the tradition. Other writers mentioned in relation to Forster include Rudyard Kipling, Samuel Butler, Herman Melville, H. G. Wells and Virginia Woolf. Critics are invariably attuned to Forster's social satire but his exact relation to realism remains the subject of debate. Forster himself claimed to have learnt from Jane Austen's comedy and Proust's psychological realism. Forster's realism, and its relation to symbolism, is discussed by S. V. Pradham in 'A Passage to India: Realism Versus Symbolism, A Marxist Analysis', Dalhousie Review, 60 (1980), pp. 300–17. Pradham argues that the conflict between realist and non-realist modes in A Passage to India emanates from Forster's 'alienation from the reality he has chosen to depict. [. . .] He cannot see it or is not interested in seeing it as a concrete totality moulded by social historical determinants. Given this radical limitation abstraction, psychologism, inadequate types, mystification (which occasionally presses lyricism into service and invests India with a halo of incomprehensibility) and symbolism follow' (p. 314).

2 June Perry Levine, Creation and Criticism: A Passage to India (London: Chatto and Windus, 1971), p. 128.

3 E. K. Brown, 'Rhythm in E. M. Forster's A Passage to India' (1950), in E. M. Forster, A Passage to India: A Casebook, ed. Malcolm Bradbury (London and Basingstoke: Macmillan, 1970), p. 104.

4 Reuben A. Brower, 'The Twilight of the Double Vision' (1951), in E. M. Forster, A Passage to India: A Casebook, pp. 116–17.

5 Wilfred Stone, The Cave and the Mountain: A Study of E. M. Forster (Stanford and London: Stanford University Press, 1966), p. 299.

6 Christopher Gillie, A Preface to Forster (Harlow: Longman, 1983), p. 108.

7 Pierre Macherey, A Theory of Literary Production, trans. Geoffrey Wall (London: RKP, 1978).

8 Wolfgang Iser, The Act of Reading: A Theory of Aesthetic Response (Baltimore: Johns Hopkins University Press, 1978).

9 Gillian Beer, 'Negation in A Passage to India', Essays in Criticism: A Quarterly Journal of Literary Criticism, 30 (1980), pp. 151–66.

10 Beer, p. 151.

11 Wendy Moffat, 'A Passage to India and the Limits of Certainty', Journal of Narrative Technique, 20 (1990), pp. 331–41.

12 The Manuscripts of A Passage to India, ed. Oliver Stallybrass, The Abinger Edition Series, 6a (London: Edward Arnold, 1978).

13 Robert Barratt, 'Marabar: The Caves of Deconstruction', Journal of Narrative Technique, 20 (1990), p. 127.

14 Jo Ann Hoeppner Moran, 'E. M. Forster's A Passage to India: What Really Happened in the Caves', Modern Fiction Studies, 34 (1988), pp. 596–604.

15 Beer, p. 151.

16 Beer, p. 151.

17 Beer, p. 152.

18 Beer, pp. 152–53.

19 For a discussion of the syntactic functions of negation see, for example, Edward Klima, 'Negation in English', in The Structure of Language: Readings in the Philosophy of Language, ed. Jerry A. Fodor and Jerrold J. Katz (Englewood Cliffs: Prentice-Hall, 1964), pp. 246–323.

20 Beer, pp. 153–54.

21 Gerald Graff points out the slippage between the terms indeterminacy and ambiguity, a slippage that also characterises the essays in this chapter: '[in] the past two decades, critics wishing to emphasize that element in literature that resists clear-cut definition have tended to speak of "indeterminacy" rather than of "ambiguity." Whether the new term means something significantly different from the earlier one is still in dispute, and some observers have argued that new

indeterminacy is only old ambiguity by another name. But the critics who have popularized the term "indeterminacy" insist that there are crucial differences. The most prominent of these critics are the so-called deconstructionists, who take their primary ideas from the French philosopher Jacques Derrida and the Belgian-American literary theorist Paul de Man', 'Determinacy/Indeterminacy', in *Critical Terms for Literary Study*, ed. Frank Lentricchia and Thomas McLaughlin (Chicago and London: University of Chicago Press, 1990), p. 165. The chief distinction between the New Critical concept of ambiguity and the deconstructionist notion of indeterminacy seems to be that while the former is the property of a given text, the latter has a meta-critical function, that is, it calls into question the process by which texts are interpreted. For another reading of *A Passage to India* informed by contemporary theory see Judith Scherer Herz, 'Forster's Ghosts: *A Passage to India* and the Emptying of Narrative', in *Negation, Critical Theory, and Postmodern Textuality*, ed. Daniel Fischlin (Dordrecht: Kluwer Acad., 1994), pp. 191–202.

22 Beer, pp. 155–57.
23 Beer, pp. 157–58.
24 Beer, p. 159.
25 See Jacques Lacan, *The Four Fundamental Concepts of Psychoanalysis*, trans. Alan Sheridan (New York: W. W. Norton, 1978).
26 Beer, p. 160. For more detailed accounts of the relation between writing and sexuality in Forster see, Richard Dellamora, 'Textual Politics/Sexual Politics', *Modern Language Quarterly*, 54 (1993), pp. 155–64; Donald Salter, 'That is my Ticket: The Homosexual Writings of E. M. Forster', *London Magazine*, 15 (2), [n.d.,] pp. 5–33 and Sara Suleri, *The Rhetoric of English India* (Chicago and London: University of Chicago Press. 1992), pp. 132–48.
27 Beer, p. 160.
28 Beer, pp. 162–64.
29 Beer, pp. 165–66.

30 Moffat, p. 332.
31 Moffat, p. 332.
32 Moffat, p. 332.
33 P. N. Furbank and R. J. M. Haskell, 'The Art of Fiction', *Paris Review*, vol. 1 (1953), pp. 29–41.
34 Stallybrass, pp. 242–43.
35 Levine, p. 92.
36 Moffat, pp. 332–33.
37 Moffat, p. 333.
38 Moffat, p. 334.
39 Moffat, p. 334.
40 Moffat, p. 334. See also Steven Doloff, 'Forster's Use of Names in *A Passage to India*', *English Language Notes*, 28.4 (1991), pp. 61–62.
41 Moffat, p. 335.
42 Moffat, p. 335.
43 Moffat, p. 335.
44 Moffat, pp. 336–37.
45 Edward Said, *Orientalism* (London and New York: Routledge, 1978). See also, *The Post-Colonial Studies Reader*, ed. Bill Ashcroft, Gareth Griffiths and Helen Tiffin (London and New York: Routledge, 1995).
46 Frederick Crews, *E. M. Forster: The Perils of Humanism* (Princeton: Princeton University Press, 1962).
47 Moffat, p. 337.
48 Moffat, pp. 337–38.
49 Moffat, p. 338.
50 For another reading of the 'Temple' section see, V. A. Shahane, 'Symbolism in E. M. Forster's *A Passage to India*: "Temple"', *English Studies: A Journal of English Language and Literature*, 44 (1963), pp. 423–31.
51 Moffat, p. 339.
52 Moffat, p. 339.
53 Michael Ryan, *Marxism and Deconstruction: A Critical Articulation* (Baltimore: Johns Hopkins University Press, 1982), p. 14.
54 Barratt, pp. 127–28.
55 Jacques Derrida, 'Structure, Sign and Play in the Discourse of the Human Sciences', in *The Structuralist Controversy*, ed. Richard Macksey and Eugenio Donato (Baltimore: Johns Hopkins University Press, 1972), p. 249.

56 Barratt, pp. 128–29.

57 Barratt, p. 129.

58 Katherine N. Hayles, *Chaos Bound: Orderly Disorder in Contemporary Literature and Science* (Ithaca: Cornell University Press, 1990), p. 181.

59 Barratt, pp. 129–30.

60 Ryan, p. 14.

61 Ryan, p. 14.

62 Jacques Derrida, *Speech and Phenomena* (Evanston: Northwestern University Press, 1973), pp. 142–43.

63 Jacques Derrida, *Positions* (Chicago: University of Chicago Press, 1981), p. 267.

64 Ryan, p. 11.

65 Hayles, pp. 182–83.

66 Ryan, p. 10.

67 Moffat, p. 334.

68 In his reading of Adela, Barratt seems to follow Ted E. Boyle's notion that 'in the caves, the subconscious, the irrational, the emotional, the very soul of India wins out over the conscious, the rational, the intellectual – all that Adela has been taught by Western society', Ted Boyle, 'Adela Quested's Delusion: The Failure of Rationalism in *A Passage to India*', *College English*, 26 (1965), p. 479. Despite his reference to the Derridean trace, which owes so much to and also revises Freud's theory of the unconscious, Barratt does not engage with the psychoanalytic implications of the Cave. The association of the female figure with the irrational has also in turn been subject to deconstruction by feminist critics. See, for example, Jane Ussher, *Women's Madness: Misogyny or Mental Illness?* (New York and London: Harvester Wheatsheaf, 1991), p. 68.

69 Barratt, pp. 130–32.

70 Paul B. Armstrong, 'E. M. Forster and the Politics of Interpretation', *Twentieth Century Literature: A Scholarly and Critical Journal*, 38 (1992), p. 371.

71 Ryan, p. 24.

72 Ryan, p. 25.

73 Jacques Derrida, 'Signature Event Context', *Glyph*, 1, (1977), p. 41.

74 Derrida, 'Signature', p. 195.

75 Barratt, pp. 132–34.

76 Henry Stapp, 'S-Matrix Interpretation of Quantum Theory', *Physical Review*, D3 (1971), p. 1303.

77 Barratt, p. 134.

78 Lionel Stevenson, 'The Earnest Realists', in *The History of the English Novel*, ed. Lionel Stevenson (New York: Barnes, 1967), II, pp. 87–102.

79 P. N. Furbank, *E. M. Forster: A Life* (London: Secker and Warburg, 1977) II, p. 125.

80 Furbank, p. 125.

81 Louise Dauner, 'What Happened in the Cave? Reflections on *A Passage to India*', in *Perspectives on E. M. Forster's A Passage to India*, ed. V. A. Shahane (New York: Barnes, 1968), p. 52.

82 For various psychological explanations of Adela's hallucinations, see G. K. Das, *E. M. Forster's India* (Ottowa: Rowman, 1977), p. 82; V. A. Shahane, *A Passage to India: A Study* (Delhi: Oxford University Press, 1977), pp. 31–32 and Claude J. Summers, *E. M. Forster* (New York: Ungar, 1983), pp. 212–13.

83 Moran, pp. 596–97.

84 Stone, p. 17 and 'The Caves in *A Passage to India*', *A Passage to India: Essays and Interpretations*, ed. John Beer (New York: Macmillan, 1985), pp. 300–01.

85 *E. M. Forster: An Annotated Bibliography of Writings About Him*, ed. F. P. W. McDowell (Dekalb: Northern Illinois University Press, 1976), p. 413.

86 Barbara Rosecrace stresses the degree of control Forster, as narrator, exerts in *A Passage to India* in *Forster's Narrative Vision* (Ithaca: Cornell University Press, 1982). For further analysis of the novel's structure, see Hugh McClean, 'The Structure of *A Passage to India*', *University of Toronto Quarterly*, 22 (1953), pp. 157–71; Gertrude M. White, '*A Passage to India*: Analysis and Revaluation', *PMLA*, 68 (1953), pp. 641–57 and Glen O. Allen, 'Structure, Symbol and Theme in *A Passage to India*', *PMLA* 70 (1955), pp. 934–54.

87 Moran, p. 598.

88 Moran, p. 598.

89 See also Benita Parry, *Delusions and Discoveries: Studies on India in the British*

Imagination 1880-1930 (Berkeley: University of California Press, 1972), pp. 129–41 and S. Gopolan, _Outlines of Jainism_ (New York: Halsted, 1973).

90 Moran, p. 598.

91 Benita Parry, 'A Passage to India: Epitaph or Manifesto?', in _E.M. Forster: A Human Exploration_, ed. G.K. Das and John Beer (New York: New York University Press, 1979), p. 135.

92 Moran, p. 600.

93 Moran, pp. 600–02.

94 Chaman L. Sahni, _Forster's_ A Passage to India: _The Religious Dimension_ (Atlantic Highlands: Humanities Press, 1981).

95 Moran, p. 602.

96 Moran, pp. 602–03.

CHAPTER FOUR

1 See, for instance, Louise Dauner, 'What Happened in the Cave? Reflections on _A Passage to India_', _Modern Fiction Studies_, 7 (1961), pp. 258–70 and Bonnie Blumenthal Finkelstein, _Forster's Women: Eternal Differences_, (New York: Columbia University Press, 1975).

2 For an interesting exploration of the figure of the female hysteric, see Clare Kahane, _Passions of the Voice: Hysteria, Narrative, and the Figure of the Speaking Woman, 1850–1915_ (Baltimore: Johns Hopkins University Press, 1995).

3 Wilfred Stone, _The Cave and the Mountain: A Study of E.M. Forster_ (California: Stanford University Press, 1966), p. 335.

4 Frances L. Restuccia, '"A Cave of My Own": E.M. Forster and Sexual Politics', _Raritan_, 9 (1989), p. 110.

5 Vron Ware, _Beyond the Pale: White Women, Racism and History_ (London and New York: Verso, 1992), p. 37.

6 Elaine Showalter, 'A Passage to India as "Marriage Fiction": Forster's Sexual Politics', _Women and Literature_, 5 (1977), pp. 3–16.

7 Showalter, p. 3.

8 Showalter, p. 3.

9 Showalter draws here on 'The Subjection of Women', in _Essays on Sex_

Equality, ed. Alice S. Rossi (Chicago: University of Chicago Press, 1970), p. 218.

10 Showalter, p. 4.

11 In Steiner's reading of this text the imperial power structure of _A Passage to India_ serves as 'a brilliant projection of the confrontation between society and the homosexual'. George Steiner, 'Under the Greenwood Tree', _New Yorker_, 9 October 1971, p. 166.

12 Showalter, p. 4.

13 Showalter, p. 4.

14 Showalter, pp. 4–5 and Stone, p. 324.

15 Showalter, pp. 5–6.

16 _The Plays of Hubert Henry Davies_ (London: Chatto and Windus, 1921), I, p. 100. Adela is much more aggressive in the earlier drafts of the novel, suggesting a more pronounced parallel between Forster's central female figure and the 'New Woman'. See Oliver Stallybrass, 'Forster's "Wobblings": The Manuscripts of _A Passage to India_', in _E.M. Forster: A Passage to India, A Casebook_, ed. Malcolm Bradbury (London and Basingstoke: Macmillan, 1970), pp. 32–43.

17 Stone, p. 327.

18 Quentin Bell, _Virginia Woolf_, (London: Hogarth Press, 1972), II, p. 133.

19 See also Finkelstein, p. 117. As Finkelstein notes, '[i]mperialism pervades this novel. Against a backdrop of oppression and manipulation of Indians by their British rulers, a parallel domestic imperialism emerges: Indian men oppress their women, while British women manipulate their men'.

20 Showalter, pp. 6–7.

21 Showalter, p. 7.

22 Showalter, p. 8.

23 Showalter, p. 8.

24 Showalter, p. 8.

25 E. Martelli, _The Key of Progress: A Survey of the Status and Conditions of Women in India_, ed. A.R. Caton (London: Oxford University Press, 1930), p. 116.

26 Caton, p. 120.

27 Showalter, pp. 8–9 and Caton, pp. 83–107.

28 Showalter, p. 9.

29 Showalter, pp. 9–10.

30 Showalter, p. 11.

31 Although Showalter is not usually associated with feminism in its more radical manifestations, this view seems to chime with those promoted by Andrea Dworkin in *Intercourse* (London: Secker and Warburg, 1987).

32 Finkelstein makes the interesting suggestion that the 'animal thing' that hits them is Adela's repressed sexuality. But her analysis emphasises Adela's realisation of her 'major character defect . . . an undeveloped heart'. This seems like an extreme case of blaming the victim. See Finkelstein, pp. 130–34.

33 Showalter, pp. 11–12.

34 Showalter suggests that the guilt of both Aziz and Fielding 'may also have a source in the homosexual aspect of their relationship'. See Showalter, p. 16.

35 Showalter, p. 12.

36 For an informed account of the psychology of sexual violence, see Susan Brownmiller, *Against Our Will: Men, Women, and Rape* (New York: Bantam, 1976).

37 Showalter, pp. 12–13.

38 Showalter, pp. 13–15.

39 Restuccia, p. 110.

40 Restuccia, p. 11.

41 For Edward Said, see especially *Orientalism* (New York: Vintage, 1978) and *Culture and Imperialism* (London: Chatto and Windus, 1993).

42 Alice Jardine, *Gynesis* (Ithaca: Cornell University Press, 1985).

43 Restuccia's reading is informed by the work of Luce Irigaray, Julia Kristeva and Hélène Cixous. For French feminist theory, see *New French Feminisms: An Anthology*, ed. Elaine Marks and Isabelle de Courtivron, trans. Keith Cohen and Paula Cohen (New York: Schocken Books, 1976). For the relationship between feminism and post-structuralism, see Chris Weedon, *Feminist Practice and Poststructuralist Theory* (Oxford: Basil Blackwell, 1987). Restuccia takes Jacques Derrida as an example of a male critic whose use of indeterminacy as a

way of theorising gender can be said to be problematic for feminists. See Derrida, *Spurs: Nietzsche's Styles*, trans. Barbara Harlow (Chicago: University of Chicago Press, 1981). Jardine's work also features prominently in Sara Mills's account of Forster's text. See 'Representing the Unrepresentable: Alice Jardine's *Gynesis* and E. M. Forster's *A Passage to India*', in *A Passage to India*, ed. Tony Davies and Nigel Wood, Theory in Practice Series (Buckingham: Open University Press, 1994), pp. 121–43. Mills argues that the elements of *A Passage to India* that destabilise its classic realist mode might be said to 'constitute moments of gynesis'. These elements include indeterminacy, mysticism, particular female characters and 'India itself' (p. 130). Mills neatly summarises Jardine's position by stating that 'many texts written within and about the colonial situation, particularly in India, are focused around women as a problem which the text tries to resolve. Modernity is seen to be a crisis of Western culture and authority, and this can be clearly seen in novels about the loss of Britain's colonial rule. For Jardine, it would not be coincidental that many of the novels about the Empire are about loss, and that loss seems to be displaced on to or articulated through the problem of women. She sees these two subjects as inextricably tied within this particular moment of Western culture' (p. 130).

44 Restuccia, p. 112.

45 Restuccia, p. 112.

46 Restuccia, pp. 112–13.

47 Restuccia, pp. 114–16.

48 Restuccia, p. 117.

49 Restuccia, p. 117.

50 Restuccia, p. 117.

51 Restuccia, pp. 117–18.

52 Restuccia, p. 118.

53 Restuccia, p. 118.

54 Restuccia, pp. 118–21.

55 Restuccia, pp. 121–23.

56 Restuccia, p. 123.

57 Restuccia, p. 123.

58 Restuccia, p. 123.

59 Restuccia, pp. 123–24

60 Jardine, p. 25.

61 Jardine, p. 25.

62 Restuccia, pp. 125–27.

63 Eve Dawkins Poll, 'The Colonization of the Ingenue in E.M. Forster's *A Passage to India*', *SPAN: Journal of the South Pacific Association for Commonwealth Literature and Language Studies*, 38 (1994), pp. 46–64.

64 Insofar as she deploys the work of Bhabha, Poll uses it to demonstrate the workings of the colonial stereotype rather than the 'type' that is represented through the female ingenue. See Homi K. Bhabha, 'The Other Question: Difference, Discrimination and the Discourse of Colonialism', in *Literature, Politics and Theory: Papers from the Essex Conference 1976–1984*, eds Francis Barker *et al.* (London: Methuen, 1989). In addition to Bhabha's work, Poll also draws extensively on other readings of Forster's text that view it from a feminist and post-colonial perspective. These readings of the text are more readily integrated into the overall argument. The criticism that features predominantly in Poll's essay includes Benita Parry, 'Passage to More than India', in *Forster: A Collection of Critical Essays*, ed. Malcolm Bradbury (New Jersey: Prentice Hall, 1966), pp. 160–74; Jenny Sharpe, 'The Unspeakable Limits of Rape: Colonial Violence and Counter-Insurgency', *Genders*, 10 (1991), pp. 25–46; and Brenda R. Silver, 'Periphrasis, Power, and Rape in *A Passage to India*', *Novel: A Forum on Fiction*, 22 (1988), pp. 86–105.

65 Poll, p. 46.

66 Poll, p. 46.

67 Poll, p. 46.

68 Poll, p. 52.

69 Poll, p. 47.

70 Poll, pp. 52–54.

71 Alison Sainsbury, 'Married to the Empire: The Anglo-Indian Domestic Novel', in *Writing India 1757–1990: The Literature of British India*, ed. Bart Moore-Gilbert (Manchester and New York: Manchester University Press, 1996), p. 182.

72 Abdul R. JanMohamed, 'The Economy of the Manichean Allegory: The Function of Racial Difference in Colonialist Literature', *Race, Writing and Difference*, ed. Henry Louis Gates, Jr (Chicago: University of Chicago Press, 1985), p. 85.

73 Poll, pp. 54–56.

74 Poll, p. 57.

75 Poll, p. 57.

76 Hazel V. Carby, 'On the Threshold of Women's Era: Lynching, Empire, and Sexuality in Black Feminist Theory', in *Race, Writing and Difference*, p. 309.

77 Carby, p. 309. Poll's strategy of drawing parallels between racial politics in an American context and those which operate within the imperial system is clearly problematic. For more on this, see, for example, *The Discourse of Slavery: Aphra Behn to Toni Morrison*, ed. Carl Plasa and Betty J. Ring (London and New York: Routledge, 1994).

78 Kumkum Sangari and Sudesh Vaid, 'Recasting Women: An Introduction', in *Recasting Women: Essays in Gender*, ed. Kumkum Sangari and Sudesh Vaid (New Jersey: Rutgers University Press, 1990), p. 10.

79 Poll, pp. 58–61.

CHAPTER FIVE

1 Jeffrey Meyers, 'The Politics of *A Passage to India*', *Journal of Modern Literature*, 1 (1971), pp. 329–38.

2 Lionel Trilling, *E.M. Forster: A Study* (London: Hogarth Press, 1969), p. 129.

3 K.W. Gransden, *E.M. Forster* (London: Grove Press, 1962), p. 85.

4 Meyers, p. 330.

5 E.M. Forster, 'Reflections on India', *Nation and Athenaeum*, 30, 21 January 1922, p. 615.

6 Meyers, p. 331.

7 Meyers, p. 332.

8 Meyers, p. 333. Meyers's italics.

9 Louis Snyder, *The Imperialism Reader* (Princeton: Princeton University Press, 1962), p. 420.

10 Meyers, p. 333.

11 Meyers, p. 333.

12 E.M. Forster, 'India and the Turk', *Nation and Athenaeum*, 30 September 1922, p.845.

13 E.M. Forster, *The Government of Egypt* (London: Labour Research Department, 1920).

14 E.M. Forster, 'E.M. Forster on his Life and Books', *Listener*, 61, 1 January 1959, p.11.

15 E.M. Forster quoted in *E.M. Forster: A Tribute*, ed. K. Natwar-Singh (New York: Harcourt, Brace and World, 1964), p.xiii.

16 Nirad Chaudhuri, 'A Passage to and from India', *Encounter*, 2, June 1954, p.19.

17 Meyers, p.334.

18 Meyers, p.337.

19 Quoted and translated from Bengali (1873) by Nirad Chaudhuri, 'On Understanding Hindus', *Encounter*, 24, June 1965, p.21.

20 E.M. Forster, 'Reflections on India', pp.614–15.

21 Quoted in Archibald Thornton, *The Imperial Idea and its Enemies* (London: [n. pub.] 1959), p.306. Meyers's italics.

22 Quoted in Arthur Koestler, *The Lotus and the Robot* (London: Hutchinson, 1960), p.280.

23 Meyers, pp.335–36.

24 Meyers, p.336.

25 Vinoba Bhave, *In Defence of Colonies* (London: [n.pub.] 1957), p.5.

26 Norman Palmer, 'Indian Attitudes toward Colonialism', in *The Idea of Colonialism*, ed. Robert Straus-Hupe (New York, 1958), p.277.

27 John Beer, *The Achievement of E.M. Forster* (London: Chatto and Windus, 1962), p.135. Beer is quite wrong when he says, '[t]here is never any doubt that they (the Indians) need the justice and fair administration that the British give them.'

28 Meyers, pp.336–38.

29 Jenny Sharpe, 'The Unspeakable Limits of Rape: Colonial Violence and Counter-Insurgency', *Genders*, 10 (1991), pp.25–46. For additional readings of Forster's imperial discourse see M.M. Mahood, *The Colonial Encounter: A Reading*

of Six Novels (London: Collings, 1977), pp.65–91; Hunt Hawkins, 'Forster's Critique of Imperialism in *A Passage to India*', *SAB*, 48.1 (1983), pp.54–65; Brenda R. Silver, 'Periphrasis, Power and Rape in *A Passage to India*', *Novel: A Forum on Fiction*, 22.1 (1988), pp.86–105; and Jeffrey Heath, 'A Voluntary Surrender: Imperialism and Imagination in *A Passage to India*', *University of Toronto Quarterly: A Canadian Journal of the Humanities*, 59 (1989–90), pp.287–309.

30 Sharpe, p.26.

31 Sharpe, p.26.

32 Sharpe, p.25.

33 Sharpe, p.25.

34 Sharpe, p.25.

35 *Colonial Discourse and Post-Colonial Theory: A Reader*, ed. Patrick Williams and Laura Chrisman (New York and London: Harvester Wheatsheaf, 1993), p.4.

36 Sharpe engages specifically with Elaine Showalter's '*A Passage to India* as "Marriage Fiction": Forster's Sexual Politics', *Women and Literature*, 5.2 (1977), pp.3–16 and Silver. Critics who presume Adela's accusation of rape to be a sign of her sexual desire and/or repression include Benita Parry, in *Delusions and Discoveries: Studies on India in the British Imagination* (London: Allen Lane, 1972), pp.294–95, Barbara Rosecrace in *Forster's Narrative Vision* (Ithaca: Cornell University Press, 1982), p.207 and David Rubin, *After the Raj: British Novels of India Since 1947* (Hanover: University Press of New England, 1986).

37 Sharpe, p.27.

38 Sharpe, p.30.

39 Sharpe, p.30.

40 Pat Barr, *The Memsahibs: The Women of Victorian India* (London: Secker and Warburg, 1976), p.143.

41 Sashi Chaudhuri aptly captures the heterogeneity of the rebellion in his description of its popular base: '[t]he villagers impeded the march of the British avenging army by withholding supplies and information which they freely gave to the rebel forces; wage earners vented their rage on the system of foreign

exploitation by a wholesale destruction of the British-owned factories; the social destitutes to whom borrowing was the only means of livelihood turned against the bankers, *mahajans* (capitalists) and usurers, the class protected by the British courts; the priests and prophets preached *jehad* against the *feringhis*; and other elements of society, not always amenable to law and order, broke out into uncontrollable fury, attacked police and revenue establishments, destroyed government records and court-buildings and telegraph poles, in fact everything which could remind them of the English.' Sashi Chaudhuri, *Theories of the Indian Mutiny 1857–59* (Calcutta: The World Press, 1965), p. 1.

42 Sir John Kaye, *Kaye's and Malleson's History of the Indian Mutiny of 1857–8* (London: Longmans, Green, & Co, 1898), II, p. 299.

43 Barr, p. 113.

44 *The Times* (London), 6 August 1857.

45 *News of the World*, 19 July 1857.

46 The source of a news story was never identified as rumour. Rather, the term was reserved for the stories circulating among the Indian populace, which predicted the end of British rule. As Ranjit Guha points out, the systematic dismissal of word of mouth transmissions as rumour and superstition negates the mobilising power of oral reports in pre-literate societies. See Ranjit Guha, *Elementary Aspects of Peasant Insurgency in Colonial India* (Delhi: Oxford University Press, 1983), pp. 220–77.

47 Sir George Campbell, *Memoirs of My Indian Career*, ed. Sir Charles E. Bernard (London: Macmillan, 1893), I, p. 400; Christopher Hibbert, *The Great Mutiny, India 1857* (London: Penguin, 1980), p. 213.

48 Sharpe, pp. 31–33.

49 Sharpe, p. 33.

50 Sharpe's discussion of rape as a violence that reproduces the gender roles of women is indebted to Monique Plaza's, 'Our Damages and Their Compensation, Rape: The Will Not to Know of Michel Foucault', *Feminist Issues*, 1 (1981), pp. 25–35.

51 Sir Colin Campbell, *Narrative of the Indian Revolt from its Outbreak to the Capture of Lucknow* (London: George Victers, 1858), p. 20.

52 This is the term that Plaza uses for the sexual positioning of the rape victim, which can include men.

53 Letter dated 4 August 1857, in the letters of Colonel Hugh Pearce Pearson, MSS Eur C231 (London: India Office Library).

54 Sharpe, pp. 33–35.

55 Sharpe, p. 35.

56 Elizabeth Cowie, 'Woman as Sign,' *m/f*, 1 (1978), pp. 49–63.

57 *An Englishwoman in India: The Memoirs of Harriet Tytler, 1828–1858*, ed. Anthony Sattin (Oxford: Oxford University Press, 1986), p. 160. This is one of the few women's diaries to have been recently reprinted.

58 An exception is Margaret Strobels' 'Gender and Race in the Nineteenth- and Twentieth-Century British Empires', which is attentive to the contradictions of the European woman's privileged yet subordinate role in colonial society, in *Becoming Visible: Women in European History*, ed. Renate Bridenthal *et al.* (Boston: Houghton Mifflin, 1987), pp. 375–96.

59 Campbell, *Memoirs*, p. 231.

60 Sashi Bhusan Chaudhuri has chronicled instances in which the British reprisals identified as acts of revenge in *Kaye's and Malleson's History of the Indian Mutiny* often took place before the massacres to which Kaye alludes. Sashi Bhusan Chaudhuri, *English Historical Writings on the Indian Mutiny, 1857–1859* (Calcutta: World Press, 1979), pp. 106–07.

61 Michael Taussig explains reversals of this kind as 'a colonial mirroring of otherness that reflects back onto the colonists the barbarity of their own social relations, but as imputed to the savagery they yearn to colonize'. Michael Taussig, *Shamanism, Colonialism, and the Wild Man* (Chicago: University of Chicago Press,

1987), p.134.

62 Cited by Francis Cornwallis Maude and John Walter Sherer, in *Memoirs of the Mutiny* (London: Remington and Company, 1894), I, p.71.

63 Cited by Kaye, p.300.

64 Bernard Cohn, 'Representing Authority in Victorian England', in *The Invention of Tradition*, ed. Eric Hobsbawm and Terence Ranger (Cambridge: Cambridge University Press, 1984), p.179.

65 Inscription on the well at Cawnpore, cited by Vincent Smith, *The Oxford History of India* (Oxford: Clarendon Press, 1923), p.719.

66 Sharpe, pp.36–38.

67 Sharpe, p.38.

68 Sharpe, p.38.

69 Sharpe, p.39. The effects of the Amritsar Massacre were not felt in England until several years later. In 1919, the events at Amritsar received little attention in the British press and were largely ignored by the intelligentsia. Upon examining the 'charges that have been brought against the English as a nation', however, Forster does refer to the massacre as one of those indefensible 'examples of public infamy'. 'Notes on the English Character' (1920), in *Abinger Harvest* (London: Edward Arnold, 1936), p.13.

70 Sharpe, pp.39–41.

71 Silver, p.86.

72 Pierre Macherey, *A Theory of Literary Production*, trans. Geoffrey Wall (London: Routledge and Kegan Paul, 1978), p.94.

73 Sharpe, pp.41–42.

BIBLIOGRAPHY

Works cited

Glen O. Allen, 'Structure, Symbol and Theme in *A Passage to India*', *PMLA*, 70 (1955), pp. 934–54.

Paul B. Armstrong, 'Reading India: E. M. Forster and the Politics of Interpretation', *Twentieth Century Literature: A Scholarly and Critical Journal*, 38 (1992), pp. 365–85.

Bill Ashcroft, Gareth Griffiths and Helen Tiffin, ed., *The Post-Colonial Studies Reader* (London and New York: Routledge, 1995).

Pat Barr, *The Memsahibs: The Women of Victorian India* (London, Secker and Warburg, 1976).

Robert Barratt, 'The Caves of Deconstruction', *Journal of Narrative Technique*, 23 (1993), pp. 127–35.

Gillian Beer, 'Negation in *A Passage to India*', *Essays in Criticism: A Quarterly Journal of Literary Criticism*, 30 (1980), pp. 151–66.

John Beer, *The Achievement of E. M. Forster* (London: Chatto and Windus, 1962).

Khani Begum, 'E. M. Forster's and David Lean's (Re) Presentations and (Re) Productions of Empire', *West Virginia University Philological Papers*, 40 (1994), pp. 20–29.

Quentin Bell, *Virginia Woolf: A Biography* (London: The Hogarth Press, 1972).

Homi K. Bhabha, 'The Other Question: Difference, Discrimination and the Discourse of Colonialism', *Literature, Politics and Theory: Papers from the Essex Conference 1976–1984*, eds Francis Barker *et al.* (London: Methuen, 1989), pp. 148–72.

Vinoba Bhave, *In Defence of Colonies* (London: n. p., 1957).

Daniel Born, 'Private Gardens, Public Swamps: *Howards End* and the Revaluation of Liberal Guilt', *Novel: A Forum on Fiction*, 25 (1992), pp. 141–59.

Ted E. Boyle, 'Adela Quested's Delusion: The Failure of Rationalism in *A Passage to India*', *College English*, 26 (1965), pp. 478–80.

Macolm Bradbury, 'Two Passages to India: Forster as Victorian and Modern', *E. M. Forster, A Passage to India: A Casebook*, ed. Malcolm Bradbury (London and Basingstoke: Macmillan, 1970), pp. 224–43.

Reuben A. Brower, 'The Twilight of the Double Vision', *E. M. Forster, A Passage to India: A Casebook*, ed. Malcolm Bradbury (London and Basingstoke: Macmillan, 1970), pp. 114–31.

E. K. Brown, 'Rhythm in E. M. Forster's *A Passage to India*', *E. M. Forster, A Passage to India: A Casebook*, ed. Malcolm Bradbury (London and Basingstoke: Macmillan, 1970), pp. 93–113.

Susan Brownmiller, *Against Our Will: Men, Women, and Rape* (New York: Bantam, 1976).

Peter Burra, 'Introduction to the Everyman Edition' (1934), reprinted in Appendix 2 of *A Passage to India*, ed. Oliver Stallybrass (London and New York: Penguin, 1989), pp. 319–33.

Sir George Campbell, *Memoirs of My Indian Career*, ed. Sir Charles E. Bernard (London: Macmillan, 1893).

Hazel V. Carby, 'On the Threshold of Women's Era: Lynching, Empire, and Sexuality in Black Feminist Theory', *Race, Writing and Difference*, ed. Henry Louis Gates, Jr (Chicago: University of Chicago Press, 1985), pp. 301–16.

A. R. Caton, ed., *The Key of Progress; A Survey of the Status and Conditions of Women in India* (London: Oxford University Press, 1930).

Nirad Chaudhuri, 'A Passage to and from India', *Encounter*, 2 (June 1954).

Sashi Chaudhuri, *Theories of the Indian Mutiny 1857–59* (Calcutta: The World Press, 1965).

John Colmer, 'Promise and Withdrawal in *A Passage to India*', *E.M. Forster: A Human Exploration, Centenary Essays*, ed. G. K. Das and John Beer (New York: New York University Press, 1979), pp. 117–28.

Elizabeth Cowie, 'Woman as Sign', *m/f*, 1 (1978), pp. 49–63.

Frederick C. Crews, *E.M. Forster: The Perils of Humanism* (Princeton, New Jersey: Princeton University Press, 1962).

G. K. Das, *E.M. Forster's India* (Ottowa: Rowman, 1977).

Louise Dauner's 'What Happened in the Cave? Reflections on *A Passage to India*', *Modern Fiction Studies*, 7 (1961), pp. 258–70.

The Plays of Hubert Henry Davies (London: Chatto and Windus, 1921).

Tony Davies, *Humanism* (London and New York: Routledge, 1997).

Tony Davies and Nigel Wood, ed., *A Passage to India*, Theory in Practice Series (Buckingham: Open University Press, 1994).

Richard Dellamora, 'Textual Politics/Sexual Politics', *Modern Language Quarterly: A Journal of Literary History*, 54 (1993), pp. 155–64.

Jacques Derrida, *Positions* (Chicago: University of Chicago Press, 1981).

—— 'Signature Event Context', *Glyph*, 1 (1977), pp. 172–97.

—— *Speech and Phenomena* (Evanston: Northwestern University Press, 1973).

—— *Spurs: Nietzsche's Styles*, trans. Barbara Harlow (Chicago: University of Chicago Press, 1981).

—— 'Structure, Sign and Play in the Discourse of the Human Sciences', *The Structuralist Controversy*, ed. Richard Macksey and Eugenio Donato (Baltimore: Johns Hopkins University Press, 1972), pp. 247–72.

Steven Doloff, 'Forster's Use of Names in *A Passage to India*', *English Language Notes*, 28 (1991), pp. 61–62.

Andrea Dworkin, *Intercourse* (London: Secker and Warburg, 1987).

Bonnie Blumenthal Finkelstein, *Forster's Women: Eternal Differences* (New York: Columbia University Press, 1975).

P. N. Furbank, *E.M. Forster: A Life* (London: Secker and Warburg, 1977).

P. N. Furbank and R. J. M. Haskell, 'The Art of Fiction', *Paris Review*, vol. 1 (1953), pp. 29–41.

Philip Gardner, *E.M. Forster: The Critical Heritage* (London and Boston: Routledge and Kegan Paul, 1973).

Christopher Gillie, *A Preface to Forster* (Harlow: Longman, 1983).

S. Gopolan, *Outlines of Jainism* (New York: Halsted, 1973).

Gerald Graff, 'Determinacy/Indeterminacy', *Critical Terms for Literary Study*, ed. Frank Lentricchia and Thomas McLaughlin (Chicago and London: University of Chicago Press, 1990), pp. 163–76.

K. W. Gransden, *E. M. Forster* (New York: Grove Press, 1962).

Ranjit Guha, *Elementary Aspects of Peasant Insurgency in Colonial India* (Delhi: Oxford University Press, 1983).

Hunt Hawkins, 'Forster's Critique of Imperialism in *A Passage to India*', *SAB*, 48 (1983), pp. 54–65.

Katherine N. Hayles, *Chaos Bound: Orderly Disorder in Contemporary Literature and Science* (Ithaca: Cornell University Press, 1990).

Jeffrey Heath, 'A Voluntary Surrender: Imperialism and Imagination in *A Passage to India*', *University of Toronto Quarterly: A Canadian Journal of the Humanities*, 59 (1989–90), pp. 287–309.

Judith Scherer Herz, 'Forster's Ghosts: *A Passage to India* and the Emptying of Narrative', *Negation, Critical Theory, and Postmodern Textuality*, ed. Daniel Fischlin (Dordrecht: Kluwer Acad., 1994), pp. 191–202.

Christopher Hibbert, *The Great Mutiny, India 1857* (London: Penguin, 1980).

Eric Hobsbawm and Terence Ranger, eds, *The Invention of Tradition* (Cambridge: Cambridge University Press, 1984).

Wolfgang Iser, *The Act of Reading: A Theory of Aesthetic Response* (Baltimore: Johns Hopkins University Press, 1978).

Abdul R. JanMohamed, 'The Economy of Manichean Allegory: The Function of Racial Difference in Colonialist Literature', *Race, Writing and Difference*, ed. Henry Louis Gates, Jr (Chicago: University of Chicago Press, 1985), pp. 78–106.

Alice Jardine, *Gynesis* (Ithaca: Cornell University Press, 1985).

Clare Kahane, *Passions of the Voice: Hysteria, Narrative, and the Figure of the Speaking Woman, 1850–1915* (Baltimore: Johns Hopkins University Press, 1995).

Sir John Kaye, *Kaye's and Malleson's History of the Indian Mutiny of 1857–8* (London: Longmans, Green, & Co, 1898).

Laura Kipnis, '"The Phantom Twitchings of an Amputated Limb": Sexual Spectacle in the Post-Colonial Epic', *Wide Angle: A Film Quarterly of Theory, Criticism and Practice*, 11 (1989), pp. 42–51.

Arthur Koestler, *The Lotus and the Robot* (London, 1960).

Jacques Lacan, *The Four Fundamental Concepts of Psychoanalysis*, trans. Alan Sheridan (New York: W. W. Norton, 1978).

F. R. Leavis, *The Common Pursuit* (London: Chatto and Windus, 1952).

June Perry Levine, 'An Analysis of the Manuscripts of *A Passage to India*', *PMLA*, 85 (1970), pp. 284–94.

—— *Creation and Criticism: A Passage to India* (London: Chatto and Windus, 1971).

Pierre Macherey, *A Theory of Literary Production*, trans. Geoffrey Wall (London: Routledge, 1978).

M.M. Mahood, *The Colonial Encounter: A Reading of Six Novels* (London: Collings, 1977), pp.65–91.

Elaine Marks and Isabelle de Courtivron, eds, *New French Feminisms: An Anthology*, trans. Keith Cohen and Paula Cohen (New York: Schocken Books, 1976).

Hugh McClean, 'The Structure of *A Passage to India*', *University of Toronto Quarterly*, 22 (1953), pp.157–71.

F.P.W. McDowell, ed., *E.M. Forster: An Annotated Bibliography of Writings About Him* (Dekalb: Northern Illinois University Press, 1976).

Jeffrey Meyers, 'The Politics of *A Passage to India*,' *Journal of Modern Literature*, 1 (1971), pp.329–38.

Wendy Moffat, '*A Passage to India* and the Limits of Certainty', *Journal of Narrative Technique*, 20 (1990), pp.331–41.

Jo Ann Hoeppner Moran, 'E.M. Forster's *A Passage to India*: What Really Happened in the Caves', *Modern Fiction Studies*, 34 (1988), pp.596–604.

K. Natwar-Singh, ed., *E.M. Forster: A Tribute* (New York: Harcourt, Brace and World, 1964).

Benita Parry, '*A Passage to India*: Epitaph or Manifesto?' *E.M. Forster: A Human Exploration*, ed. G.K. Das and John Beer (New York: New York University Press, 1979), pp.129–41.

— *Delusions and Discoveries: Studies on India in the British Imagination 1880–1930* (Berkeley: University of California Press, 1972).

— 'Passage to More than India', *Forster: A Collection of Critical Essays*, ed. Malcolm Bradbury (New Jersey: Prentice Hall, 1966), pp.160–74.

— 'The Politics of Representation in *A Passage to India*', *A Passage to India: Essays in Interpretation*, ed. John Beer (London: Macmillan, 1985), pp.27–43.

Carl Plasa and Betty J. Ring, eds, *The Discourse of Slavery: Aphra Behn to Toni Morrison*, (London and New York: Routledge, 1994).

Monique Plaza, 'Our Damages and Their Compensation, Rape: The Will Not to Know of Michel Foucault', *Feminist Issues*, 1 (1981), pp.25–35.

Eve Dawkins Poll, 'The Colonization of the Ingenue in E.M. Forster's *A Passage to India*', *SPAN: Journal of the South Pacific Association for Commonwealth Literature and Language Studies*, 38 (1994), pp.46–64.

S.V. Pradham, '*A Passage to India*: Realism Versus Symbolism, A Marxist Analysis', *Dalhousie Review*, 60 (1980), pp.300–17.

Frances L. Restuccia, '"A Cave of My Own": E.M. Forster and Sexual Politics', *Raritan*, 9 (1989), pp.110–28.

Barbara Rosecrace, *Forster's Narrative Vision* (Ithaca: Cornell University Press, 1982).

Alice S. Rossi, ed., *Essays on Sex Equality* (Chicago: University of Chicago Press, 1970).

David Rubin, *After the Raj: British Novels of India Since 1947* (Hanover: University Press of New England, 1986).

Salman Rushdie, 'Outside the Whale', *American Film*, January–February 1985, pp.16–18.

Michael Ryan, *Marxism and Deconstruction: A Critical Articulation* (Baltimore:

Johns Hopkins University Press, 1982).

Chaman L. Sahni, *Forster's A Passage to India: The Religious Dimension* (Atlantic Highlands: Humanities Press, 1991).

Edward Said, *Orientalism* (New York: Vintage, 1978).

—— *Culture and Imperialism* (London: Chatto and Windus, 1993).

Alison Sainsbury, 'Married to the Empire: the Anglo-Indian Domestic Novel', *Writing India 1757–1990: The Literature of British India*, ed. Bart Moore-Gilbert (Manchester and New York: Manchester University Press, 1996), pp.163–87.

Donald Salter, 'That is my Ticket: The Homosexual Writings of E.M. Forster', *London Magazine*, 15 (2), pp.5–33.

Kumkum Sangari and Sudesh Vaid, 'Recasting Women: An Introduction', *Recasting Women: Essays in Gender*, ed. Kumkum Sangari and Sudesh Vaid (New Jersey: Rutgers University Press, 1990), pp.1–25.

Anthony Sattin, *An Englishwoman in India: The Memoirs of Harriet Tytler, 1828–1858* (Oxford: Oxford University Press, 1986).

V.A. Shahane, *A Passage to India: A Study* (Delhi: Oxford University Press, 1977).

V.A. Shahane, ed., *Perspectives on E.M. Forster's A Passage to India*, (New York: Barnes, 1968).

V.A. Shahane, 'Symbolism in E.M. Forster's *A Passage to India*: "Temple"', *English Studies: A Journal of English Language and Literature*, 44 (1963), pp.423–31.

Jenny Sharpe, 'The Unspeakable Limits of Rape: Colonial Violence and Counter-Insurgency', *Genders*, 10 (1991), pp.25–46.

Elaine Showalter, '*A Passage to India* as "Marriage Fiction": Forster's Sexual Politics', *Women and Literature*, 5 (1977), pp.3–16.

Brenda R. Silver, 'Periphrasis, Power, and Rape in *A Passage to India*', *Novel: A Forum on Fiction*, 22 (1988), pp.86–105.

Vincent Smith, *The Oxford History of India* (Oxford: Clarendon Press, 1923).

Louis Snyder, *The Imperialism Reader* (Princeton: n.p., 1962).

Oliver Stallybrass, 'Forster's "Wobblings": The Manuscripts of *A Passage to India*', *E.M. Forster: A Passage to India, A Casebook*, ed. Malcolm Bradbury (London and Basingstoke: Macmillan, 1970), pp.32–42.

Oliver Stallybrass, ed., *The Manuscripts of A Passage to India*, The Abinger Edition Series, 6a (London: Edward Arnold, 1978).

George Steiner, 'Under the Greenwood Tree', *New Yorker*, October 9, 1971, pp.158–69.

Lionel Stevenson, 'The Earnest Realists', *The History of the English Novel*, ed. Lionel Stevenson (New York: Barnes, 1967) II, pp.87–102.

Wilfred Stone, *The Cave and the Mountain: A Study of E.M. Forster* (Stanford and London: Stanford University Press, 1966).

Robert Straus-Hupe, ed., *The Idea of Colonialism* (New York, 1958).

Sara Suleri, 'The Geography of *A Passage to India*', *E.M. Forster: Modern Critical Views*, ed. Harold Bloom (New York: Chelsea, 1987), pp.169–75.

—— *The Rhetoric of English India* (Chicago and London: University of Chicago Press, 1992).

Claude J. Summers, *E.M. Forster* (New York: Ungar, 1983).
Michael Taussig, *Shamanism, Colonialism, and the Wild Man* (Chicago: University of Chicago Press, 1987).
Archibald Thornton, *The Imperial Idea and its Enemies* (London: n.p., 1959).
Lionel Trilling, *E.M. Forster: A Study* (London: The Hogarth Press, 1969).
Jane Ussher, *Women's Madness: Misogyny or Mental Illness?* (New York and London: Harvester Wheatsheaf, 1991).
Vron Ware, *Beyond the Pale: White Women, Racism and History* (London and New York: Verso, 1992).
Chris Weedon, *Feminist Practice and Poststructuralist Theory* (Oxford: Basil Blackwell, 1987).
Gertrude M. White, 'A Passage to India: Analysis and Revaluation', *PMLA*, 68 (1953), pp.641–57.
Patrick Williams and Laura Chrisman, eds, *Colonial Discourse and Post-Colonial Theory* (New York and London: Harvester Wheatsheaf, 1993).

E.M. Forster

Novels
Where Angels Fear to Tread (London: Blackwood, 1905).
The Longest Journey (London: Blackwood, 1907).
A Room with a View (London: Edward Arnold, 1908).
Howards End (London: Edward Arnold, 1910).
A Passage to India (London: Edward Arnold, 1924).
Maurice (London: Edward Arnold, 1971).
All of the above texts are available in Penguin editions.

Stories
The Celestial Omnibus and Other Stories (London: Sidgwick and Jackson, 1911).
The Eternal Moment and Other Stories (London: Sidgwick and Jackson, 1928).
The Life to Come and Other Stories (London: Edward Arnold, 1972).
Arctic Summer and Other Fiction (London: Edward Arnold, 1980).

Non-fiction
Pharos and Pharillon (London: Hogarth Press, 1923).
Aspects of the Novel (London: Edward Arnold, 1927).
Goldsworthy Lowes Dickinson (London: Edward Arnold, 1934).
Abinger Harvest (London: Edward Arnold, 1936).
Two Cheers for Democracy (London: Edward Arnold, 1951).
Marianne Thornton, 1797-1887, A Domestic Biography (New York: Harcourt, Brace & Co., 1956).
The Hill of Devi (New York: Harcourt, Brace & Co., 1983).

Selected articles

'Reflections on India', *Nation and Athenaeum*, 30 (21 January 1922).

'India and the Turk', *Nation and Athenaeum*, 31 (30 September 1922).

'Indian caves', *Nation and Athenaeum*, 37 (11 July 1925).

'The Individual and his God', *Listener*, 24 (5 December 1940).

'The Art and Architecture of India', *Listener*, 50 (10 September 1953).

'E.M. Forster on his Life and Books: An Interview Recorded for Television', *Listener*, 1 (January 1959).

ACKNOWLEDGEMENTS

The editor and publishers wish to thank the following for their permission to reprint copyright material: Penguin Books (for material from *The Common Pursuit*); The Hogarth Press (for material from *E.M. Forster*); Macmillan (for material from 'Two Passages to India: Forster as Victorian and Modern'); *Journal of Narrative Technique* (for material from 'A *Passage to India* and the Limits of Certainty' and 'Marabar: The Caves of Deconstruction'); *Modern Fiction Studies* (for material from 'E.M. Forster's *A Passage to India*: What Really Happened in the Caves'); *Women and Literature* (for material from 'A *Passage to India* as "Marriage Fiction": Forster's Sexual Politics'); *Journal of Modern Literature* (for material from 'The Politics of *A Passage to India*'); *Genders* (for material from 'The Unspeakable Limits of Rape: Colonial Violence and Counter-Insurgency').

There are instances where we have been unable to trace or contact copyright holders before our printing deadline. If notified, the publisher will be pleased to acknowledge the use of copyright material.

The editor would like to thank Mary Ring and L.B.B. for their assistance during the preparation of this manuscript.

Betty Jay is a Lecturer in English at Royal Holloway, University of London. She is co-editor of *The Discourse of Slavery: Aphra Behn to Toni Morrison* (Routledge, 1994) and is currently completing a book on Anne Brontë for the Writers and their Work Series (Northcote House).

INDEX

THE ICON *CRITICAL GUIDES* SERIES

NEW TITLES FOR SPRING 1999

George Eliot
Middlemarch
The Mill on the Floss
Adam Bede
Edited by Lucie Armitt
ISBN 1 84046 040 7

Nathaniel Hawthorne
The Scarlet Letter
Edited by Elmer Andrews
ISBN 1 84046 041 5

T.S. Eliot
The Waste Land
Edited by Nick Selby
ISBN 1 84046 039 3

Elizabeth Gaskell
Mary Barton
North and South
Edited by Alison Chapman
ISBN 1 84046 037 7

William Faulkner
The Sound and the Fury
As I Lay Dying
Edited by Nicolas Tredell
ISBN 1 84046 036 9

Printed in the United States
72863LV00002B/10-12